PICNICS
And
PORCUPINES

GREAT LAKES BOOKS

A complete listing of the books in this series can be found online at
wsupress.wayne.edu.

Editor
Thomas Klug
Sterling Heights, Michigan

PICNICS ~AND~ PORCUPINES

Eating in the Wilderness of
Michigan's Upper Peninsula

CANDICE GOUCHER

Wayne State University Press
Detroit

ISBN 9780814351543 (paperback)
ISBN 9780814351550 (e-book)

Library of Congress Control Number: 2024930907

Cover art by Penn Weldon (pennweldonart@gmail.com).
Cover design by Philip Pascuzzo.

Publication of this book was made possible through the generosity of the Friends of the Great Lakes Books Series Fund.

Wayne State University Press rests on Waawiyaataanong, also referred to as Detroit, the ancestral and contemporary homeland of the Three Fires Confederacy. These sovereign lands were granted by the Ojibwe, Odawa, Potawatomi, and Wyandot Nations, in 1807, through the Treaty of Detroit. Wayne State University Press affirms Indigenous sovereignty and honors all tribes with a connection to Detroit. With our Native neighbors, the press works to advance educational equity and promote a better future for the earth and all people.

Wayne State University Press
Leonard N. Simons Building
4809 Woodward Avenue
Detroit, Michigan 48201-1309

Visit us online at wsupress.wayne.edu.

To my mother, Hyla Rae Hamel

CONTENTS

LIST OF RECIPES

The Picnic Potato Salad

Berry-Picking Pick-nicking (1935)

Some More Picnics (1927–1930s)

Governor's Picnic (1953)

Midcentury Modern Beached Picnic (1960s)

Church Picnic (1960s)

Yoopers vs. Fudgies Picnic (c. 1977)

ACKNOWLEDGMENTS

As the great-granddaughter of an early pioneer in the eastern Upper Peninsula of Michigan, I was born in Sault Ste. Marie, in traditional Anishinaabeg territory, before paved roads connected Cedarville to "the Soo." Even after my family moved away, I returned to the Upper Peninsula (UP) dozens of times over the course of more than fifty years, picnicking as a toddler and again with a toddler of my own. I am grateful to my extended family, who remained enthusiastic and patient fans of my historical interests, especially John and Jeri Griffin, Brenda DeRosha, Sally Nye, Tom and Deb Nye, Susan Rutledge, the late Elda Nye, the late Joyce Pines, the late Arlo Hamel, Alana Kemper, Kay Radtke, Kosa Goucher-Lambert, Kimberly Lockwood, and the late Hyla Hamel Goucher. Members of this tribe at times simply listened and at times provided me with room and board; they shared summer picnics, photographs, postcards, books, videos, hikes, stories, boat rides, bicycles, snow boots, memories, donuts, and their love of local lore. I also acknowledge the Anishinaabe and other Indigenous people, who journeyed through centuries of changing foodways and called the Upper Peninsula their home. I hope this project helps to make visible their struggles before and after my family's ancestors arrived. Like any other long-plowed research project, this field's furrows have also benefited from the assistance of numerous librarians and museum staff, especially at the Benson Ford Research Center Reading Room, the Henry Ford Museum, the Les Cheneaux Historical Museum and Library, Mackinac Island State Parks, and the Opie Library Archives at Michigan Technological University, Houghton. Special thanks to Leslie M. Behm and Peter Berg at the Michigan State University

Library, Special Collections, and Jeremiah Mason at the Keweenaw National Historical Park. Thank you to Alyssa Sperry for bibliographic assistance at the University of Oregon. I am indebted to editors Sandra Korn and Tom Klug for their enthusiastic guidance, to copyeditor Sandra J. Judd, and to the manuscript's reviewers, who saw the project as world history and provided invaluable suggestions for its revisions. Thanks to photographer Jack Deo of Superior View, to Harrison Higgs at Washington State University, Vancouver, and to the talented Penn Weldon, who helped visualize the project's components.

Although I spent a lot of time working with words, I have also learned directly from the wilderness, where I savored outdoor meals in the Porcupine Mountains, in Ironwood, in the Keweenaw Peninsula, at the Pictured Rocks National Lakeshore, at Tahquamenon Falls, at Detour Village, on Marquette Island, on Mackinac Island, in the environs of Cedarville and Hessel, and in places, on paths, and at shores in between. I have been privileged to watch porcupines, beavers, moose, and deer, to see the fish jumping in the lake, and to hear the call of the sandhill crane at sunset. I have tasted more than my share of pasties and whitefish dinners. I have listened to the lapping waters of the lakes and seen the northern lights. I have glimpsed the wild iris, butterfly migrations, and lightning bugs at dusk, and I have smelled the scent of sweetgrass along a wooded path. My personal memories thus are intertwined with the paths of the historical events described in this book. I invite readers to take delight in these social and natural landscapes, relish past picnics, and be inspired to create their own. The environmental writer Robert Macfarlane observed that "Paths are the habits of a landscape. They are acts of consensual making. It's hard to create a footpath on your own."[1] Together, then, by continuing the traditions of "picnics and porcupines," perhaps it will be possible for us to protect both the culinary heritage and the wilderness resources for the journeys of future generations.

INTRODUCTION

There is no landscape that is not obscure, underneath its
pleasing transparencies, if you speak to it endlessly.
—Édouard Glissant, *The Thinking of the Opacity of the World*[1]

A picnic near the shores of Lake Michigan is the opening scene of the short film *Powers of Ten: A Film Dealing with the Relative Size of Things in the Universe and the Effect of Adding Another Zero* (1977), made by the globally influential modern American designers Ray and Charles Eames.[2] In the film, two picnickers are viewed from above by the camera held at a distance of one meter. Then, every ten seconds the camera moves away: first ten meters, then one hundred meters, one thousand meters, ten thousand meters, and so on. At one million meters, the entire Great Lakes and clouds are visible, and at one hundred million meters, the motion of the stars can be seen. The film carries us from the everyday picnic blanket on the lakeshore to the visible edge of the known cosmos. As we travel exponentially away from the picnic, human activity is gradually lost to sight, replaced by other perspectives, including regional, continental, planetary, and cosmic.

Scale matters in history too. This book that you are reading considers history at the scale of an individual life in a single moment, the enjoyment of a summer picnic in 1911, captured in a black-and-white photograph of my grandmother. The picnic photograph is viewed by her granddaughter (a historian), who examines the event at multiple scales, including microhistorical levels of individual biography, family lore, and regional history, as well as from within the Big History levels of the environment and global history. The various dimensions of the photograph reveal the continuum between the social world of human activity (the picnicker) and the natural world (the world of the porcupine viewed from a distance). In the 1970s, Ray and Charles Eames used the shared and fundamentally global relationships revealed by their film to argue about more than perspective. As were the underlying concerns of the Eameses' film, the endpoints of this book's historical analysis are intentionally the ecological relationships that can be reconstructed along the way.[3]

A picnic is comprised of elements of people, food, and place. Like any culinary event, the picnic embraces all the senses, from taste and smell to sight, touch, and even sound. Food history is at once the account of a startlingly intimate experience of foods that enter the individual human body and the simultaneous connections that link people to their environments. Another way to say this is to emphasize that a picnic is also a place, and its spatial identity inside a landscape matters. The social and natural worlds meet and conspire to make shared meals possible and meaningful. Their paths and intersections are the subject of any history of food, but they gain greater prominence when the shared meals take place outdoors.

The full sensory spectrum of the picnicker has informed the book you are holding in your hands. As with the picnickers, my scenic gaze has been on the specific local foods rooted in the landscapes of the Upper Peninsula (the UP) of Michigan. The project began with a photograph of a grandmother I never met holding a watermelon slice at a picnic in July 1911, long before I was born. It has considered the changing menus of picnics, including local foods and the countless "foreign" foods that were invented, borrowed, and introduced via global trade and migration. In uncovering the patterns of interaction that changed over time, I have used visual resources and material culture, including photographs, films, sketches, cartoons, advertisements, maps, and postcards, to demonstrate how the grasp of the modern world has shaped and reshaped a regional identity. I have listened to the soundscapes of the forests, informed by the memory found in the music of lumberjacks and the musical instruments of Victorian lady picnickers, as well as the calls of wild birds and other critters of the natural world. The lapping of lake waters along the shoreline was inescapable, and the deep silences of the woods were remarkably persistent. To reconstruct the life of the picnic, I have read letters, scientific reports, books, articles, diaries, cookbooks, and recipes gleaned from a variety of sources.

Cooking food from historical recipes and meals described in the past has provided further historical evidence of the tastes and smells that were integral to the picnic experience. Indigenous peoples, early adventurers, miners, lumberjacks, industrialists, scientists, writers, artists, conservationists, ordinary families, and extraordinary tourists ate outdoors, as did my grandmother, often holding food in their hands, on the edge of the wilderness. Their lives literally touched the forests and lakes, creating a culinary past that reveals the wilderness home of the porcupines and picnickers alike. In the ebb and flow of access to its reaches, I found that the human narrative crossed paths with nonhuman species, since both experienced more than a century of dramatic globalization, technological revolutions, and cultural interactions. Inexorably, the project became more than a narrative of family and food in the Great Lakes. Its global framework explicates connections between local, regional, and global foodways. In this way, it also contributes to world history, US history, and environmental history.

EATING OUTDOORS

This book is a history of the shifting concept and experience of the picnic—an outdoor repast that connects people to specific places in a landscape.[4] The concept and experience of this landscape, the edge of the elusive wilderness, were similarly dynamic, as one version of "wilderness" was transformed into another. While the naming of an *outdoor* (rather than indoor) meal as a "picnic," perhaps evolving from the French "pique-nique," probably dates to the beginning of the nineteenth century, eating outdoors has a much more primordial past that is deeply ingrained in the DNA that makes us human. Shared, cooked food in a communal environment provided our ancestors with the common cultural element from which humanity evolved. It is the continuing essence of a global food history. Enormous piles of oyster, snail, and clamshells or collections of the bones of butchered large and small mammals and birds shared around a firepit are all that remain from what we can imagine of prehistoric picnics. Modern picnics record the movement of peoples from their original picnic grounds along pathways that reached into every corner of the planet and met in the Upper Peninsula, where they created one picnic diaspora after another, remembering some traditions and forgetting or inventing others.

The shared landscape of the UP picnic was inevitably placed near or within what people called and/or imagined to be "wilderness." This landscape of forest and water was not unchanging, and other scholars have noted many of its forces of transformation across the centuries.[5] In particular, historian William Cronon called attention to the ironic fact that the wilderness was a profoundly human creation, its memories a cultural invention.[6] If that were so, then what did the edge of the wilderness represent? The conservationist Aldo Leopold (1887–1948), who spent childhood summers in the eastern UP, viewed the region as "a phenomenon of edges."[7] The ecological consciousness that arose in the wake of Leopold's writings furthered an awareness of borderlands between the natural and human-built, culminating in the work by Robert Michael Morrissey.[8] The transitional spaces between habitats were called ecotones. These were meeting places for the advantageous access to multiple environments, mosaics, and patchworks of bioregions. Entangled histories of human and nonhuman would follow.

Indigenous peoples formed their own concept of the landscape even as they fully captured its natural resources, including copper, wood, bark, and a variety of gathered and hunted foods. Indigenous land use altered and transformed the region through seasons of cultivation and harvest, through hunting and gathering practices, and through mining, travel, and settlement, amidst centuries of adaptations to the instability of climate and the presence of microenvironments.[9] In seventeenth-century America, the invaders imposed another concept of wilderness as "a dark and dismal place where all manner of wild beasts dash about uncooked."[10] Cooking and eating outdoors were seen as ways to bring civilization to the wild place, the place of porcupines on the forest's edge. The history of the picnic thus needs to be understood in close association with the transformations of the region's forests, wetlands, and lakes. Some of these changes were the consequence of climate and geography. Eventually, they were also brought about by the forces of the Anthropocene, the current geological era that marks a period in which the planet's climate, landscapes, and environments have been dominated by human activity. In our search for its history, we can look to actions by the nomadic and settled residents of the region, not just its prominent visitors who wrote literary or scientific interpretations of their personal observations.

The idea of approaching the untamed wilderness as emblematic of the conquest of Nature, in opposition to Civilization, is a view found in many cultures. The anthropologist Claude Lévi-Strauss, himself a vegetarian, used this Nature/Culture dichotomy to think about raw versus cooked food as useful categories common to all societies. Indigenous peoples separated deep forest from edge of forest in their languages, a meaningful difference that they also used to conceptualize foodways.[11] And the early Euro-Americans made comparisons between their own homes in France (Alexis de Tocqueville, a visiting political writer) or England (Charlotte O'Brien, a wife and mother resident on Mackinac Island) and other distant landscapes when they encountered the Great Lakes region and ascribed to it a "wilderness" designation. By the nineteenth century, the "wilderness" was already farmed and mined by Indigenous peoples and European immigrants. Yet O'Brien brought along her monogrammed silverware and Tocqueville would go on to write his influential political science treatise *Democracy in America* (1835) using the destruction of the wilderness as proof of the inevitable formation of a new nation-state. If the lumberjack's wilderness was a hypermasculine space, the picnic on its edge was feminine, even family friendly, and a site of healing and sublime transcendence. That edge of the wilderness itself was similarly a cultural invention.

The wilderness landscape became a memory of what once had been densely forested and bountiful in wildlife. Some later semblances of its wild memory might be preserved and curated as a woodsy parklike setting for outdoor meals. Invented tropes suggested the healing balm of the wilderness experience for the tourists tempted away from the increasingly urban pace of modern life. The very same trains that carried picnickers on Sundays transported the timber and ores extracted from the wilderness the remainder of the week. Because the focus of this book is the culinary history of a specific and unique American landscape, the changing wilderness of the Upper Peninsula of Michigan, the picnic's past is also an environmental narrative. By focusing on a single landscape, I can trace the transformation (and mostly the loss) of the forest itself and the creation of a modern concept of wilderness as it emerges in the North American imagination and popular culture. The forested landscape of the twentieth century was far removed from its primeval and ancient origins in the last glaciation. Scientific studies of the landscape have revealed how the forest itself changed over time. Perhaps twelve thousand years ago, the forest was spruce, then, as the climate shifted, the vegetation expressed itself in a mosaic of pine and oak, and then hemlock dominated maple and beech by about three thousand years ago.

In contrast to the term "landscape," which suggests a picturesque, postcard view as seen from a distance, "wilderness" encompasses the place of both the human and nonhuman elements jointly engaged by the outdoor experiences of the Upper Peninsula. Yet its conceptualization changes over time and across cultures. Similarly, food historians have looked at meals as select opportunities to examine the past with a close-up lens, one that views the most intimate of human actions when food gains access inside cellular levels of the individual body. By the nineteenth century, the habits of food brought the world to the table. Just as any world history must toggle between the global and the local, humans also were inseparable from the rest of the natural world. People engaged with the trees, birds, animals, fish, rocks, plants, and water, and they did so under conditions that were decidedly global. The porcupines in the book's title remind us that the natural ecology of the picnic reflected these complex sets of human and nonhuman relationships. At the same time, the porcupine is both a prickly reminder and a symbol of the underlying ecology. Accordingly, this study has considered the plight of both picnickers and porcupines across time because both traveled regularly to the feeding sites of their choosing on the forest edge, and both were engaged in the ecology of picnic meals in a shared landscape of meaning.

For some residents of the UP—voyageurs, miners, loggers—ordinary meals were necessarily consumed outdoors. For others—summer tourists or laborers seeking a moment of leisure—picnics were social occasions that symbolized both freedom and belonging. Picnic meals varied greatly, from time of day to the choice of foods. While acknowledging that cultural differences have flavored the picnic experience, historians have not examined the institution's features, which also may have changed over time.[12] Food historians have documented how meals can provide glimpses into the daily lives of people, revealing their predilections for pursuing individual taste preferences and managing the contradictions of ethnicity, class, race, and gender against the memories that particular foods evoke. Picnics are no different. Indeed, they remained at the heart of historical memory in the twentieth century.

THE GLOBAL DIASPORA OF PICNICS

The UP's changing wilderness owes much to global forces, despite the region's claim to remoteness or pristine wildness. Climate change altered the glacial retreat, creating lakes, swamps, and successive forest mosaics. In the Anthropocene, humans have altered climate itself. Human migrations brought the original settlers, and they continued to add to the diversity of residents in modern times. This narrative invites us to apprehend the impact of imperialism, the colonial appropriation of land and conquest of people, industrialization, urbanization, warfare, ideologies of inequality and cultural superiority, and new technologies, including steam power and the automobile's internal-combustion engine, among the many global forces and events that were critical in shaping the region's past and present. Eating outdoors also happened against a single, stunning panorama in which Indigenous peoples became subject to the forces of global change. French, British, and American imperialism brought to the Upper Peninsula early voyageurs and settlers, scientists, philosophers, and conservationists, who considered the region's beauty and potential for learned admiration, exploitation, settlement, preservation, healing, and sometimes plunder. In his landmark study, John Knott has used literature to map these transformations of forests in the popular imagination.[13] This study of food and environment adds the interplay of both individual and global contexts in which to comprehend those transformations.

While marketing the UP region from the nineteenth century onward emphasized a soul- and health-affirming mystique and balm characteristic of the remote *American* "wilderness," its past was not yet narrowly regional nor was it truly national. Immigrants had arrived with their individual food-ways, including those of Central Algonquian (Anishinaabe/Ojibwe),[14] French, English, and various African groups, as well as those of Croatian, Slovenian, Hungarian, Italian, Irish, Scottish, Finnish, Swedish, Russian, and German speakers. Eventually, an American national identity was forged with food. More importantly, the identity of the UP also remained globally and region-ally demarcated. For example, the Cornish pasty was brought from England to the Upper Peninsula (and to Montana and Mexico) by nineteenth-century miners. Locally, it was revered by British immigrants, rejected by others, and embraced as the food of acculturation by yet other ethnic groups. As late as the 1970s, the pasty was not remembered by Finnish immigrants and their descendants in association with the Cornish, but rather it was foreign to them because it was "American."[15] The semantic shift in foods as "ethnic" or "American" has been part of the evolving language of food and identity, and of picnics themselves.

The Upper Peninsula was thus a complex mosaic of linguistic and cultural influences in which the picnic played a critical social role. The picnic tableau helped de-emphasize some cultural differences, giving a commonality of shared place, if not always a shared diet. The significance of this diasporic wealth was that it was not subjected to the urban-dependent process of acculturation and homogenization so typical of the American experience. Other historians have studied the creation of regional cuisines, but not as the exclusive product of rural America. As Ron Takaki pointed out long ago, "the study of the past can provide collective self-knowledge," but it can also reflect the historian's own understanding of the world, a "different mirror."[16] The Upper Peninsula was not an urban cauldron. The lack of play of urban dynamics across the Upper Peninsula permitted a slower evolution of regional identity, one that emphasized the ever-changing landscape and all it had to offer to a lesson of persistence. The unfolding of a regional identity was above all linked to the activities of the outdoors: hunting, fishing, and picnicking. For this reason, the outdoor meals best captured the foods that could be easily transported to express aspects of identity. Transportation technologies are key elements in the picnic's history.

Recognition of a regional cuisine has been a long time in the making. Aside from some geographically limited community cookbooks beginning in the late nineteenth century, there are few sources that might be considered as regional treatments of food history. Nature and Culture both found their allies. Fortunately, government support of naturalists, writers, and artists left behind some key sources for reconstructing the environmental and cultural pasts across the United States. Recreational areas began to be preserved as early as 1872, with the National Park Service coming into being in 1916 and the UP's Hiawatha National Forest in 1931. Between about 1933 and 1945, the Civilian Conservation Corps initiated a program of forest restoration, tree planting, and wildlife habitat improvement in the UP.[17] Heritage recovery efforts also extended to cultural spheres.

Established by Franklin Delano Roosevelt in 1935, the Federal Writers' Project was another part of the New Deal's Works Progress Administration (WPA) and meant to support Americans in the Great Depression. As part of a project called "America Eats," writers were sent across the nation to record local foodways. Mark Kurlansky's *The Food of a Younger Land* (2009) has chronicled some of the WPA accounts by grouping them regionally ("The Midwest Eats").[18] Around the same time, in the 1930s, cartoonist William Donahey and his wife, Mary Dickerson, assisted in compiling and editing a cookbook entitled *The Cooking Pots of Grand Marais* (1976 reprint), a slim volume that contained the foodway reminiscences of locals in Grand Marais.[19] The more recent book by Larry B. Massie and Priscilla Massie, *Walnut Pickles and Watermelon Cake: A Century of Michigan Cooking* (1989), surveyed a wider field: Michigan state cookbooks and recipes from the 1820s onward, including a few from the UP. While the compilers pronounced the recipes' multicultural characteristics, they did not attempt to historicize them.[20] Individual food items have not received much attention by historians. Much has been written about the popular "pasty" from Cornish heritage in the Copper Country, yet scant historical research provides a foundation for examining change over time, even for this legendary regional food icon.

Popular writing and local lore suggest the twentieth-century formation of a Northwoods, "Yooper" cultural character. The rural Yooper identity and the term itself derived from the understandings associated with being resident in the UP (i.e., being a "UP-er" or "Yooper") year-round, not only in the season of picnics. The UP is again grouped with five other states in the culinary treatment of the "Upper Great Lakes" in Katherine S. Kirlin and Thomas M. Kirlin's Smithsonian *Folklife Cookbook* (1991).[21] Retired historian Russell M. Magnaghi has two recent and relevant books on the UP's past, *Prohibition in the Upper Peninsula: Booze & Bootleggers on the Border* (2017) and *Upper Peninsula of Michigan: A History* (2017), although foodways are not highlighted in the latter.[22] Women are widely associated with the preparation of food, so they should be expected to wield the greater historical agency. However, the hypermasculine environments of mining, logging, hunting, and fishing meant a more complex and calibrated play of historical roles. The practice of gendering the past has been late to arrive in the UP, and little attention has been paid to how local foodways document gender dynamics in any of these histories.

The popularization of the picnic in Western culture parallels the settlement of the Great Lakes region. The popular *Beeton's Book of Household Management* (1861) makes suggestions for elite English picnic fare, some of which advice (bringing champagne, lobster, and lamb) would have been inappropriate for much of the UP's history.[23] The first cookbook devoted entirely to the picnic was Linda Hull Larned's *One Hundred Picnic Suggestions* (1915), which addressed the author's acute awareness of the automobile's impact by dividing recipe sections into "For the Picnic Basket" and "For the Motor Hamper."[24] May E. Southworth's *The Motorist's Luncheon Book* (1923) offered menus to be prepared on a campfire before reaching that "woodsy paradise." Southworth's advice on emergency supplies notably included chocolate.[25] Later in the twentieth century, major food writers thought quite a lot about picnics, even if historians did not. These writers included James Beard (1903–85) and M. F. K. Fisher (1908–92), both influential American food critics and fans of the picnic and eating outdoors.[26] A bonfire full of barbecue cookbooks and outdoor eating menus followed this era. A few more recent cookbooks have examined picnic foods exclusively: Jeremy Jackson's *Good Day for a Picnic: Simple Food That Travels Well* (2005) devotes twelve pages to the picnic's history (followed by recipes), and Marnie Hanel et al., *The Picnic: Recipes and Inspiration from Basket to Blanket* (2015), demonstrate that picnics are alive and well in the twenty-first century.[27]

Surprisingly, histories of the picnic are very rare. Walter Levy's *The Picnic: A History* (2014) focuses on picnics in England, Europe, and the United States, as seen through literature and cinema.[28] It is a romp through the picnic's past, with summaries of eras suggestively revealed through the population of fictional characters. Recently an entire book was devoted to the symbolic and political meaning of a single nineteenth-century picnic.[29] The place of the picnic was not a timeless world outside of history. By linking picnics to specific historical places, people, and eras, this project aims to reveal an understanding of how global forces first created and then undermined the regional identity of Upper Peninsula foodways and that they did so in relation to the changing conceptualization of the wilderness itself.

When the disappearing wilderness was gone, it still had to be imagined. A significant part of the exercise of reimagining the wilderness was conjuring its tastes: maple, spruce, venison, and whitefish could sample the old meaning of wilderness flavors and thereby create new connections. Like the twentieth-century practice of "sampling" music that reuses existing recordings to create new work, the sampling of earlier foods created a common experience of place-contingent tastes. By definition, this wilderness was the opposite of civilization and also simultaneously served as a tamed cultural refuge for the benefits of civilization, offering improved health, wealth creation, and recreational opportunities for many. Against the initial backdrop of the wilderness landscape, this book examines the more recent foods of its picnickers on the edge of once-forested tracts, in grassy fields and on rocky shores, spread on picnic blankets and makeshift tables fashioned from tree stumps, boulders, and even concrete.

The Porcupine and the Picnic

The other key facet of this project has been to examine the place of the picnic in the natural world. The edge of the forest is shared by picnickers and many creatures, but none is so persistently present as the porcupine. The porcupine is a creature of the wilderness edge. The animal's unique relationships with place are employed in this study both as part of the scientific observations of picnic habitats and metaphorically to reflect the changes that occur over time. The porcupine follows the same paths daily on the forest's edge before venturing farther into the wilderness in search of food and comfort.

The porcupine is not only a harbinger of the changing technology but also a victim of the gradual loss of picnic habitat. At the same time, unlike many other species, the porcupine can make behavioral adjustments, adaptations to the region's environmental crisis. Other nonhuman species are glimpsed within the era, including various species of fish, butterflies, and birds. Canals, dams, steam power, iron roads, gasoline engines, electricity, and bridges connect the global advance of transportation innovations to the local destiny of picnics. Throughout, both porcupines and picnickers continued to seek the same places on the edge of the dwindling woods and settled lakeshore properties.

THE ANATOMY AND METHODOLOGY OF PICNICS

Reconstructing the menus from typical and actual picnics across the eras has required the curation of foods, recipes, and landscapes as coequal artifacts of the picnic. Baskets, lunch pails, and bags of charcoal briquettes also have informed the sensibility of this collect-and-carry operation. Among the book's picnic participants are famous picnickers: a scientist, a labor activist, an author, a lumberjack, an industrialist, a conservationist, and a politician, among others. There are also unknown ones, the unidentified picnickers who boarded steamships or jumped on picnic trains to find that perfect spot. Dozens of signature recipes are included in this book: each chapter provides picnic menus that lend thematic shape and specific flavors to the remembered meals. The menus reproduce historical "receipts" (the old-time term for recipes) from early regional cookbooks and other historical accounts and provide some original recipes that were inspired by the historical contexts of the recreated picnics, as well as adaptations of traditions. Any associated historical references to specific picnickers or picnics from the era at hand have been noted in the picnic and recipe headnotes.

More than a century of memorable people gathered for the picnics described herein. The recipes provide a way to sample their historical experiences. Their inclusion is meant to encourage the reader to consider fully, with all the senses, the changing picnic fare, past and present. Together they also explain the changing foodways over which local and global constraints reigned. They document the culinary styles and taste preferences that were elaborated as a consequence of these forces. In this way, the reader also is invited to picnic and taste the past as an alternative way of considering the histories of food and place.

The methodologies employed include the analysis of a vast range of written and nonwritten sources. They include the perspectives of individual biography in the form of written and spoken word, curated photograph, postcard, letter, recipe, and diary. They include the hallmarks of popular culture, from songs to cartoons, movies to advertisements. They range from scientific studies to creative writing, from invisible, edible memories to the inedible and physical markers of the past. These methodologies originate in multiple disciplines, but they all weave narratives that require a global framework.

A Road Map for the Themes of the Book

Following this introduction, the book's thematic parts are arranged roughly chronologically, in an overlapping historical narrative that reveals the impact of changing technology and other global forces on real and romanticized "picnicscapes" (a term I employ to describe the visible and invisible connections between picnic and place) and actual picnic events. Chapters use visual keys to open and introduce the chapter's thematic focus and central narratives: a photograph, an illustration, or perhaps a visually rich description captured from oral memory serves to anchor the reader in the relevant context. Chapters also contain a pairing of their historical essays with sets of picnics and specific recipes relevant to the era and theme.

Chapter 1 examines briefly the global and American history of the picnic, focusing on the late nineteenth and twentieth centuries, before and after the year of my grandmother's picnic. Chapter 2 places the porcupine at the picnic table, revealing the encounters between picnicker and porcupine, stand-ins for the human and nonhuman, across time as the wilderness begins to shrink in response to deforestation and exploitation. The next three chapters consider different modes of transportation. Chapter 3 discusses how early picnickers reached picnic sites on foot and by boat. The era's earliest opportunities for syncretism, borrowing, and culinary transformation suggested the initial interplay of local and global dimensions in the past, including science and pseudoscience. The chapter opens with a canoe journey, marked by an iron frying pan tied to the boat's hull. When European travelers first arrived in the UP, they encountered wilderness areas and forest civilizations unlike their own. They came with global desires that would increase global inequalities and promote the UP as a local cache of wilderness resources for mining, timber, fishing, and tourism. They built their new order on the foundations of global migration attracted to edible landscapes, a feat that required extensive cultural synthesis and adaptation. We can call the shared meals outdoors "picnics," although they were often far from gay and pleasurable frolics. They reinforced the social interactions and cemented relationships between people and the waters and forested lands held in common. The early encounters were recorded in travel narratives and scientific studies, in archaeological excavations and even religious tracts, which reveal notable experiences of dining on the edges of the forest and lake. The scientific limitations of knowledge were situated amidst the popular perceptions of endless availability, another characteristic imposed on the wilderness landscape. While the earliest meals outdoors required traveling across waterways, these culinary encounters gave way to shared foodways, borrowing, and adaptation, culminating in global and regional identities.

Chapter 4 examines the full impact of global imperialism as reflected in the region's plundered past and its reliance on trains. Both mining and intensive logging of the Upper Peninsula in the long century between about 1820 and 1920 brought about changes to its landscapes, foods, and inhabitants. This impact was both cultural and environmental. Between 1905 and 1917, Sunday picnic trains carried picnickers along iron roads to prescribed picnic destinations. Technologies, migrations, languages, and social lives were inscribed on the wilderness. Expressions of disparities and differences also may be found in the drinking and dining habits of immigrant populations. They are inherent in the relationships of exploitation and plunder that were forged by early capitalist development.

Chapter 5 focuses on the era of the automobile, when tourism gradually replaced the extractive industries, redefining the regional identity in terms of "wilderness" restoration and recreation. The chapter opens with the disembarkation of an automobile on a shoreline that lacked roads. The commodification of the picnic also emerged in the era between about 1895 and 1935, which witnessed the arrival of automobilism. Whereas eating outdoors and picnicking had occurred earlier, in these eras the picnic was fully embraced as a cultural phenomenon, a "craze" eventually reached by cars, roads, and bridges. Against the background of changing technologies and engineered landscapes, a regional identity was taking shape as tourism almost fully replaced extractive industries.

Finally, chapter 6 revisits the picnicscapes inherited by the region's most recent generations of inhabitants. The essence of these curated places arises from preceding historical decisions about both where and what to eat, decided by the politics of the picnic and individuals within its landscape. The politics of the picnic can be found in the legislation culminating in the Wilderness Act of 1964 and shaped by a growing consensus around public policy. Picnicscapes in the legally protected wilderness were not identical to the curated landscapes or marketed settings in which the UP's picnics took place in the prior century. Their contours were not simply unspoiled, pristine natural worlds left behind. They were continuously shaped by the twentieth-century availability of global foods, economic and social factors globally rendered, and responses to the many environmental challenges for both the picnic and its wilderness landscapes experienced locally. Profound transformations were brought about by the introduction of steamships, trains, and automobiles, the construction of the monumental Mackinac Bridge, and countless paved roads and rest stops with picnic tables that cut through the heart of dynamic ecologies.

The book thus provides a pioneering overview of the picnics and landscapes of the Upper Peninsula in a world historical context. The Upper Peninsula at the turn of the twentieth century had become a distinctively global community, primarily comprised of immigrants attracted to the region's industries of mining, fishing, and logging. When these industries declined, they gave way to others—especially tourism, which celebrated the combined cultures of picnics reached by boat, train, and automobile. Over the centuries, the picnic was also the vehicle that connected immigrants and visitors to their new homes in an unfamiliar place, partly imagined, under assault, yet ultimately surviving. The foods and meals shared outdoors were essential components in the complicated process of attaining a regional and national identity, both helping to define and being defined by the unique paths of the picnic through the "wilderness" of Michigan's Upper Peninsula.

1

THE PICNIC

It is a cardinal belief with every man, woman, and child that
a picnic includes pretty nearly the most perfect form of human
enjoyment . . . but the great charm of this social device is undoubtedly
the freedom it affords. It is to eat, to chat, to lie, to talk, to walk,
with something of the unconstraint of primitive life. We find a
fascination in carrying back our civilization to the wilderness.
—Anonymous, *Appleton's Journal*, 1869

Wish you could take a walk with us on this beautiful island.
Ella thinks it is the prettiest spot she has ever seen.
—Unsigned, postcard from Mackinac Island c. 1910[1]

INTRODUCTION

The journey began and ended with a picnic. I had turned the page of a family album of photographs and saw my grandmother's grinning face as she held a slice of watermelon at a summer picnic in 1911. Grandma Gertrude Doretta [neé Meyer] Hamel, known as "Gertie," had just turned nineteen. She was fashionably attired in a long white dress. She posed in the page's photographs with ten other women perched on a picnic blanket, then frolicking on a seesaw. They lined up in rows of hungry guests, women standing and seated side by side, cheek by jowl, each one of them triumphantly holding an individual slice of watermelon.

Gertie's handwriting across the top of the album page declared that this picnic had taken place in "July 1911," "at Bois Blanc," a small island on Lake Huron in the Straits of Mackinac, about twelve miles from the even smaller but more famous Mackinac Island, and five miles from the place in the Lower Peninsula (Rogers City) where Gertie had lived since about 1901.[2] It was and is a place the locals call "Boblo." Another, renowned "Bob-Lo Island" is situated in the Ontario, Canada, waters of Lake Huron, near the mouth of the Detroit River, more than three hundred miles away. That locale was eventually Michigan's own "Coney Island," an amusement park connected by steamship to the upper Midwest. The other Boblo was also visited by Gertie and friends in the summer of 1915, and the small photos on another album page are marked "Boblo, July 17, '15."

There were other picnics, outings in rowboats and canoes, at the edge of the lakeshore and near the woods, immortalized in the album's photographs. I never met my Grandma Gertie. She died when my mother was a small child. But I marveled at how closely my mother resembled the woman in the picnic photograph, and I casually wondered what else Grandma Gertie had eaten at her island picnic more than a century before. The seemingly simple question about Gertie's picnic menu took me a decade to answer. This book presents what I discovered along the way about the American picnic and its place in individual and collective memory of a changing landscape.

THE HISTORY OF THE PICNIC

It turns out that no truly global history of the picnic exists, and there is not even full agreement about its definition. The picnic has come to refer to "an outing or occasion that involves taking a packed meal to be eaten outdoors," thus embracing essential issues of food history, transportation, and a certain sociability inside a landscape.[3] Should every social meal that is carried outdoors be called a picnic? Probably not. The word itself has unknown origins. Picnics evolved into unique social repasts eaten outdoors, but in some respects, they shared similarities with the characteristics and ingredients of other historical

RIGHT: Gertrude "Gertie" Meyer, c. 1910.
BOTTOM: Gertie's July 1911 picnic on "Bois Blanc" Island from the Hamel family album. She is seated in the front row, far left. Collection of the author.

meals. Walter Levy's *The Picnic: A History* (2013) is a fascinating exploration of the Western world's picnics in art, music, film, and literature.[4] The picnic has a deep and wide geographical past. In ancient Persia, picnics involved frolicking emperors, hunting groups in the countryside, and lovers in gardens. In Japan, elaborate picnic boxes were multitiered lacquered treasures that were presented as wedding gifts to the married couple. I soon discovered that picnics were to be found in many world cultures from which migrants carried their social spirit and practiced their culinary flavors far from home.

All historical meals, including the picnic, reflect the social and economic contexts of the menu's foods. Foods were prepared according to shared cultural tastes and traditions. Whether the sojourners arrived in their new homes in the Americas by boat, train, or automobile, their meals also would reflect the unique and dynamic environments of their new landscapes. The forces of globalization wrought changes in taste, foods and ingredients, and their preparation, preservation, and transportation. The same global network of meals and memories altered many other aspects of the diverse cultural lives of the modern world. The search for Grandma Gertie's picnic menu led me to explore the global and local ingredients of the twentieth-century picnic and revealed key features that reflect the much broader social and environmental contexts of the picnic meal. In fact, the close examination of picnics in one place, the Upper Peninsula of Michigan, across a broad slice of time, gradually became a window on both the ecological and the cultural transformations of the landscape across generations. Historians could "read" about the history of the world by studying the food on any modern plate, including the picnic plate.

The picnic wasn't invented in the twentieth century, although that is surely when it reached the pinnacle of its American popularity and cultural status. By the early part of the nineteenth century, the English already had borrowed the French word for picnic and made it their own. The decidedly French origin of "pique-nique" is obscure (the French verb *pequer* means "to bite"). Its earliest mention in print is in 1692. Originally the term seems to have referred to an indoor, rather than an outdoor, meal that consisted of shared components. It was something like a potluck to which guests brought their own wine. English picnickers also took the picnic outside. They made it bigger and better by staging the picnic within the natural world. They prescribed bills of fare and offered recipes, and then they brought the picnic tradition to the Americas. In England, Isabella Beeton's best-selling

Beeton's Book of Household Management (1859–61) offered general advice for the organizer responsible for an English picnic for forty persons, recommending "A joint of cold roast beef, a joint of cold boiled beef, 2 ribs of lamb, 2 shoulders of lamb, 4 roast fowls, 2 roast ducks, 1 ham, 1 tongue, 2 veal-and-ham pies, 2 pigeon pies, 6 medium-sized lobsters, 1 piece of collared calf's head; 18 lettuces, 6 baskets of salad, 6 cucumbers." And that didn't begin to describe the fruits, pastries, breads, and drinks; her "things not to be forgotten" included condiments: "a stick of horseradish, a bottle of mint sauce well-corked, a bottle of salad dressing, a bottle of vinegar, made mustard, pepper, salt, good oil, and pounded sugar."[5] On the other side of the Atlantic, the English and European picnic came under the influence of a mixture of new environments and far greater cultural diversity.

Settling Down for the American Picnic

Around the mid-nineteenth century, the North American picnic had learned to mimic its English and other European counterparts in new environments. Settlers in New England built towns and farms, and they went on picnics. In natural clearings that were otherwise not active agricultural fields, picnickers found sites in which to gather for picnics. Picnics were held in the cultivated places of memory, in public parks and cemeteries, where the ancestors were acknowledged and invited, as well as in curated places in the accessible countryside, seashore, and lakeside. Where deforestation had taken its toll, the would-be picnickers created sacred groves of trees in cleared lands that became monuments to the changing landscape. Picnics became intergenerational perennial family events, church socials, and opportunities for political campaigning and commemoration. At the Tranquility Grove in Hingham, Massachusetts, the Great Abolitionist "Pic Nic" of August 2, 1844, was held to commemorate the tenth anniversary of abolition in the West Indies and to urge the end of slavery in the United States. Local women prepared an astonishing abundance of food, and even more was brought by visitors from Boston and the other surrounding counties: "bread of all kinds, cakes, pies, tea, coffee, cream, lemons, sugar, boiled ham, neats' tongues, fowls, fruits of all sorts, raisins, fresh vegetables, and flowers."[6] It was recalled as a "monster picnic" by one participant.[7] The picnic food was accompanied by music and prayers, and the day's antislavery speeches were witnessed by an estimated crowd of as many as ten thousand picnickers.

In the UP, the picnic may have been brought from afar, but even its earliest iterations reflected the social engagement of new arrivals within the local landscape, once home to Anishinaabe people. Since the sixteenth and seventeenth centuries, the French had dominated the woods and waters of the region as a colonial power before giving way to the British. Annual summer gatherings around the time of the wild rice harvest brought Indigenous families and groups together for community feasting in outdoor camps. At the 1763 picnic celebration of King George III's birthday, local Anishinaabe people joined in with a game of *baggataway* (a precursor to lacrosse), which they used to stage the capture of the British Fort Michilimackinac. Although King George III would become known as the monarch who lost America, on this occasion the land was quickly reclaimed by British soldiers. Twenty years later, the region was made part of the United States, its territories delineated by an international agreement called out in the 1783 Treaty of Paris. Picnics weren't always as revolutionary as the eighteenth-century event, but they did reflect the changing tapestry of culinary tastes and political traditions.

Indigenous peoples were unable to stop the forces of colonization, as first the French and British and later the Americans encroached on their territories. When statehood was negotiated in 1836–37, Michigan became the twenty-sixth state, through which the Upper Peninsula was annexed as part of the United States. Although the region's forts, waters, and woods had changed hands, the quintessential picnic social persisted through political chessboards, conquests, and changing global powers. Waves of immigrants assisted in the lucrative exercise of global economic growth, from the mining and timber industries to the settlement of the northern wilderness. This disappearing wilderness was a testimony to "progress" and the obligation of civilizations to conquer and destroy what was wild.

PICNICS AS SITES OF MEMORY

Picnics were occurring more frequently as greater numbers of women and their families moved to the Upper Peninsula. The physical features and even the place-names of sites could evoke historical memories. The word "Mackinac" (sometimes spelled "Mackinaw") may come from the Ojibwe word "Michin-nimakinong," which refers to the special connection to land or place, or perhaps from the word that means Great Turtle.[8] On Mackinac Island, Charlotte Tull O'Brien (1812–55) was one of the early women who were resident at the island's fort. Born in England and married to the American fort's British chaplain, she spent long periods of time alone with her children. These days must have reminded Charlotte of her own childhood, when she went fishing in brooks and wandered in the forest around Walthamstow, a London borough comprised of the Waltham Forest and surrounding wetlands, today a nature preserve. On Mackinac Island, her days alone would be punctuated by summer strawberry-picking and picnics near the woods. In a letter to her husband, John, Charlotte described a Fourth of July picnic on nearby Round Island, also in the Straits of Mackinac. In 1848, she wrote that, despite being in a gay party of fifteen picnickers with loads of picnic food, she sorely missed the chaplain:

We started at 2 o'clock in a large batteau [flat-bottomed boat] . . . & we really had a pleasant trip. & such delicious cake, & ice cream, & charlotte ruse, & strawberries & coffee, & almonds & raisins, & wine & B, & lemonade and such quantities of chicken & tongue, & sandwiches, & oceans of cream for all!! all that was wanted was you, yes you . . . at any rate, it raised for a while my sad spirits, and for the dear children it was all unmixed delight.[9]

The menu for Charlotte's picnic included foods that originated far from the UP, including wheat flour, almonds, raisins, coffee, lemons, chicken, beef, wine, and cream—indeed, this might easily have been a picnic back home in Waltham Forest. It also included the ubiquitous picnic food: the simple sandwich, meat, cheese, or other fillings held together by two slices of bread. The picnic experience, by definition, was pleasurable. It was supposed to be fun and effortless, though in truth it could require a great deal of effort and preparation to achieve its element of gaiety. The picnic meal was also a welcome respite to the daily workaday grind of pioneer life, even for an upper-class resident. And although their menus may have celebrated a shared identity emerging far from its home, these early picnics were filled with elitist longings for other vistas and the missing social connections that all immigrants left behind. At the same time, picnics were social gatherings that created new lineages of memory.

In the following generation, the picnic settled down and became an American repast. If possible, it was even more popular at the turn of the late nineteenth and early twentieth centuries. As a social occasion, the classic picnic was informal but also traditional. The notion of enjoying a picnic conjured up not only eating outdoors but also gathering casually in a somewhat spontaneous or impromptu manner. The American chef James Beard put the contradiction perfectly well when he noted that the "oceans" of picnic fare must contrast with daily food, just as the scenic landscapes of the picnic contrasted with the dining room at home.[10] An American picnic had evolved into traveling food, the portable feasts associated with an outing. In addition to being traveling occasions, some picnics were annual or commemorative events. Others were frequent gatherings, but only in the warm summer months.

The simplicity of picnics grew familiar over time, although the description may belie the fact that women's unpaid labor on the home front was a characteristic of gender and other inequalities in the early twentieth century. Elite women and even some middle-class women relied on servants. Rural women did not. Classic picnic foods would come to include fresh and pickled fish, cold fried chicken, deviled eggs, cakes and sweets, bread, and all sorts of sandwiches, all homemade. All the foods together had to amount to abundant contributions for the ravenous hunger expected of picnickers. As Beard astutely noted, "sandwiches might have been invented for this kind of portable feast."[11] The hotdog, centerpiece of the mid-twentieth-century American picnic, had appeared at the Columbian Exposition in Chicago as early as 1893, but it was a long way off from joining the list of expected picnic fare at the turn of the century.

COOKING FOR PICNICS

Searching the region's early cookbooks for picnic recipes revealed that quite a few recipes might have informed the menu of Grandmother Gertie's picnic in 1911. In northern Copper Country, where mining took hold, picnics celebrated the cultural and ethnic diversity of the immigrants. Gertie's family roots were far away in Germany, home to the Meyers only a generation before (and, much earlier, to the Sprankles). Other family ancestors hailed from English and French Canadian stock who had managed to homestead in the UP. Cookbooks across the UP represented the favorite tastes of these and other individual communities and their historical roots. Picnics celebrated both the community's individuality and its place in a larger national experiment conducted by female home cooks preparing foods for the outdoors.

Since the 1840s, the copper and iron mines had been magnets for immigrants, who brought their mining experience, skills, and culinary preferences to the far northwest region of the Keweenaw Peninsula, at the upper northwest corner of the UP. Among the earliest immigrants in the formerly British territory were English and Irish miners and other craftspeople. By the 1860s, Cornish miners from England had introduced the pasty, a baked meat pie easily held in the hand and so a favorite, hearty food suitable for portable picnics and work lunches alike. The pasty became a staple in the miners' dining pails carried underground into the early working mines near the village of Red Jacket (now called Calumet).[12] Yet images and descriptions of the early pasties are surprisingly rare, and even the miner's daily dining pail is seldom glimpsed, since the men tended to sit hunched on their pails when posing for group photographs. Early written recipes for pasties were widespread. They suggest some variations in ingredients, but their size was uniformly large and imitated their Cornish origins as work food away from home.

Although pasties are found in mining communities from Montana to Mexico, the UP versions, notable for their traditional combination of ingredients, appear to be among the earliest and most successful of the global portable foods to move beyond their original ethnic and mining communities. And they made the perfect portable picnic food, as the parallel growth of pasty shops adjacent to picnic tables attests. Mid-twentieth-century pasty recipes in the UP still instructed the baker to cut the dough into circular shapes equal to the size of dinner plates. Wheat flour and lard could be obtained in the grocery stores in the towns of Laurium and Calumet, where beef and pork were also sold in salt barrels. The miner's cottage typically had a garden for growing the potatoes, turnips, rutabagas, carrots, and/or onions. Gardens also became medicine chests, providing herbs and plants for traditional healing practices. Sharing familiar foods from home was a means by which newcomers felt comforted in a strange place.

Attaining the familiar tastes with ingredients from a new continent was not a straightforward task. The butter or lard behaved differently. Even the flour did not perform in a similar manner.[13] Yet somehow the early cooks adapted old recipes to create familiar tastes. Writing to relatives back home in Cornwall, Jinny Penhale described the reception she had received in the Keweenaw Peninsula in the 1850s in terms of the following foods: "A tastie stew," "oggon," "caake," a baked pasty, coffee, and tea, which "made us appy right away."[14] Not all of the miners appreciated the Cornish pasty for their dinner, however. Croatians, who first arrived in large numbers after 1881, called the Keweenaw town of Calumet "New Lipa," as it was becoming their largest settlement in the United States. At least one Croatian miner publicly ridiculed the pasty as "Cousin Jack (the nickname for an Englishman) crap" (*Cuz me drek*).[15] Other ethnic groups added their own twists to the pasty's recipe, such as the Finnish substitution of rutabaga or carrot for potato around the 1860s. The Finns had retained their own name for the Copper Country, Kuparisaari (Copper Island), another sign of their cultural reluctance to become fully assimilated. Finnish handheld savory pies included

Early group of iron miners with dinner pails. Courtesy Jack Deo/Superior View.

the *Karjalanpiirakat* and the *kalakukko*, a fish-stuffed rye bread. To a "Cornish" fish pie the Finns would add cream poured through the steam hole. If the nineteenth-century cookbooks lacked recipes for the pasty of their new homes, the twentieth century brought a full embrace of the customary fare.[16] In contrast to the Cornish, who became the early bosses in the mines, Croatians and Finns sometimes assumed roles of labor activists, challenging the disparities created by industrial capitalism. Among the most famous was Big Annie, a celebrated labor organizer within the mining community of the UP's Copper Country.

BIG ANNIE'S BIG PASTY FIGHT (1913)

At over six feet, "Big Annie" was easily recognized as she led public marches in support of the thirteen thousand striking miners while carrying a ten-foot flagpole with a large American flag waving high over the summer skies of 1913. Workers marched to protest the introduction of the one-man drill, a technological innovation that was destined to cut the labor force. Ana Klobuchar Clemenc (1888–1956) was the daughter of Slovenian immigrants in Calumet (also called Red Jacket), in the UP's Copper Country, a region rich in mining resources and rife with hardship, deplorable conditions, and injustice by the early twentieth century. Her father was a miner, her mother a cook. She married a copper miner.[17] Daughter "Big Annie" was immortalized in the lyrics of "1913 Massacre," written and performed by folksinger Arlo Guthrie. "Look what your greed for money has done," implored Big Annie and Guthrie of the mine owners, who sought profits over safety. Big Annie became the founding president of the Women's Auxiliary No. 15 of the Western Federation of Miners. She and other union organizers held picnics and other events to raise money for members or to fund activities, such as the publication of newspapers. Clemenc was arrested for union activities on September 11, 1913, when she confronted men in the street carrying their metal pails. The pails usually contained a meal of a meat pie or "pasty" (and so presumably they indicated the men were strikebreakers on their way to or from work).[18] She was also one of the organizers of the tragic Christmas party to distribute food and holiday sweets for striking miners and their families at the Italian Hall in Calumet, Michigan, in December 1913, where more than seventy people (mostly children) were killed in a stampede caused by anti-union "thugs." As Annie herself claimed, "we were not fighting with the law but for our bread."[19] Big Annie has been described as an "American Joan of Arc," and her portrait hangs today in the Michigan Women's Hall of Fame.

Big Annie's labor organization was not the only women's group in town. Other women's groups also gathered in the communities of the Copper Country, including the Calumet Women's Club, founded by ten of the community's elite, upper-class women and chartered in 1901 with a philanthropic mission.[20] In 1903, the club invited welfare pioneer Jane Addams of Hull House, a settlement house for women and children in Chicago, to give an inspirational public lecture in support of the care of the poor at the Northern Michigan General Hospital. Addams would go on to win the Nobel Peace Prize. There were also numerous fraternal and benevolent societies that formed the basis for Cornish, Scandinavian, German, Irish, Italian, Polish, and Slovenian social events, including picnics and communal activities, such as winemaking. The various formal women's associations more commonly formed along ethnic rather than class lines. Women helped celebrate and maintain diverse culinary traditions through their published cookbooks, through weekly and monthly luncheon meetings, and in the group picnics they held.

Women picnicking in Laurium Park. Courtesy Keweenaw National Historical Park.

THE LANGUAGE OF MEMORY

Distinctive ethnic groups brought specific foods, which were fitted into the pattern of familiar taste preferences and identified in the specific languages of the homeland brought to the UP. My own great-grandmothers and their descendants were known for their German cakes and a large variety of cookies, including molasses cookies shaped like Santas and given as gifts at Christmastime, and the springerle and pfeffernuesse, with anise seed and lemon, whose recipes are preserved in a family heirloom cookbook.[21] Ethnic associations helped enable the replication of familiar foodways, shared resources and memories, and stamped group identities in periods of adjustment. Initially mostly men arrived as laborers, then later sent for their wives and families. Groceries stocked the highly desirable ingredients, but the isolation caused by frozen lakes and long winters made the UP behave like a remote island, leaving cooks inaccessible and alone. All families relied on the foods of the forest and lake. As individuals intermarried, the lines of heritage became blurred.

Church cookbooks helped bring the language of home to the picnic of life, and their foods participated in the sacred act of remembering. Church and community cookbooks were often compiled as fundraising ventures for local charities and social causes. Cookbook sales supported social welfare projects in the wider community and the construction of church buildings themselves. Finns, Slavs, and Italians may have been united in their support of the Western Federation of Miners and their union strike for better wages, safer conditions, and collective bargaining rights, but their allegiances to different churches sometimes reinforced rather than cut across ethnic lines. Slovenians ate and sang at Saint Joseph's. The Methodists included Cornish families, as well as Finns and Swedes. Croatians built the wood-framed St. John the Baptist Church on Seventh Street in Calumet in 1901. There were six Roman Catholic churches, including Saint Mary's, built in 1897 by the Italian residents, but St. John's opening celebration enjoyed a truly multicultural parade of Cornish musicians, Irish riflemen, and French Canadians, all of whom celebrated the patron saint of miners, St. Barbara.

Cookbooks celebrated the unique cuisines of their religious congregations. The recipes show both overlap and distinctive characteristics. Assertion of ethnic identities was possible, as the region spawned grocery stores that stocked their key ingredients. In the many specialty shops, bakeries, and butcher shops that appeared in the region, shoppers were able to buy a diverse array of items made locally and imported from around the world, such as Kosher meats, saffron cakes and saffron bread, ice cream, curry powder, coffee, salted fish, oysters, and Cuban rum. They could expect the clerks in stores to speak their native languages.[22]

Among the most enduring church cookbooks was *Copper Country Cookery* (1902), compiled by the Ladies' Aid Society of the Laurium Methodist Episcopal Church, which was designed and built by Wells D. Butterfield and boasted a "spacious dining hall and kitchen" funded by the cookbook's editors, who were able to "lure reluctant quarters from masculine pockets."[23] This cookbook incorporated earlier recipes from the Calumet Women's Club, with borrowings from the ever-popular Miss Parloa. Parloa, the Boston author of multiple cookbooks, including *Camp Cookery* (1878), gave practical advice for cooking in a remote area. For example, she recommended the provisions for camping, a list that might also have described the outfitting of required supplies, not unlike those needed for the larder of UP homes or picnics:

> When it can be obtained take Hecker's prepared flour, wheat, rye, Indian, or Graham. From this you will always be sure of good bread and griddle-cakes. Salt pork, smoked ham, bologna sausage, eggs, dried beef, salt fish. Game, fresh fish, and fresh meat are supposed to be obtained in the vicinity of camp. Pilot bread, crackers. Canned fruit and vegetables, where fresh cannot be obtained. Potatoes, beans, onions, Indian meal, molasses, sugar, salt, pepper, mustard, vinegar, butter, coffee, tea, chocolate, rice, oat-meal, baking soda, ginger, spice, soap, parafine [*sic*], candles, and kerosene oil.

Parloa went on to describe the essentials:

> The Essential Utensils are tin kettles with covers, coffee-pot, spiders with covers, gridiron, pans, basins, tin cups, pails, cans, knives, forks, spoons, lanterns, bags, ropes, strings, thread, needles, matches, shovel, axe, hammer, nails, slicking plaster, Jamaica ginger, fishing tackle, gun and ammunition, towels, stockings, and flannel garments. Each and every one of these articles may be found serviceable. The value of a match, a string,

knife, a pin, or a pinch of salt, can never be realized, until in the woods or on the water the need of them has been felt. Parties scorning the idea of bothering with so many things when simply going out to *rough it*, will find it better to see that everything is provided before starting; even then, they will find camp life rough enough.[24]

Despite the surrounding lakes with their own delicacies available in large quantities, Parloa's authoritative recipe for cooking oysters was included by the local women in *Copper Country Cookery*, as was a recipe for "Little Pigs in Blankets," oysters wrapped in bacon and cautiously fried. This recipe was attributed to Mrs. W. J. Webb, but derived from Parloa's version.[25] Surrounded by abundant fresh fish locally, the UP residents were oddly not unlike other nineteenth-century Americans in their love for oysters from afar. These oysters were harvested in large numbers on the East Coast (perhaps 160 million pounds between 1880 and 1910). The Atlantic oysters then were shipped to the UP on ice, and they were also available in tins. They were cheap and clearly trendy.[26]

Other recipes in *Copper Country Cookery* provide evidence of the mingling of Cornish (pasties, scones, "London muffins") and Finnish (fried and baked cheese, *leipajuusto*) traditions. Salted cod, a maritime staple, united most of the community, who enjoyed eating rice and cod croquettes and fish balls. Recipes also reflected the mixing of global goods and readily available, locally sourced ingredients, such as a cake frosting made of both pulverized cane sugar from the tropics and locally produced maple syrup.[27] In the same year that *Copper Country Cookery* appeared, Adelaide Keen published her *With a Saucepan Over the Sea; Quaint and Delicious Recipes from the Kitchens of Foreign Countries* (1902), recognizing the "Out of Many, One People" process of becoming one American table. The successful book suggested the popularity of the interest in and embrace of multiethnic foodways. Yet Keen's recipe book simultaneously reflected the recognition of an "American" and "foreign" divide.[28] In the words attributed to Mark Twain, perhaps a more pragmatic attitude was possible, as "part of the secret of success in life is to eat what you like and let the food fight it out inside."[29]

Other community or church and charity cookbooks intentionally called attention to the multiple ethnic identities of their parishioners at the turn of the century. The *Superior Cook Book* (1905) was prepared by the members

First M. E. Church, Larium, Mich.

Postcard of the Laurium Methodist Episcopal Church (built 1902). Courtesy Keweenaw National Historical Park. MethodistChurchEarly.jpg.

of Grace Church's Women's Auxiliary in Ishpeming.[30] Its global reach was astonishing, with recipes ranging from Mrs. Tonnesen's "Norwegian Fish Balls" and "Oysters a la Kalamazoo," Mrs. Needham's sacrilegious "English Mince Meat Without Meat," and two recipes for "Yorkshire Pudding," to Mrs. Klenner's "Liver Dumplings, German, and Kartoffle [Potato] Torte." Additionally, there were recipes from India and "Indians," suggested by entries for curry sauce, Minnehaha cake, and succotash. Alongside locally originating recipes for planked and pickled whitefish was a recipe for unattainable fresh Atlantic sole by "Oscar" of the Waldorf Astoria. Some of the required foreign ingredients could be locally sourced. Available at Peter Koski & Co. in Ishpeming was a full line of "Fancy and Staple Groceries, Dry Goods, Fresh and Salt Meats."[31] In the 1896 community of Red Jacket, the Vertin Brothers department store similarly sold all manner of ingredients to spice up a monotonous fare, including whole peppers, ginger root, Lea & Perrin sauce, pickles, chowchow, Heinz's ketchup, H. Wichert's pepper sauce, and horseradish by the pint.[32] After all, as the church women in Laurium claimed in their cookbook, "[the] civilized cannot live without cooks."[33] And many of these cooks commanded purchasing power.

Churches were not the only sites of cultural interaction, nor were they the only cause for community picnic gatherings. Masonic lodges welcomed men of different religions, but not races. The Lake Superior Masonic Lodge No. 67 in Ewen and No. 101 in Marquette were chartered in 1854 and 1858, respectively. They offered fraternal meetings for white Masons with repasts of food and drink, as well as annual picnics for their families. Other associations enhanced the historical visibility of global connections by providing opportunities to share heritage foods. The Italian Mutual Benefit Society was formed in 1889, thirty years after the arrival of the first family from Italy. Soon there were Italian boardinghouses and pasta "factories," supplying "Pasti all'italiani" to hotels and retail shops.[34] Daughters of Italy and Daughters of the Eternal City (Rome) appeared as well. By 1910, there were nearly twenty such lodges and mutual aid societies spread across the UP. The ethnic enclaves also picnicked together. Community picnics reinforced a sense of belonging and celebrated locally sourced foods from back home.

The early census data make clear that there were enclaves of language speakers living together across the UP. Hotels, boardinghouses, and associated taverns also accommodated specific ethnic preferences and targeted separate racial groups. The 1860 census reveals that in Marquette, a group of persons marked on the census's racial category as "B" for "Black" and "I" for "Indians" were living together at Hotel Barney's Exchange. African Americans frequently were listed as cooks or barbers in the columns describing their occupations and race. They hailed from Pennsylvania, North and South Carolina, Indiana, Kentucky, Maryland, and Virginia. Black barber Charles Baker resided at Barney's with his Indigenous American wife and their three children. A few African Americans lived as servants with white families, such as George Shiras's photographic assistant Samson Noll (described in the next chapter). An unusually large number of Blacks also appear as cooks on the 1860 census for other parts of the UP, including five in Houghton: George Cook, the two Wilsons, Daniel Reed, and John Anderson. The first African American cookbook was published in Paw Paw, Michigan, about this time (in 1866), and it is likely that Southern food enjoyed a pleasurable reputation throughout the territory.[35] Southern food traditions spread through cookbooks and via people's oral traditions that also preserved recipes. The Houghton men probably had followed the railroad, perhaps as porters and cooks, as it extended African American migration beyond urban centers into the northern woods of the Upper Peninsula at the time of the Civil War. Their unique recipes inspired later generations of picnickers, seeking the comforts of fried chicken, smoked ham, sweet potato anything, and lemonade.[36]

THE PICNIC'S WATERMELON

Another early picnic gathering on Mackinac Island reflected the picnic's commonplace character after the 1880s and the central role played by the watermelon forever afterward. That picnicker was Harold Dunbar Corbusier, who was a small boy when his father moved the family to take up a position as physician at the island's American fort. Harold's childhood diary depicts the frequent spring and summer picnics, where "everyone has a tremendous appetite."[37] Some of those picnics followed the gathering of maple sap in the woods on the west side of the fort. Other picnics required the hire of a boat or canoes to travel to less accessible shores or other islands, including the Les Cheneaux Islands in Lake Huron. In the summer of 1884, Harold described, in the language, spelling, and grammar of a child, just such an August picnic, where "we hired a boat from Davis an [sic] rowed around to the other side of the Island past arch rock and had picnic. We went in wadeing [sic] as it was very warm. We took a big watermelon with us buried it in the san [sic] to keep it kool [sic]."[38] Such intimate occasions for gathering together family and friends contrasted with the more public social meetings at the early island hotels being built for visiting picnickers.

By the time of the young Corbusier, many of the imported picnic ingredients had been embraced as standard local fare. For example, the watermelons he carried and cooled in the beach sands along the lakeshore had been shipped from the Southern fields where they were grown. The fruit traveled north on trains as far as the Great Lakes and then was brought to the UP on steamers and smaller boats throughout the summer season. As Mark Twain noted in his *Puddn'head Wilson* (1894), where he extolled its virtues, "The true southern watermelon is a boon apart and not to be mentioned with commoner things. It is chief among this world's luxuries, king by the grace of God over all the fruits of the earth. When one has tasted it, he knows what the angels eat."[39] The lake ice prevented the deliveries of food and other supplies in the winter months, so only the warmth of the late spring and summer brought the return of true picnic fare and the ingredients for weather-dependent social gatherings.

In virtually all types of weather, the early picnics included tea and/or coffee, as many of the early photographs attest. These hot drinks were considered essential provisions that fueled the long and strenuous workdays. The picnic ingredients and many other commodities consumed in nineteenth-century meals connected the Upper Peninsula to the Caribbean and South America, Asia, or Europe through a global marketplace. In contrast, maple syrup was collected locally and frequently substituted for the expensive, tropical sugar in recipes and in the teacup. Global foods were imported and embraced locally. Besides watermelons, many nonlocal foods regularly found their way to the UP, altering the parameters of local and seasonal fare.

Other picnic selections were determined by the food trends of the day. Pickles and jams carried flavors in an otherwise monotonous and bland diet before refrigeration. In the twentieth century, technologically processed foods would replace preindustrial delights. Most women grew kitchen gardens of vegetables and herbs. They made their own pickles by canning at home. Near the end of the nineteenth century, the industrialization of the food industry spilled over

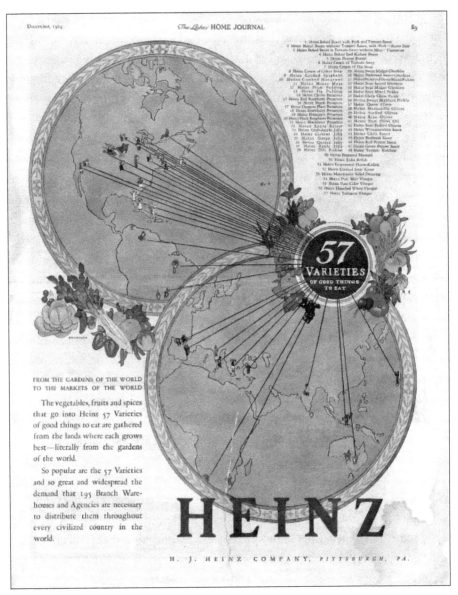

Heinz advertisement showing their global reach, *Ladies' Home Journal*, 1924. Courtesy H. J. Heinz Company Records, MSS 057, Detre Library & Archives, Senator John Heinz History Center, Pittsburgh, PA.

onto the picnic blanket. Everything from mass-manufactured marshmallows to bottled condiments, pickles, and packaged meats soon became available to the daily diet of Americans.[40] Foods now came in tin cans, which the archaeology of picnic sites would confirm. As the H. J. Heinz Company's Heinz 57 Varieties of Good Things to Eat professed in a 1924 advertisement in the *Ladies' Home Journal*, their "vegetables, fruits, and spices . . . are gathered from the lands where each grows best—literally from the gardens of the world."[41] From the gardens of the world to the markets of the world, manufactured products traversed national boundaries. Baked beans, ketchup, and chowchow pickles were popular canned or bottled products, reflecting the movement of foodstuffs and tastes along global maritime routes. The Heinz Company's products would be distributed globally, "throughout every civilized country in the world." The Heinz 57 Varieties advertisement's map of global food connections proudly proclaimed the imperial origins of the familiar in faraway lands from Africa, Eurasia, and Australia to the Americas.

Not only was global trade delivering a greater variety of foods than ever before but, importantly, the population of picnickers had also changed dramatically by the early twentieth century. Populations had increased as immigrants to the Upper Peninsula followed in the wake of mining, logging, and homesteading opportunities well underway. For example, in the generation between 1850 and 1880, the population of Marquette, the region's largest community, rose from 136 to 25,394, and it reached 46,739 by 1910, when the growth leveled off. The census records also document the arrival of immigrants to the UP from all parts of the globe, although some categories (such as "Hungarian") were imprecise indications of ethnicity and locality on modern maps. The picnickers and foods reflected the mobility of individuals, the fluidity of ethnic designations that were transnational, and the shifting nation-state boundaries themselves. The nation's culinary diasporas were being created, and their members also went on picnics.

THE OTHER INGREDIENTS OF THE PICNIC

The ingredients of the individual picnic were also shaped by the purely practical need for mobility. Picnic foods were transported from fields to markets, then from markets to homes and from homes back to picnic fields. Foods that traveled well were selected. Picnickers were advised to "Make it strong and keep it light, for an ounce in the morning weighs a pound at night."[42] The new science of home economics gave advice on the "well-selected picnic basket" that held both foods and equipment.[43] Ordinary foods and special picnic fare were both welcome. While processed foods were available at the end of the nineteenth century, they didn't entirely replace homemade versions. At the end of the century, even canned mackerel was advertised using the trope of picnic scenes,[44] but home cooks were encouraged to find the time to make their own "Tomato Catsup."[45] Turn-of-the-century local cookbooks carried globally inspired recipes for curry and rice, as well as India relish; they also touted German potato salad and frenchified recipes (always with classic sauces).[46] In contrast, picnic foods relied on the twin poles of simplicity of ingredients and ease of transportability. Mostly precooked foods were brought to turn-of-the-century picnics. Smoked and pickled foods were also popular in an age without refrigeration. In the early twentieth century, recipes for macaroni salad were added to those for hot dishes, with macaroni and dairy products (milk and cheese) commonly appearing in cookbooks. By about 1913, cooks flavored the cold pasta salad with celery, pimento olives, sour pickles, onions, hard-boiled eggs, and salad dressing.[47] Stuffed eggs (also called deviled eggs) used butter rather than mayonnaise as an early-twentieth-century binding element in their popular recipes. In *Copper Country Cookery* (1902), Laurium cooks were advised to slice the boiled eggs in half and "put the halves together" again after stuffing them.[48]

Sandwiches were among the stalwarts of picnics, being easily prepared, crowd-pleasing, and mobile foods. This remained true in the twenty-first century, when *Food & Wine* magazine declared sandwiches still to be "the centerpiece of a picnic spread."[49] However, the choice of specific sandwich ingredients in the early twentieth century might look odd to modern cooks: onions, radishes and butter, chocolate, preserves, and all manner of pickles were common. Even their breads displayed the range of both local and foreign-derived flavors, from saffron to corn and graham flours. In this way, sandwiches became the quintessential picnic fare, defying the fact that not only the foods but also the picknickers were required to travel far to reach their picnic sites.

TRAVELING FOR A PICNIC

My grandmother and her friends would have walked, rowed boats, or taken a ferry from their island and mainland homes to reach their picnic destination in July 1911. Beginning in the nineteenth century, the UP began to welcome a temporary population of leisure travelers and tourists seeking the scenic beauty and health benefits of its restorative wilderness. Despite the severe changes in the natural landscape wrought by the logging and mining of the early migrants, the UP still offered enough of its remaining forests, lakes, and unpolluted air and made them accessible to those sick and weary of gritty city life. Steamers linked up with rail lines and carried the escaping urbanite passengers and their trunks from Down Below cities to coastal docks Up North, where locals met them with music and food in the summer months.[50] Many of the early tourists traveled by train to lake ports and boarded overnight steamers headed for Mackinac Island. From there, some vacationers traveled on smaller vessels to other destinations in the UP. Early hotels and exclusive clubs appeared along the lakeshores to cater to the leisure time and hunting and fishing interests of guests. The locals, including a cadre of African Americans, worked for the tourists and summer guests, as guides, housecleaners, and cooks, or by delivering groceries and supplies, until the automobile and roadside motels put an end to the exclusive lakefront hotel establishments and made steamer service redundant.[51]

THE EARLY SUMMER HOTELS

Although an array of earlier hotels had been built to accommodate temporary travelers in Sault Ste. Marie, St. Ignace, Marquette, and a few other UP places, the most lavish of hotels appeared at the end of the nineteenth century. Built in 1887, the Grand Hotel on Mackinac Island was a destination reached by steamer. Steamboats had been inaugurated in 1819, and they gradually brought greater ease of movement for visitors and residents alike. Guests had been traveling to Mackinac Island for "health and refreshment" since the 1820s.[52] Until 1895, the strategic island also was home to the British and then American fort and hosted a significant military presence. Even in the 1840s, its village was not much more than a few wooden homes with cedar bark roofs, an Indian dormitory, the office and home of the territory's Indian agent (Henry Schoolcraft), the mission church, a school, the American Fur Company's retail shop, fishing docks, and icehouses. Other businesses included several modest guesthouses and hotels. Still, despite this miscellany of establishments, there was an allure, romantic and picturesque scenery, and "no finer climate in the world."[53] One traveler, having

Selling picnic baskets and *makaks* to the tourists on Mackinac Island, c. 1905. Photograph courtesy of Library of Congress, LC-D4-33745.

voyaged by canoe around Lake Superior eating mostly pork and dough boiled in a kettle on its sandy shores, arrived on Mackinac Island in 1846 and prophetically surmised its potential as "indeed one of the most unique and delightful places in the world . . . [which] will soon be the fashionable resort of summer travelers."[54]

Urban wealth Down Below came at the cost of gloomy and polluted cities at the end of the nineteenth century. Tiring of the city sidewalks, the leisure classes of Detroit, Cleveland, Pittsburgh, and Chicago eagerly boarded trains to reach the floating hotels that would carry them to the Upper Peninsula in the season of navigation, the summer. While writers extolled the "tonic character of its climate," visitors sought both health and pleasure.[55] On Mackinac Island, the Grand Hotel offered both. Visitors enjoyed summer breezes on the longest hotel porch in the world. Guests rode horseback, mounted bicycles, rented canoes and rowboats, and hiked to island picnics. Dances, drinking, and gambling filled the moonlit nights on the island. Room rates started at three dollars per night.

TALL TALES, POSTCARDS, AND SOUVENIRS

Visiting picnickers also sought mementos of their stays. The availability of curiosities was mentioned by Henry Rowe Schoolcraft, a member of an 1820 scientific expedition that reached the Great Lakes in early June.[56] In 1841, a Swedish traveler observed maple sugar, wild rice, and baskets decorated with porcupine quills being offered to steamboat passengers from a single shop at the Mackinac Island wharf.[57] In 1847, island souvenirs were "agates and pebbles of loveliest hue."[58] By 1890, the locally made "Indian curiosities" were now sold near the docks, in shops, and even from a stall on the grounds of the Grand Hotel. They included woven mats, corn husk dolls, and birch, sweet-grass, and porcupine-quill baskets. Miniature *makaks* (small birch food baskets) filled with maple sugar and large picnic baskets were offered to tourists eager to experience the local life, especially the food scene outdoors. Although plenty of American flags waved in the island breeze, the souvenir and grocery shops also sold global goods shipped in from around the world. Not much food was grown on the island itself, which was less than four square miles in size, but "fruits and nuts in season" were promised. The "Oriental Novelties," "Indian

Curiosities," and other "assortment of Fancy and Goods too numerous to mention" were claimed to have sold "like hot cakes" to the tourists.[59]

There were also visual mementos, photographs and postcards that were eagerly sought after. Invented in 1861, the postcard became a popular item for communication via postal carriers. Eventually, it was also a means of advertising the features of a place. The postcard's so-called golden age (1907–15) witnessed a flurry of images being exchanged by travelers and tourists. Following in the footsteps of earlier nineteenth-century artists who had produced sketches, paintings, and engravings of the local scenery, photographers made certain scenes iconic, through repetition and the creation of postcards sold to tourists by local businesses. They produced influential images in work that was patronized by the visitors, who posed for individual and group portraits. The increasing popularity of postcards paralleled the growth of tourism.

One of the earliest photographic artists to set up a studio, the professional photographer William H. Gardiner, arrived on Mackinac Island in the 1890s. Over the course of the next four decades, he returned every summer from his winter home in Florida to document the island's activities, including its picnics.[60] Introduced by Eastman Kodak in 1900, the Brownie box camera brought the notion of the snapshot to the masses, including my young Grandma Gertie. Still, many people turned to professional images for more satisfying mementos. The Detroit and Cleveland Steam Navigation Company advertised their "Lake Tour to Picturesque Mackinac" in a passenger guidebook: roundtrip transportation between Cleveland and Mackinac Island, ten meals at fifty cents each, and accommodations in an upper berth cost eighteen dollars per person in 1884.[61] Mackinac Village was described as "a perfect curiosity in itself," while its local features, Arch Rock and Sugar Loaf Rock, "alone possess attractions sufficient to justify a visit to Mackinac Island."[62] They were already iconic vistas thanks to early paintings and engravings widely published and the thousands of postcards and photographic portraits in circulation.

Portrayed as the ideal response to the "high pressure of American life," the lake tour also suggested the destination of picturesque Mackinac was the grandest and most romantic "return to Nature."[63] At the same time, it was readily admitted that most of the ancient forests were already gone from the island, having been replaced by young growth.[64] The wood for building and various other uses on Mackinac came from other places, including Bois Blanc

Island, where my grandmother's 1911 picnic took place.[65] The revelation of deforestation didn't stop the flow of visitors. Around 1908, Gardiner produced a thirty-four-page brochure that featured his photographs and played up the island's historical significance: *Mackinac Island: The Ancient Michilimackinac.*[66] By 1910, postcards were particularly important advertisements for the tourist attractions of the Upper Peninsula. Images with iconic poses by and on top of natural wonders like Arch Rock were recognizable trophies for tourists and picnickers alike from the late nineteenth and early twentieth centuries onward.

The tourism craze spread from Mackinac to other islands. Whereas Mackinac Island residents in the 1880s might head by rowboat or canoe to the Les Cheneaux Islands and "intend to find a lonely island & camp there," a string of cottages and hotels were being built there as well.[67] These new establishments marked local know-how, from food to fishing. The locals possessed specialized knowledge about a place based on their familiarity with the ever-changing off-season rhythms. They maintained personal connections through family memories of their participation in social occasions like picnics. A round of picnics followed the tourists everywhere they traveled. And, in return, residents of the Les Cheneaux Islands rowed to Round Island or Bois Blanc for their own picnics. Eventually the locals also opened their own hotels and welcomed the tourists attracted to their scenic vistas. One of the grandest of the early hotels in Cedarville was the Islington. Built in 1897, the hotel quickly became a showplace, where guests dressed up for dinners of whitefish and lake perch that had been caught in nets earlier in the day. Lunchtimes and teatimes found the guests having informal picnics and playing games on manicured lawns and lakefront beaches. Nearby, the Cedar Inn, once called "Hodeck House," competed for another share of the market. Originally, the building was a log-hewn boardinghouse built in the 1890s in "Swedish fashion." Adorned with a décor inspired locally and globally, with its stuffed birds, "Oriental" and deerskin rugs, and Chinese lanterns, the Cedar Inn became known for Sunday roast duckling dinners.[68] Guests could sit in rocking chairs on the wide porch, from which they enjoyed the view of Cedarville Bay.

Even smaller establishments organized fishing and other activities for their guests. One of those guests was Robert Heuck, who recalled the central role that picnics played in the social life of Les Cheneaux summers at the turn of the century. According to Heuck's account,

Picnics at the Snows really started as fish shore dinners. Perch of three-quarters to a pound were common. We never took anything on our own picnics except a frying pan, coffee pot, bacon, bread, coffee, cream, and sugar. The only picnic I recall that was with sandwiches, hard boiled eggs and a few trimmings was the Big One [forty people at McGulpins around 1902]. . . . The launches Heuck and Islington, with two tows, carried the crowd. We would tow a rowboat, let members fish for an hour or so, then pick them up and tow them to the picnic. They would clean the fish while they were being towed.[69]

The fishing grounds then could turn up more than one hundred perch in less than an hour, to the delight of all of the hungry picnickers.

Picnickers were both observers and participants. They consumed the panoramic views of iconic scenes like Arch Rock on Mackinac Island and Pictured Rocks National Lakeshore on Lake Superior. They curated the landscape that surrounded them. The Upper Peninsula was comprised of so many more scenic vistas than the popular Mackinac Island and Pictured Rocks—Drummond Island, Bois Blanc, Beaver Island, Isle Royale, the Les Cheneaux Islands (thirty-six islands in all), Picnic Rock, Tahquamenon Falls, the Porcupine Mountains,

Postcard of the Islington Hotel and dock. Courtesy Les Cheneaux Historical Association, Cedarville, MI.

and dozens more scenic shorelines and viewpoints—and nearly all welcomed visitors for more than a century of well-honed hospitality. From the end of the nineteenth century, the UP's picnickers were mostly born on other continents. Did Croatian immigrants stand above the Pictured Rocks and remember Plitvice Lakes and the waterfalls and woodlands of their homes across the Atlantic? Did French immigrants ponder the cliffs of Étretat in Normandy or the French Canadian Niagara when they gazed out at Arch Rock? Did Cornwall's rugged clifftops and coves come to the minds of English sojourners who boarded the picnic boats and trains remembering the scenes they left behind? The region's landscapes were theaters of memory, inviting sentimental longing for the past, as well as offering new attachments to the lands and lakes belonging to an uncertain future. Picnic meals were comprised of more than foods. They were both the meals and the memories that carried residents and tourists to this unique and special place, the fragile wilderness of the Upper Peninsula. The next chapter explores the changing landscapes of its picnics through the lives of picnickers and the habitats of fellow residents from the animal kingdom: the porcupines.

FINDING WORDS AND WATERMELONS

There is something about a picnic that levels the social playing field, acknowledging that basic truth: memory is hunger and shared memory is the stuff of food history.[70] Watermelons were popular picnic fare even as far north as the UP. The watermelon fruit (*Colocynthis citrullus* and *C. lanatus*) was first domesticated in central and southern Africa. Watermelon then spread to other parts of the African continent and beyond Africa to Eurasia, eventually arriving in the Americas in the post-Columbian era. Grown from seeds brought by enslaved Africans and European sailors, watermelon was particularly well suited to the climate and soils of the American South, and it became associated with rural stereotypes of African Americans. Racist depictions of watermelon crops appeared after the Civil War and later resurfaced in the early twentieth century.[71]

I found a watermelon postcard among my grandmother Gertie Hamel's treasured mementos and images left behind by a tragically short life (she died at age forty-five, leaving four children, including my mother, who was six years old). I set it aside from the other sources and facets of this project. The postcard was embarrassingly racist and sat stubbornly on the corner of my desk, painfully contrasting with the gaiety of typical picnic and other photographs I had encountered in my research. Its imagery depicted a field of oversized, giant watermelons, amidst small and childish African American field workers engaged in eating or cutting the fruit. A white man in a horse-drawn wagon observes the activity as if assuming the role of a plantation overseer or field driver, conjuring up the legacy of enslavement. The card is titled "Carving One of Our Watermelons" (c. 1909) and was reproduced by the Martin Post Card Company. The Martin company became well known for its use of trick photography to create millions of exaggerated ("tall-tale") scenes of animals, fish, and giant vegetables, from pumpkins to peaches, corn to cabbages, scenes that seemed to confirm the myth of abundance associated with American life and picnics. The genre of exaggerated postcards made William Martin a millionaire.

"Dear Gertie," reads the message on the back of the postcard, "You said in your letter about a picture. I lost that one and am sending a card of myself in exchange." The card's handwritten note is signed "Henry" and it is dated and postmarked October 28, 1910, the autumn before the photograph of my grandmother's watermelon picnic.[72] I searched for a Henry among the possible men living in or near Rogers City at the time. Roy Henry Young was about the right age, and he was working in a photographic studio in Sault Ste. Marie, on Lake Superior. Gertie had kept a 1913 photograph of Young, who was also a part-time

Exaggerated postcard of a watermelon field. Martin Post Card Company, 1909. Collection of the author.

lumberman. He was a friend of Gertie's eventual husband, Robert Hamel, whom she married in 1916. Besides, he went by the name "Roy." Henry Hoeft was a bit young. Born in 1897, he would have been just thirteen years old at the time. Gertie also had a cousin Henry Meyer.

Who was Henry? He was most likely Henry Walter Uhl, the thirty-year-old photographer. The Uhl Studio operated between c. 1910 and 1920 in Rogers City, where Gertie lived with her family. The studio occupied the same building (203 North Third Street) and was next door to the Hoeft Department Store, where Gertie worked as a "sales lady" (the occupation listed on her marriage certificate). Another page of her album's photographs shows her posing inside and on the boardwalk in front of the store. At Hoeft's, she worked alongside Uhl's wife, Edna May Hoeft, whom he married in September 1908. As a photographer, Henry Uhl would have had access to any number of popular photographic postcards. The card was mailed in Detroit to Gertie, who was visiting nearby Fair Haven at the time. Why did he choose an image of the watermelon field, an image historians view today as racist? Was it meant to conjure memories of a picnic?

Other scholars have considered closely the meaning of some of the racist associations with watermelon and other foods. Kyla Wazana Tompkins suggested that "to taste food, and to taste certain forms of desire, is to experience that which cannot yet be put into words."[73] Indeed, opposition to such imagery has a long history. An attempt to initiate a "Colored American Day" at the 1893 World's Columbian Exposition in Chicago by giving out two thousand free watermelons had been a badly misguided answer to the African American boycott of the world's fair.[74] In the case of my grandmother's postcard, the card was chosen and sent, creating a conversation of image and word between the sender (Henry) and the recipient (Gertie). As one historian has noted, "tourists who sent postcards and recipients who received them participated in a much larger conversation about a place that went far beyond the image, title, caption, and even the brief text scribed by the sender."[75] While both Gertie Meyer and Henry Uhl married others, perhaps they once shared a picnic watermelon.

What was the impact of the conversation created by my grandmother's keepsake postcard? The same sender addressed another postcard to Gertie, this one seemingly innocuous, the next month. Dated November 1910, it began with the lament, "Why haven't you written me?" As much as it is appealing to think the awkward silence was the consequence of the offensive nature of the earlier card, it is equally difficult to imagine that racist humor cultivated by white privilege grew only in the isolation of faraway fields across the lake. It licked the shores of home Up North and echoes among the region's family memories.

Most of the early sweet pickle recipes called for a combination of whole cloves, allspice, cassia buds, a stick of cinnamon, and green ginger root. The lack of electric refrigeration and the impact of maritime tastes meant that vinegary flavors permeated the turn-of-the-century table, encompassing pickled fish, pickled vegetables, and pickled fruits and extending the summer season far beyond picnic days. Global condiments were mimicked locally to add variety to an otherwise repetitive menu, and the early cookbooks regularly included shared recipes for such condiments as chowchow, cherry ketchup, and various South Asian–inspired chutneys.

Grandma Gertie's Watermelon Pickles[76]

Ingredients

2 cups sliced watermelon rind
(the white part of the flesh
cut from a 2-pound fruit)
4 cups water
1 tablespoon plus 1 teaspoon salt
¾ cup apple cider vinegar
1 cup sugar

5 whole cloves
5 whole black peppercorns
¼ teaspoon allspice
2 teaspoons cassia buds
1 stick cinnamon
½ finger of green ginger, peeled
and finely sliced (optional)

Instructions

Prepare the watermelon by peeling the green skin and scooping out the red melon (but leaving behind a small bit of pink) for a separate occasion. The remaining pink and white flesh should be sliced into thin pieces, about 2 inches long and ⅛ of an inch thick. Boil the watermelon rind in salted water for about 5 minutes. Strain and set aside in a glass bowl.

In a heavy saucepan, combine vinegar, remaining 1 teaspoon salt, and sugar, with spices. Bring to a boil, stirring until the sugar has dissolved. Pour the liquid over the rinds. If needed, use a smaller bowl or plate to press rinds down and keep them submerged. Cover the larger bowl with plastic wrap and refrigerate overnight.

The next day, strain the liquid from the rinds back into a saucepan and bring to a boil. Pour over the rinds and repeat one more time before placing the rinds and liquid in lidded jars. Refrigerate for up to several weeks.

THE 1911 PICNIC

Picnics ended with watermelon slices, and this was true of Grandma Gertie's picnic in 1911. Nineteen years old at the time of the Bois Blanc picnic, Gertie and her friends likely brought nothing more elaborate than sandwiches and perhaps cookies or cake for the remaining part of their shared meal outdoors. One flavor that Cornish, Scandinavian, German, and other immigrants could agree on was saffron. Originating in Asia, the crocus was widely grown in other parts of Europe and even in England by the seventeenth century. Adapted from the Calumet Woman's Club *Copper Country Recipes* (ninth edition, 1979), the first recipe below can also be made into a small bread loaf to be sliced for sandwiches. It needs little more than butter and/or jam but can stand up to ham or other cold leftover meats. The saffron bread reflected the Swedish, German, and Finnish heritage of baking saffron buns for St. Lucia's Day and other holidays. Saffron was also found in Dutch and Cornish tea-cakes in the mining community of Laurium. Spicy, edible nasturtiums were popular additions to summertime sandwiches, and they also adorned the region's cakes.

Mrs. Alger Train's Saffron Buns

Saffron Buns: Leave 1 tablespoon saffron steeped in ½ cup boiling water overnight. To ¾ cup milk scalded and cooled, add 1 package dry yeast or 1 cake compressed yeast, 1 teaspoon sugar, ⅓ cup water and 1½ cups flour. Add saffron liquid and saffron. Beat until smooth.

Let stand about an hour in a warm place. Add ¾ cup sugar, 1 teaspoon salt, 1 teaspoon nutmeg, 1 teaspoon lemon extract if desired, and ½ cup melted shortening (part lard), 1 cup raisins, currants, or mixed fruit, and 3 cups flour.

Knead until smooth and elastic. Cover and let rise until double in bulk. Shape into buns the size desired and let rise until light. Bake at 350 degrees for 25 to 30 minutes.

Slice and butter, adding jam, thinly sliced onions or ramps, pickles, or nasturtium flower petals for a sweet and peppery twist that also matches the bread's bright, orange color.

Great-Grandmother's "Sound of Stars" Cake[77]

Minnehaha was the name given to the beloved figure in Henry Wadsworth Longfellow's famous epic poem *The Song of Hiawatha* (1855), inspired by his friend Henry Rowe Schoolcraft's romanticized stories of the Upper Peninsula and Schoolcraft's wife Jane, known as *Bamewawagezhikaquay*, "Woman of the Sound the Stars Make Rushing Through the Sky," and the granddaughter of an Ojibwe chief.[78] This family recipe once was called "Minniehaha Cake." A ship named *Minnehaha* sank in Lake Michigan in 1893, and a recipe for Minnehaha cake also appeared that year in the Chicago *World's Fair Recipe Book* (1893).[79] Gertie's mother, Ella, passed down her cake recipe to women in the family, including to Gertie's niece Joyce Meyer Pines. Joyce recalled that Ella Sprankel Meyer, a mother of eleven children, baked this cake nearly every weekend to offer to the visiting family and friends, who stopped by the Second Street house in Rogers City where Gertie grew up. A recipe for "Minnehaha Cake" attributed to Mrs. George Bamford and made with egg whites only also appears in the *Superior Cook Book* (1905), where the recipe inadvertently omits the cake's flour.[80] Great-grandmother Ella reportedly made date, raisin, and lemon fillings to spread between the layers of her cake. Boiled icing with maple syrup and candied ginger might also adorn the cake top.

Ingredients

Cake
½ cup butter
1½ cups sugar
2 eggs plus 2 more egg whites,
    separated and beaten
    (reserve yolks for filling)

1 cup milk
2½ cups flour
½ teaspoon salt
2 teaspoons baking powder
1 teaspoon essence (vanilla)

Filling/Icing

½ cup date syrup
1½ cups maple syrup (or omit date
   syrup and use 2 cups
   maple syrup)

2 egg yolks (see above), well beaten
   for about 5 minutes
¼ cup candied ginger (ground or in
   pieces) or nuts for the topping

Instructions

Cream butter and sugar; add eggs. Stir in milk. Gradually add the sifted dry ingredients and, finally, vanilla. Bake at 350 degrees in two 9-inch layer pans for about 30 minutes.

Bring the syrup to 240 degrees (using a candy thermometer, let the syrup reach just the soft ball stage). Very slowly add syrup to the egg mixture. Beat until thick and fluffy. This is enough frosting for a two-layer cake. Decorate with candied ginger, which provides a starry twinkle to the cake top.

Aunt Eileen's Easy Bars

Eileen Meyer Radtke (1913–89) was Gertie's youngest sister. She carried on the family tradition of weekly baking of sweet cookies and cakes, greeting visitors with the tin filled with a variety of goodies she always kept on hand in her Rogers City home.

Ingredients

1⅓ cups brown sugar
1 stick butter
2 eggs
1 cup flaked coconut or chocolate (or
   butterscotch) bits or dates and nuts

1½ cups flour
2 teaspoons baking powder
½ teaspoon salt
1 teaspoon vanilla essence

Instructions

Cream the sugar and butter. Add eggs, one at a time. Add the chosen filling. Stir in dry ingredients. Add vanilla. Spread in a greased 9 × 13 pan and bake at 350 degrees for 20 minutes. Cut into squares after cooled.

2

THE PORCUPINE

All this wildness
embeds itself
in one bristling dot,
ledger's entry
in a bank of forest,
punctuation
of the truest economy.
—Naila Moreira, "Porcupine"[1]

It was an improbable nighttime scene at the turn of the twentieth century. A newfangled camera. Two men, one black and one white, paddling together across Whitefish Lake in a canoe. An intricate system involving a kerosene lantern, trip wires, and magnesium. Flashes in the darkness revealing secrets of the black night: this one, an albino porcupine; another one, three wide-eyed deer leaping. Near Marquette, in Michigan's Upper Peninsula, the photographic assistant Samson Noll, a former slave from Virginia, worked alongside Pittsburgh naturalist George Shiras III, the first to photograph wildlife at night using a technique learned through Noll from Ojibwe hunters.[2]

Noll cooked the camp breakfast the next morning for Shiras, who later extolled the virtues of Noll's culinary talents, saying Noll "knew the secrets of the wilderness."[3] In turn-of-the-century parlance, was this not a racist characterization common to the time—the person of color equated with the antithesis of "civilization," thus forever associated with "wilderness"? Yet the photography assistant Samson Noll was remarkable. He was one of many African Americans who came north during Reconstruction, reinventing himself as opportunities allowed. Hunter and guide, Noll was the cook creating for a wilderness party his very own "poetry of ham and eggs" and other delectable meals, as photographer Shiras recorded: "[On] July 7, 1894 . . . [f]or breakfast we had, among other delicious things, the fish which we had caught. Again, were we inspired with ardent admiration for Samson, the cook."[4] Noll was also the bridge between Shiras and the nighttime secrets of the wilderness. Whose wilderness was this, captured by day and night, with gun, fishing line, camera, and cooking pot?

All picnics connected diners to a place in the landscape. This basic feature of the picnic begs the question of how picnickers also curated the landscape of their repasts. In the Upper Peninsula, the picnics danced with the edge of the wilderness. As I looked at imagery of the classic picnic through time, I realized

Albino porcupine on a floating log at night, Whitefish Lake, Lake Superior region, Michigan, July 1, 1905. Photograph by George Shiras III, 1905. Courtesy DeVos Museum of Art, Marquette.

almost all historical picnic scenes I encountered, including those of my grand-mother, were either on the lakeshore or in clearings adjacent to the woods, also the favorite habitats of the porcupine. These were very specific Up North landscapes, and they turned out to be the only places where porcupines were routinely sighted historically. My own first glimpse of the small and spiky, quilled creature had been next to the woods in Hessel Bay at dusk. I remember its quills made the animal seem much larger to my four-year-old eyes than it really turned out to be.

There, *near* the forest, were the places in the landscape where picnickers and porcupines met. The New World porcupine is a species that today and long ago favored wooded areas, showing adaptations for arboreality.[5] The porcu-pine of northern Michigan spends roughly half of the time in treetops.[6] The quills of the porcupine suggest the animal's evolutionary specialization was also well suited for open spaces, where some form of defense against predator carni-vores would be required equipment. In the UP, the porcupine's predators were the fisher, coyote, and bobcat. The albino porcupine was a genetic anomaly, but like any and every porcupine, it represented the forest edge in its unique way. Shiras observed his special porcupine:

> When alarmed and on the defensive, the porcupine raises the quills with the long hairs of the body at right angles to the skin, just as the hair rises on the neck of an angry dog. With its back humped the creature becomes a mass of bristling weapons, so that most of its enemies give it a wide berth. It appears at such times much larger than it really is.[7]

The quills not only deceive its would-be predators but also protect the porcu-pine from attacks from behind and above. Porcupines typically live in dens that are securely inside caves, hollow trees, or logs, traveling to food trees at dusk and nighttime. Among the first night photographs anywhere in the world, the black-and-white images of an albino porcupine on a floating log, were taken by Shiras, who visited the porcupine's habitat between 1897 and 1904. The photographer went back to view his porcupine repeatedly. Later scientific studies have suggested that porcupines live about six to ten years in the wild and between six and twenty-two years in captivity.[8] Shiras was not the first nor would he be the last to capture the essence of this unusual animal on the edge of the forest. And shifting porcupine populations were not the only signals of the changes in the picnic's landscape.

At the Edge of the Woods

Generations of Indigenous people observed the porcupine of the Upper Peninsula before my pioneering great-grandparents arrived. For them, the porcupine was associated with the edge of the forest, the transition between human habitation and deep wilderness. The porcupine or *gaag* (in Ojibwe; pl. *gaagwag*) was a fellow inhabitant, and its presence was a harbinger of the altered landscape. Weighing in at about twenty pounds, the North American porcupine (*Erethizon dorsatum*) was a medium-sized rodent, usually considered an herbivore (at times, they did gnaw on bones), eating a range of plants, barks, pine needles, grasses, leaves, seeds, stems, and berries. Although slow moving, porcupines employed their coats of long, sharp quills to their advantage by contracting muscles that caused the quills to bristle and stand up when threatened. Native peoples used the thirty thousand or more quills on each animal they harvested to decorate birch bark and woven basket containers, as well as to adorn deerskin leather garments. They made hair combs from the underside of the porcupine's tail and used the quills in the tapping of maple sugar. Indigenous people also consumed the porcupine for medicinal purposes and as meals of roasted and stewed meat, particularly during times of famine. The habitat of the porcupine was on the edge of the forest, in hollow trees or rocky areas. Ojibwe-speakers discriminated between being "*in* the wilderness" (*bagwaj*) and *on its edge* (*jigaakwaa*), by or near the woods.[9] The forest's porcupine was most often glimpsed on its edge.

Ojibwe also discriminated between their own and other human foodways, which they believed belonged to different environments. They and other Algonquian speakers conceptualized the food they ate in terms of proximity to lake and tree. Indeed, there were some people known as "Tree-eaters," who were believed to consume primarily bark and nuts.[10] To enter dense woods (*zagaakwaa*) could mean that one was approaching hard times. According to Roger Williams, in his *A Key into the Language of America* (1643), the first printed treatise on Algonquian languages, the question "what will you eat" (*Teaqua-cummeich*) could be well satisfied with a picnic of sorts. Williams described the Algonquin cooks around Narragansett as such: "Every man carrying a *little Basket* of this [Parch'd meal] on his *back*. . . . With a *spoonful* of this *meale* and a *spoonful* of water from the *Brooke*, have I made many a good dinner and sup-per."[11] Awareness of surroundings and classification of the foodways in environmental terms resulted in the mobility of meals that permeated the region's most ancient cultures. What they held in common with modern picnics ensured their survival across the centuries.

Like the modern picnicker, the porcupine was also a truly global critter, native to Africa and found in Eurasia, as well as in the Americas. The Old World (Hystricidae) and New World (Erethizontidae) branches are not closely related, although all porcupines have the peculiar feature of quills, their coats of thickened spines. In the Brazilian biodiversity hotspot of the northeastern Atlantic region, a new species of porcupine in the genus *Coendou* was discovered in 2013.[12] In the three New World genera (*Coendou*, *Chaetomys*, and *Erethizon*), there are currently sixteen species. The easternmost appearance of the Old World porcupine is on the island of Flores, the second largest island in the Indonesian province of East Nusa Tenggara. This porcupine (*Hystrix javanica*) shares its habitat with the Nage people, who have created their own folk taxonomy of the natural world. Gregory Forth's anthropological study *Why the Porcupine Is Not a Bird* (2016) explored the observations of the Nage that include classification of the porcupine as both mammal and bird, the latter due to its spiritual associations and the somewhat peculiar aspects of morphology and behavior. Porcupines are also considered by the Nage to have connections with "inverted" beings, who do things opposite to humans.[13] Although they are wild animals, they are believed to be the domesticates of spirits (*nitu*), and thus they are also paired with human domestic counterparts, the sheep, goat, and pig. The Nage observe that the lack of tail, lack of fur (the quills do not replace fur), and other characteristics contradict their mammalian status and provide porcupines with a birdlike identity expressed in linguistic terms, referring to male and female as cock and hen. While the porcupine has a global distribution, its meanings were understood in decidedly local terms. The species found on Flores does not climb trees, but nonetheless is associated with the in-between world that the UP porcupines were similarly observed to inhabit.

Early Scientific Observations

The earliest scientific investigation of the North American porcupine was recorded in the work of the French surgeon Michel Sarrazin, who was stationed with the French Royal forces in Québec in the late seventeenth and early eighteenth centuries. His report on the "*porc-epic*" was submitted to the Académie royale des sciences by his patron, René-Antoine de Réaumur, in 1727.[14] While a few earlier travelers had observed the animal informally (including noting its importance as an Indigenous food source during famines), Sarrazin embarked on the first full-blown scientific study that disproved that porcupines "throw" their quills. His observations also included the animal's grazing, lifespan, and gestation. He utilized field observations and dissection and compared the North American porcupine with its African counterparts. Indeed, an inventory of his personal library revealed that he was well informed about the global dimensions of natural history, including the work by the fellow correspondent in Africa.[15] Sarrazin's study has been heralded by modern scientists as an "astonishing paper, inventive in its experimental approach and filled with details of the taxonomy, anatomy, and natural history."[16]

Later scientific observers did not fail to notice and record the peculiar porcupine found in the Upper Peninsula. Henry Schoolcraft (1793–1864) was the earliest geographer and ethnologist in the region. Part of the Lewis Cass expedition, Schoolcraft served as their geologist, attempting to trace the nearly two thousand miles of land and water across the Great Lakes and down the Mississippi River. When Henry Schoolcraft journeyed by canoe along Huron's shores in 1820, he glimpsed a large porcupine in "summer dress" and noted that its meat was "said to be delicious, and to resemble young pig in flavor."[17] Schoolcraft was later assigned to Sault Ste. Marie as the first Indian agent of the US government. Although trained as a scientist, his observations of the porcupine did not extend far beyond the dinner table.

On his midcentury scientific journey, the world's most famous geologist, Jean Louis Rodolphe Agassiz (1807–73), observed closely both the porcupine and its environment of forest and lake. By this time, the scientist was among the world's most influential scholars of natural history and held a post at Harvard University, where he founded the Museum of Comparative Zoology. Louis Agassiz took credit for exploring the world's largest freshwater lakes when he observed Lake Superior as a counterpart of the wider, ancient landscape. An expert on fossil fish, Agassiz primarily would be known for his geological work to understand glaciation as a force that created the habitats of fish, animals, and forests. However, his legacy also revealed the opportunities afforded well-educated white male scientists to travel, experience, observe, and describe the world, from the perspective of a narrative they built with profoundly racist underpinnings. Later research by Agassiz fell short when it came to human observations. Traveling to Brazil, Agassiz collected thousands of specimens and amassed photographs of bodies he believed supported his racial gaze and poly-genist views that each race was created separately, and blacks were inherently barbarous. A key figure in the rise of the racial thinking that became funda-mental to the construction of medical and scientific knowledge and pseudo-scientific claims of white supremacy, Agassiz traveled a world torn asunder by slavery and empire.[18] He categorized its inhabitants and features as products of a long history, where place and climate shaped the local outcomes. Cling-ing to views that were stridently opposed to Darwinism, he called Indigenous people "savages" and "half-breeds," but also "indominable, courageous, [and] proud," in their positioning in nature.[19] After the visit to the wilderness of Lake Superior, Agassiz commissioned a notorious collection of photographic images of enslaved men and women on a South Carolina plantation and eventually journeyed to Lake Superior's tropical counterpart in Brazil, where he photo-graphed local people he would classify and categorize. Once again, his empha-sis on the specifics of discrete geographical and temporal distributions failed to see the unity of humanity.[20]

In the Great Lakes, Agassiz surmised that the origins of bodies of water and land were associated with the ancient melting of great ice sheets. As an anti-Darwinist, Agassiz was intensely interested in the complexity of the region, in part as an extension of his earlier work on the Alps, where he perceived the power of the Creator. He hypothesized that the three or four ice sheets that occurred between 35,000 and 10,000 BP (that is, years Before the Present) had carved out the ancient rock and created the region's lakes. The ancient glacial mega-lake—likely seven hundred miles across in the Pleistocene and disappearing about 8,400 years ago—was named after Agassiz in 1879. Even earlier volcanic activity from the Portage Lake and Porcupine Volcanoes had left behind copper deposits. When Agassiz viewed the landscape, he noted the

Drawing of the Porcupine Mountains on Lake Superior, Seth Eastman (1854). Courtesy Wisconsin Historical Society, WHI 23365. Named because the tall pines atop rugged hillsides resemble the porcupine's silhouette, they are home to the largest surviving tract of virgin hardwoods east of the Rockies, as well as to many picnic sites within their reach.

unfolding of these geological processes through the ages. The uplift of land included the western UP's Porcupine Mountains, named after the silhouette of the mountain's pine trees that resembled the spiky back of the animal.

The final retreat of the glaciers, occurring over thousands of years and forming the present arrangement of the aptly named Great Lakes, had begun by about 7,000 years ago. Five freshwater seas and 9,500 miles of shorelines were created. This glacial retreat also produced the patterns of flora and fauna, which could be observed in the appearance and disappearance of species available by reading the fossil record and closely examining nature itself. At the place they called the "island" of St. Ignace, Agassiz and his artist-companion, John Cabot, shared a picnic, spread on their blanket on the ground in a clearing near the woods of the Huron lakeshore on July 17, 1848.[21] The clearing was the result of the construction of a small building two years earlier, and the resulting tree stumps are visible in the image Cabot created. From their vantage point, they viewed the interplay of land and water, and they collected rocks and studied them. The following week the men explored northern Lake Superior by canoe, beginning about fourteen miles from Fort William near Pie Island in Thunder Bay (today, Ontario, Canada). On the evening of July 25, 1848, the Agassiz party reported that "a porcupine was killed on the beach as we landed and proved very good meat."[22] Professor Agassiz was inspired to give a lecture that evening about the natural distribution of plants and animals, remarking that "there is no animal, and no plant, which in its natural state is found in every part of the world, but each has assigned to it a situation corresponding with its organization and character."[23]

The idea that the Upper Peninsula was an island had some early traction and persisted through the emphases of language and observation. The word "peninsula" actually means an "almost island" and comes from the Latin words *paene* (almost) and *insula* (island). As early travelers noted, Michigan's Upper Peninsula was a stretch of land *almost* completely surrounded by water. Thus, nearly every scenic vista included the waters of the Great Lakes as viewed from the shoreline and other (smaller) islands. Indeed, my grandmother's picnic island of Boblo—only thirty-four square miles in area—was an ideal island for the porcupine. Even the small Bois Blanc Island contained valuable woods and six lakes of its own. And the edge of its forest was "almost" wilderness.

As early as 1669, the waters of the Great Lakes appeared to outsiders "like two seas, so large are they."[24] Indeed, the lakes seemed to behave like the ocean, to which the miniscule rising and falling of their tidewaters, the enormous waves (in actuality, oscillating seiches) caused by barometric pressure and winds, and the many shipwrecks can attest. And the Upper Peninsula behaved like an island, which rode the sea like a ship in water. Sure, its western edge was surrounded by a sea of trees, tethered to Wisconsin, so technically the UP was not a true island. If glaciers had scoured the land, creating freshwater lakes large enough to exhibit a tidal pull but considered by scientists to be nontidal, both the lands and the lakes had gained in the process magnetic qualities of their own, drawing visitors repeatedly to their reaches.[25] Before 1957, most people came to the UP by boat, canoe, or steamship. Like other islands on the planet, the region was a crucible of creolization, a meeting place of different nationalities, cuisines, and personalities. Even while losing its wilderness, it was gaining its own accent, what would become over time its "Yooper" qualities, a product of and play on the culture of the Upper Peninsula. By the twentieth century, the region would also boast its unique foodways that were a culinary amalgam of adaptation and mixing, its elements imported, borrowed, and invented. The island mentality afforded the appearance of inaccessibility and isolation, as much as it heeded cross-cultural and cross-species encounters. There were some constants: the forest and the lakeshore, always accessible. And almost every scenic vista potentially included the curious, salt-seeking porcupine.

OTHER VISIONS OF THE PORCUPINE

The recognizable features of the porcupine were recorded by the most renowned illustrator of the natural world: John James Audubon (1785–1851). Born in Haiti, the enslaver Audubon turned to the illustration of animals after he completed his more famous treatise on North American birds. In his *The Viviparous Quadrupeds of North America* (1845–54), Audubon presented the *Hystrix dorsata*, first classified by Linnaeus (1758) and by Cuvier (1823) and drawn from nature.[26] Audubon's porcupine sits astride a tree limb and displays his rodent teeth, claws, fur, substantial tail, and quills. Among the twentieth-century illustrators of the porcupine was the artist-naturalist Louis Agassiz Fuertes (1874–1927), who produced several sketches and ink drawings (1915–20) of the animal. Fuertes was named by his Puerto Rican father, himself a pioneering engineer at Cornell University, after the famed naturalist Louis Agassiz, who had died the previous year. Fuertes was unrelated, except by occupation. Although known primarily for his illustrations of birds, Fuertes traveled widely as a naturalist (including to Abyssinia, Alaska, the American Southwest, and the Caribbean), and his keen observations and fine paintings describe a range of other animals in the wild. The porcupine image published in Palmer's *Field Book of Nature-Study* (1928), like ones from earlier centuries, shows the gnawing creature on the ground with his back humped up, a defensive posture.[27] The artist's earlier color print (1918) poses *Erethizon dorsatum* on a tree branch, his sharp paw grasping the tree bark he has already attacked. It was very much the same pose observed by Audubon.

City slickers also captured the porcupine. By the 1920s, porcupines were residents of the nation's city zoos, which presented the creatures as an

The North American Porcupine, an Italian engraving by Innocente Alessandri, *Descrizioni degli animali* . . . (Venice: Carolo Palese, 1772), vol. 2, plate 87. Courtesy Biodiversity Heritage Library/Smithsonian. www .biodiversitylibrary.org/item/130590#page/103/mode/1up.

exotic species housed next to monkeys and lions. The artist Alexander Calder made a series of sketching trips to the Bronx and Central Park Zoos in New York City in 1925–26. Based on observations, Calder's drawings in India ink described the essentials of the porcupine's shape and movement nonetheless, "rendering them with economy and flair," using his signature "rapid, shorthand technique" that would form the basis of modernist abstraction.[28]

Other researchers eventually discovered that the porcupine does not torpedo its quills at an attacker, confirming the conclusions made earlier by Michel Sarrazin. Rather, the animal does a dance to rattle them. Once bristled and erect, the barbed weapons become a danger to the enemy. Sometimes the porcupine lashes out with its tail or even charges backward. In his essay "An Astonished Porcupine," naturalist John Burroughs observed the surprise of a porcupine who had encountered an enemy against which these tactics did not work.[29] Burroughs notes the similar observation of naturalist Charles Roberts: "[The porcupine] did not care who knew of his coming, and he did not greatly care who came. Behind his panoply of biting spears, he felt himself secure, and in that security, he moved as if he held in fee the whole green, shadowy, perilous woodland world."[30] Because the quills easily detach from the porcupine's body, they enter the skin of predators, usually driven in by force (the force of the attacker). The barbed shape of the quills, with sharply pointed ends, makes them painful to remove. After they are dropped by the porcupine, the quills grow back just like hair.

Illustrations based on the sketches made by scientist-artists, who had spent time making observations in the field, gave way to photographic renderings. The porcupine photographs of George Shiras reflected another level of close observation and the unique nighttime images of a mostly nocturnal animal. Photographs would eventually replace illustrations and field sketches as the definitive guide to forest wildlife, and Shiras was a key player in this transition. Shiras was in pursuit of a rare, albino specimen. The typical porcupine uses its black-and-white markings, which function as part of a warning system to would-be predators.[31] The white of their quills and the white stripe down its back are fluorescent in the darkness. Other warning signals include the loud clattering of teeth and the release of a glandular odor to repel the unwanted visitor. Shiras used special techniques to "hunt" nocturnal animals, including the elusive porcupine, with his camera.[32] While Shiras could not have known about the animal's fluorescent pigments that lit up the scene at Whitefish Lake on July 1, 1905, his gambol with the porcupine was part of a larger commitment to the protection of the species and its wildlife environment during his career. The publication of seventy-four photographs by *National Geographic* in 1906 used groundbreaking techniques to capture the images on his glass plate negatives. They have been described as "poetic" and containing both a beauty and an "eeriness" that render them unforgettable.[33]

THE PORCUPINE'S HABITAT

The forest was home to other gnawers and destructive mammals, such as the beaver and muskrat. Both porcupine and beaver are part of the scientific order of Rodentia, with long incisors as one indicator of their rodent status. Only the beaver and the South American capybara are larger rodents. Whereas the porcupine left telltale gnaw marks in the bark of trees, the beaver often consumed entire trees by cutting through to the wood beyond the surface. Its behavior fascinated scientists, including geologist Louis Agassiz's son Alexander Agassiz (1835–1910), who had become interested in the mining operations in Calumet. In 1871, the younger Agassiz became a principal investor and president of the Calumet and Hecla Mining Company. But Alexander Agassiz was a scientist at heart, and he searched the nearby forest for an object for his scientific curiosity during the two years of his stay Up North. For Alexander, the town of Calumet in 1867 was still a "rough primitive community with little to offer in the way of comfort beyond the bare necessities of life. The 'hotel' was scarcely more than a log cabin on the edge of a primeval forest rising directly behind it."[34] When Mrs. Agassiz strolled through the town with one of her small children, she was compelled to wear a revolver strapped to her waist. Despite the dangers and challenges, her young husband was determined to make a go of the mining operations there to be able to support his scientific research.

Alexander Agassiz's investigations in the area's natural history included study of the beavers he had observed to have migrated great distances from their dams. Agassiz estimated some of the colonies of beavers were nearly a thousand years old. Some of their ponds covered forty acres, whereas the meadows created by forest clearing equaled two hundred to three hundred acres in their expanse. Unfortunately, before Agassiz could publish his own observations, Lewis H. Morgan's book *The American Beaver and His Works* (1868) appeared to take the wind out of his sails. Morgan had used his connections with the directors of the railroad company building the track to the iron mines to access the beavers in this once untouched wilderness, "his [the beaver's] native wilds." Each summer, beginning in 1855, Morgan had been based in Marquette, where he had watched the human community go from "a few scattering houses" to nearly three thousand inhabitants.[35] Morgan spent years measuring, sketching, and recording the building activities of the beavers.

Beavers near Lake Superior's southern shores, between the Carp River that flows into Lake Superior and the Escanaba River that flows into Lake Michigan, weighed as much as sixty pounds, compared to the dainty porcupine, who seldom weighed more than twenty-five pounds.[36] Both their population numbers and their size dwarfed the smaller porcupine, and beaver pelts had supplied the global hat-making industry with its main waterproof material for men's fancy top hats until the 1830s, when fashionable silk hats held sway. In contrast, interest in the porcupine was never commercial. Morgan had claimed the beaver "works" in the Upper Peninsula to be unsurpassed by any other beaver district in North America, a feat that also meant nowhere else was subject to more of their gnawing and damage than the UP. A single dam's construction consumed upwards of seven thousand cubic feet of wood and materials. Today the world's largest beaver lodge, constructed over generations in Alberta, Canada, can be viewed from space. Despite the obvious differences, beavers and porcupines were often looked upon as similar forces of deforestation.

George Shiras had found that the porcupine's habitat was typically the dens found in rock crevices within low outcroppings and sometimes in tree hollows.[37] These places provided winter accommodations that were relatively safe from the porcupine's predators. Especially during snowy seasons, when they were most visible if seen outside the den, porcupines stuck to the solitary and temperate den dwellings most of the time. Shiras's favorite porcupine, the white albino one, made its den in "a narrow crevice in a big, glaciated rock a short distance back on the path leading to the water."[38] Otherwise, in the late spring, summer, and early fall, the porcupines spent most of their time in trees. Each animal claimed a resting tree for daytime hours and one or more trees as feeding stations, traveling between the two places along a regular pathway. Most favored were the canopies of linden (basswood, *Tilia americana*) trees, where the porcupines consumed the bark and leaves, leaving behind a littered picnic ground of niptwigs. Niptwigs are the so-called ends of branches from which the porcupines have nibbled away all but the petioles, the stalks that attach the leaf blades to the stems. The animals begin their search for food at dusk as they travel to find sources of salt, bark, leaves, nuts, or berries, depending on the season's offerings. This explained why they were commonly viewed just before twilight. Shiras observed that:

> Even in the mid-summer, if the wind turns northerly or the air becomes damp and penetrating with the drizzling rains of such a latitude, one may look for them in vain. Whenever the soft winds blow and the setting sun leaves the darkening shore still alight in the afterglow of a summer evening, the shores of little lakes and ponds may fairly bristle with the waddling creatures.[39]

The sweet smell of the linden tree in the early summer was attractive to picnickers and porcupines alike.

As humans increasingly altered their forest abodes, the porcupine adapted by savoring the salts they brought and left behind, often inadvertently. George Shiras III had noticed how "these animals content themselves by gnawing everything containing the slightest salty flavor. . . . Even the trace of salt left on an implement by a perspiring hand attracts them."[40] These salt sources have included the sodium-rich canoe paddles and boat oars, picnic benches and picnic tables, salt residues from treating icy winter roads, treated posts, wooden buildings, outbuildings, and even certain paints on signs. The annual salt search of the porcupine replaces sodium levels depleted by winter's end. Because of the high level of interaction with the human-made world, the porcupine has been designated as proto-domesticated, meaning that the animal's learned behavior has carried across genetic changes that favor the survival of those adaptations.[41]

THE PORCUPINE'S GHOST LANDSCAPES

The forests were essential to the ecology of the porcupine, and they provided the essential vistas for picnics in the UP. The porcupine's favorite linden tree was favored for making furniture because of its straight grain, however. Settlements and clearing fields for agriculture and roads also took their toll over time. The furnaces that processed the local ores being mined and the new railroad known as the "Iron Mountain" that carried them away possessed voracious appetites for wood. In 1867, the amount of ore exported out of the UP by rail and ship totaled 270,000 tons of iron. Iron production came at a high environmental cost. Each time a train left a new mine for the first time with a carload of iron ore, it was decorated with a symbol of that maiden voyage: an entire tree tied to the top of the train like a trophy or moving grave marker.[42] The loss of forests during the nineteenth century progressed steadily, alongside the economic success and destructive deforestation wrought by the mining and timber industries. Naturalist writer Robert Macfarlane called these "ghost" landscapes.[43] Being able to see through the cleared fields to the missing trees would become part of the art of the picnic.

Picnic grounds, like cemeteries, were ways to reach back to ancestors and forgotten places. Sometimes picnic grounds and cemeteries were one and the same swath of land. The wilder landscapes whispered to picnickers and porcupines alike. The picnic grounds were gathering sites, where picnickers were surrounded by memories. The cemeteries could be picnic sites, where ancestors were remembered and families reconnected. The quills of the porcupines and the skulls of deer and moose were found on the margins of forests and along the counterpart lakeshores. My family carried a whitened moose skull all the way home from Hessel to California one summer. Back in Cedarville, the graves of my great-grandparents, my grandparents, and now my parents rest together in the Edgewood Cemetery, a small, neat tract of land with a grove of sacred trees surrounding it. The carved granite stone positioned at the resting place of my Grandma Gertie says simply "Gertrude M. Hamel, 1892 Mother 1937." This cemetery is also more literally, for forests and people, a ghost landscape as much as it is a landscape of ghosts.

Mines and timber camps occupied the wilderness regions once relegated to hunting. They reached back all the way to the time of early scientific voyageurs like Louis Agassiz and John Cabot, who were among the most experienced canoe men of the wilderness travelers, carrying "convenience and luxury . . . cooks and bakers, together with delicacies of every kind, and an abundance of choice wine for the banquets."[44] Members of the elite and exclusive Beaver Club founded in 1785 in Montreal (on the Canadian side of the border) smoked a peace pipe (calumet) that was passed around.[45] They reminisced about their fur-trading journeys in the UP while they ate local foods, including venison, wild rice, quail, partridge, bear meat, and, of course, beaver. By the 1820s, their provisions included corn, flour, and bacon.[46] In 1848, as the Agassiz party of gentlemen-scientists made their way through what they called the "Fur Countries," the lakes, rivers, and lands remained the territory of the voyageurs and trappers. A little more than a decade later, the census of 1860 showed their numbers had dwindled so that very few inhabitants still declared hunting, fishing, or trapping as an occupation. The once-lucrative occupations of hunter and guide gave way to small businesses and migrants, seasonal labor within increasingly diverse settlements. Likewise, the forests disappeared, and their disappearance was because of mining, industry, agriculture, roads, and settlement. From the days when logs were rolled to the river to the twentieth-century reliance on the railroad, the applications of new technology were critical stages of exploitation. In the words of Charles Bert Reed, writing in 1909, this classic "advancement" of "civilization" made these human actors "Masters of the Wilderness."[47]

Steam power applied to tracts of wilderness more quickly deforested the Upper Peninsula's prized hardwoods of maple and beech and decimated forests of pine.[48] Gertie's father, Ernst Meyer, worked at a sawmill in Rogers City. Her eventual husband, Grandpa Bob Hamel, was similarly one of these hewers of hardwood and the first to own a steam-powered sawmill in his portion of the UP. He was a skilled wooden boatbuilder. His son and grandson built wooden docks. Sadly, the historic loss of forest habitats required adaptations by the local artisans and picnicking humans and porcupines alike.

CONSERVATIONISTS AND COOKS

Small game had been abundant in the Upper Peninsula visited by Schoolcraft, Morgan, and the Agassiz families, but it was a lot less familiar to early cooks in the new settlements and towns that were growing rapidly in size and impact at the century's end. Across the twentieth century, early cookbooks in the Upper Peninsula commonly continued to provide recipes for preparing such wild forest meats as bear, porcupine, muskrat, raccoon, venison, and beaver. Versions of recipes for wild game appear in my family's Rogers City 1996 cookbook assembled much later. Porcupines were rare, inviting recipes that automatically substituted ground beef and added ingredients to mimic its quills.[49] While the culinary concerns noted the loss of habitat and wildlife, the first half of the twentieth century simultaneously witnessed the emergence of a new strand of scientific interest with the preservation of the wilderness as its primary goal.

By the beginning of the twentieth century, porcupines were still associated with the edge of a forest, but that forest was rapidly dwindling. As a young man, the naturalist and writer Stewart Edward White (1873–1946) worked briefly as a lumberjack in White Pine's (Ontonagon) forest in 1901. The logging camps had first begun to appear deep in the white pine and conifer woods by the middle of the nineteenth century. Their operations attracted immigrants and local laborers, who worked tirelessly and fearlessly in isolated communities. As White soon learned, the men worked in teams, in which they called out the rhythm and pace of logging in chants. In the camps, they developed their own culture, giving new terms to old and monotonous foods. The word "punk" meant bread, "red horse" was corned beef, and "sowbelly" referred to pork.[50] At night White and the other men still saw a silent parade of forest creatures, especially noting the "porcupines in quest of anything they could get their keen teeth into."[51] The focus of logging activities was seasonal. During winters, the trees were felled. Using horses and sleighs, the giant logs could be transported more easily overland through the snow and ice to reach the river's edge. Springtime thaws brought greater mobility for the logs to be moved down rivers to the shores of the Great Lakes once the ice had broken up. This was the most dangerous stage, when men known as "river pigs" guided tons of massive logs downriver. White was a lumberjack only briefly, before becoming a conservationist and writer of fiction, nonfiction, and Hollywood filmscripts. However, his sensitivity to and appreciation of the forest remained undiminished, and the porcupine population similarly persisted. White wrote in *The Forest* (1903) about this sensual balance of power:

A faint, searching woods perfume of dampness greets your nostrils. And somehow, mysteriously, in a manner not to be understood, the forces of the world seem in suspense, as though a touch might crystallize infinite possibilities into infinite power and motion. But the touch lacks. The forces hover on the edge of action, unheeding the little noises. In all humbleness and awe, you are a dweller of the Silent Places. At such a time you will meet with adventures. One night we put fourteen inquisitive porcupines out of [the lumber] camp.[52]

White unfairly took the porcupine as a symbol of destruction, when he likened the action of the lumberman to that of the animals in the forest, where "we seem to hear the ax biting the pine."[53] Deforested hills that once housed logging camps were remembered by place-names like "Hungry Hill," suggesting the voracious appetite of the industry had remained in the landscape and was somehow something natural and alive.[54] In this example, the porcupines were harbingers of environmental changes, signaling the destruction of their own habitats. In fact, the porcupine's gnawing rarely circled the tree, thus stopping short of its total destruction. Not surprisingly, the porcupine and the picnicker now shared the same space in the changing landscape.

The scientific exploration of the porcupine did not stop in the twentieth century. The important recent research by Anthony Barnosky and others at Porcupine Cave has used the remains of the porcupine (*Erethizon* spp.) and other species to reconstruct the changing paleoclimate and landscape in the Middle Pleistocene, between 800,000 and 950,000 years ago. The presence of porcupine in North American fossil remains proved to be a critical clue to reconstructing an environment with fewer trees. The world's modern expert on the North American porcupine, Uldis Roze, also followed his share of the spiky animals through deforested and diminishing stands of trees. Remarkably adaptable, the porcupine ranged widely through ancient forests and non-wooded sites, then as now a symbol of the transition between dense forest and cleared landscape.

According to Roze, the lives of porcupines are expressed through the cycles of seasons. No other person has spent more time studying them. The porcupine of my grandmother's picnic days is the only porcupine in the world that has adapted to a northern, nontropical climate. In addition to its unique relationship to the trees it climbs for leaves and bark, the UP porcupine boasts a fascinating digestive system, which stores and facilitates the fermentation of their mostly plant diet. At the junction of the large and small intestines of these animals is a sac, the saecum. This porcupine feature evolved to hold the bacteria that combines with stored food and ferments the sac's contents, holding it for stored energy over a long period of time. Water conservation is also a feature of their intestinal system, which resorbs water from leaves, allowing the animal to go days without drinking water—sometimes for as many as five days in total.[55]

The conservationist porcupines also use collaborations within their environment. At a porcupine reintroduction site in the UP, Roger Powell and Robert Brander (1977) showed that the fisher (then *Martes diluviana*) and porcupine populations interacted and stabilized in paired association with one another.[56] As deforestation was accompanied by a decline in the population of porcupines, it was assumed that loss of habitat was the cause. However, other factors also were at play, including human populations and eventually automobiles. Powell and Brander studied the adaptations of porcupines in interactions with fishers in the hardwood-hemlock forest of Upper Michigan beginning in 1969, when fishers were reintroduced.[57] Powell and Brander demonstrated that the decreased porcupine population density "will increase the fisher dependence on other food sources."[58] The fishers were successful in reducing the porcupine populations, until they both reached a stabilizing point of homeostasis.

Adaptations enabled survival. Even an albino porcupine could survive in the wild.[59] It is also possible to trace the destructive impact of porcupines on successive generations of forest.[60] Normally porcupines ate twigs, roots, stems, bark, and berries, but they also relished the salty surfaces of wooden objects that had come into contact with human sweat, from axe handles to canoe oars. This predilection brought the animals in contact with humans outdoors, both creating and being attracted to the edge of a forest. In the Upper Peninsula, porcupines themselves were an important source of food, especially during the long winters in the precontact and postcontact wilderness, when they could become famine food. In the summers they were synonymous with outdoor eating and gathering sites, as they were frequently glimpsed along the forest's edge, competing for berries, salty, sweat-soaked canoe paddles, and a special place at the picnic basket and table.

At the same time the porcupine's habitat was under attack, outsiders began to travel to the northern reaches of the Upper Peninsula by train and then steamer for vacations in the nineteenth century. One of the most impactful of these so-called summer people was Aldo Leopold, who first arrived in the eastern UP as a child with his family. Leopold (1887–1948) went on to become an American pioneer of conservation, called by some the "father" of wildlife ecology. He spent many summers in the Les Cheneaux Islands, and he was inspired by his experiences and observations in the outdoors. His father eventually purchased a summer cottage on Marquette Island in 1898, and Aldo traveled there from Iowa and Wisconsin for the remainder of his life, often enjoying six-week vacations. Aldo explored the island, producing hand-drawn maps of the trails, illustrated with sketches of trees, animals, and birds of the coastal wetlands. As an adult, he returned with his own family, eventually developing ideas about the moral responsibility of humans to protect the rest of the natural world.

Modern deforestation resulted in another kind of transition, from the era of heavily logging forests to multiple-use approaches, from private to public. By the end of the nineteenth century much of Mackinac Island already had become a park, no longer a wilderness. Its few remaining trees were protected from destruction and defacement, along with "shrubs, turf, [and] natural curiosities."[61] Furthermore, the area within the island's park would be made safe from "frays, quarrels, or disorders of any kind." Animals, game, and fish were also protected from capture. In this manner, the landscape of the porcupine and picnic were simultaneously considered by these early rules and regulations under the command of the fort's general. The early ideas in place on Mackinac Island spread across the Upper Peninsula's storied landscapes.

At the height of the Conservation Era, Congress commissioned a bureau of the federal government that would become the US Forest Service, thus creating a national body to acquire, protect, and maintain forestlands across the North American continent. During President Theodore Roosevelt's administration, lands were acquired to establish the Marquette National Forest in 1909. These acres, together with the Huron National Forest, established in 1909, were eventually combined to create the Michigan National Forest in 1915. In 1931, the combined lands of what was then called the Hiawatha National Forest touched all three of the Great Lakes and integrated national protection and local cultural use. After a century of intensive exploitation, were these lands still considered wilderness? The word "wilderness" in English comes from the Middle English "wilddeorness," meaning the place of the wild deer. Indeed, there were still wild deer and other animals that had survived across the Upper Peninsula. But this wilderness was also a cultural product, a construct of imagination. Finally, in 1964, legal recognition of the American "wilderness" was put into place with the passage of the Wilderness Act. The act recognized the need to set aside the landscapes in which humans did not dominate the natural world, where:

> the earth and its community of life are untrammeled by man, where man himself is a visitor who does not remain. An area of wilderness is further defined to mean in this Act an area of undeveloped Federal land retaining its primeval character and influence, without permanent improvements or human habitation, which is protected and managed so as to preserve its natural conditions and which . . . generally appears to have been affected primarily by the forces of nature, with the imprint of man's work substantially unnoticeable.[62]

The Upper Peninsula, like many designated wildernesses, was not "untrammeled by man." This definition overlooks the complex history of Indigenous land use and land transformation, for example, through the cultivation of wild rice in the Great Lakes region. While the wilderness might also contain features of ecological, geological, scientific, educational, scenic, or historical value, the definition became the hallmark of the natural world, its forests and waters contrasted with anything humans might conceive and create.

The forests of the UP had been greatly diminished by settlements, logging camps, mining and smelting operations, the railroad, and agricultural pursuits. By the end of the logging boom, there were almost no remnants of the original, old-growth forests. Furthermore, the period following intensive logging had left the forestland vulnerable to forest fire. Despite these losses, there remained some visible portions of the UP wilderness and its edge that still offered visitors seemingly unlimited tracts of forested hills, valleys, lakes, and streams for hunting wild deer and for freshwater fishing. That was more wilderness than many urban Americans would ever glimpse or could even imagine. Even the limited stands of secondary forest or replanted lands managed by the forest system contrasted with the sidewalk experiences of most visitors from an increasingly urbanized America. Today there are more than a dozen official, federally designated "wildernesses" in the Upper Peninsula and Great Lakes region. Despite these efforts to restore habitats, even the local memory of the forest had its limitations.

An environmentalist perspective was again summoned after decades of logging. Picnics and porcupines were linked together, not only in their shared placement and accommodations in this diminished wilderness but also in a common food chain. The functioning of the ecosystem revealed an interdependent system that relied "on the co-operation and competition of its diverse parts." In the eastern UP, Aldo Leopold summoned inspiration from a lifetime of wilderness observation and experience. Using the language of science and philosophy, he wrote that only "when we see land as a community to which we belong, we may begin to use it with love and respect."[63] Leopold would come to realize that the language of the wilderness went far beyond what was written, because "nothing so important as an ethic is ever 'written.'"[64] His ruminations sparked "the stirrings of an ecological conscience" that would usher in a new era in which the UP wilderness areas offered up their wildlife, watersheds, and forests for restoration and recreation.[65]

THE PATHWAYS OF THE PORCUPINE

The French political scientist Alexis de Tocqueville visited Michigan's Upper Peninsula in the summer of 1831, while researching his famous study *Democracy in America*. Like the other early visitors, he had traveled by canoe, by boat, and on foot. In *A Fortnight in the Wilderness*, Tocqueville noted that "at sea at least a traveler contemplates a vast horizon at which he always looks with hope. But in this ocean of trees, who can show you the way?"[66] One reliable guide turned out to be the porcupine. When the porcupine's routes were followed from tree to tree, it seems that the journeys were repeated. George Shiras had noticed this in the early twentieth century. He observed, "the animal always came down to the margin of the lake shore at the point to the left of 'a' and, after following the shore around to a point 'b,' it returned to its home in a small cave hidden alongside a deer trail."[67] Watching the albino porcupine, he noted how "its habits were clocklike in their regularity, and it followed the same route going out to forage and returning."[68] Marking the trail with their own scent, each porcupine selected pairs of trees for sleeping and eating. Such pairing is not only native to the animal's instinctive behavior but also indicative of the features of the regional landscape. These features similarly "marked" the landscape of the picnic.

GEOLOGY'S GLACIAL GHOSTS

None had more to say about the geological contours of the porcupine's land-scape than the pioneer of natural history Louis Agassiz. When the scientist first set out for the Upper Peninsula of Michigan in 1848, he had just been hired as a professor at Harvard, and he brought along a global perspective. A native of Switzerland, Agassiz had grown up among the imposing Alps, where he also had witnessed the living impact of glaciation. Louis Agassiz was destined to travel far beyond his place of birth. He studied in Paris with the naturalist and zoologist Georges Cuvier, and he wrote a brilliant treatise on fossil fish in Bra-zil. Charismatic and charming, Agassiz also was destined to travel far in life. He vehemently disagreed with Darwin's theory of evolution and held openly racist views on the "mismeasure" of man, claiming larger skulls and superiority for the European.[69] He was terribly wrong. What Agassiz seems to have gotten right were his observations of the geological landscape that would, in turn, explain the natural history of the UP, including the porcupine's favored habitat.

Agassiz argued that when the climate cooled during the planet's last ice age, the glaciers expanded southward, pushing the forests further ahead of the ice sheet known as the Laurentide. This created, among other features, an ice-dammed lake later named Lake Agassiz that was larger than the Great Lakes combined. The maximum phase of extension was known as the Porcu-pine phase of Lake Superior's paleogeography, thought to have occurred just about eleven thousand years ago.[70] At the end of this era, a warming took place between approximately twelve thousand and ten thousand years ago, when the ice sheet retreated and the forests returned to the UP. Scientists today generally agree on this enormous time scale. They think that spruce, tamarack, pine, fir, and finally maple and hemlock were able to selectively recolonize and thrive in the new patterns of soils, gravels, rocks, and hydrology left behind by the melting ice sheet. Once the weight of the ice was lifted, the earth often rose, too, in patterned elevations of mountain ranges and hills.[71] The birch and pine were "first forests"—that is, the ones that survived the frozen zones of the once-arctic north. These geological events were observed by Agassiz as he viewed the sediments, rivers, and lake ecologies of the UP region. He noted the distribution of flora and fauna and hypothesized about their formation in relation to glaciation. "The trees are not large," observed Agassiz, "usually not exceeding thirty or forty feet in height. Yet the whole effect is rich and picturesque. Here, as in all the features of the lake, the impression is a grand uniformity, never monotonous, but expressive of its unique character."[72]

These stupendous geological events were not random, Agassiz believed. Everywhere was proof of his glacial theory, the events of which had created not only the Upper Peninsula of what now belongs to the State of Michigan but also the largest collective source of freshwater in the world: the Great Lakes. Agassiz and Cabot published *Lake Superior: Its Physical Character, Vegetation, and Animals, Compared with Those of Other and Similar Regions* in 1850. The final chapter of *Lake Superior* (chapter 12) dealt with their scientific observations of the geology of the region and the copper ores it had produced. Having glorified the forests, the narrative admitted one obstacle: "Neither the love of the picturesque, however, nor the interests of science, could tempt us into the woods, so terrible were the black flies." It was from the edge of the forest that the wilderness could be glimpsed after all: "In geographical position the lake [Lake Superior] would seem naturally to lie within the zone of civilization. . . . But on the north shore we find we have already got into the Northern Regions. . . . The rivers and the islands are counterparts of each other."[73] The same forces created both. So began a kind of love-hate relationship with the wilderness that more often pushed sojourners, including porcupines, to its edge than to its center.

THE PICNIC'S SCENIC VISTAS

On Mackinac Island, a group of well-heeled tourists visited the geologic formation known as Devil's Kitchen, a favorite picnic spot described in their 1899 visitor's guidebook, as "a mass of calcareous rock cut out by the action of water and believed to resemble a Dutch Oven."[74] The very next day they found themselves as picnickers next to another of the island's natural curiosities. In awe, the travelers viewed one of the island's most prominent geological features, a limestone sea stack that had gained the name "Sugar Loaf" because it resembled the cone-shaped birch basket or *makak*, which held maple sap. For the Ojibwe, who now sold souvenirs, including *makaks* and picnic baskets to the tourists on the lake's shoreline, the same formation was believed to have once been a beehive inhabited by the Great Spirit. Its vertical column was the product of wind and sea eroding the limestone breccia across millions of years. That the early generations of both residents and guests saw their surroundings in terms of a magical outdoor food court should come as no surprise. In Lake Superior, one island looked like a giant pasty or meat pie (Le Pâté or Pie Island, near Thunder Bay). Connections to the wilderness of Michigan's Upper Peninsula were fueled by visions of

Visitors pose in front of the iconic landmark known as Sugar Loaf, Mackinac Island, c. 1890s. Courtesy Mackinac State Historic Parks.

picnics and porcupines. These were among the curated vistas the locals increasingly shared with their summer visitors, who had been invited to the wilderness edge.

While favorite picnic spots often were near the lakeshore at the edge of the woods, as scenic landscapes they shared some other characteristics with the places sought by porcupines. The ledges and rocky outcroppings favored by the four-footed animals made enviable picnic tables while commanding a view of their surroundings. The small islands in Lake Superior near Marquette are still known as Picnic Rocks. Accessible by boat or canoe, the scenic picnic places selected by picnickers and porcupines commonly established a relationship with the landscape, its wood and water. Picnickers were consuming the vision of the porcupines at the edge of the wilderness when they dined in its landscape.

"A Spirit of Picnic"

The ingredients of a picnic included more than the material elements of food, drink, and the conveniences required to create mobility, appreciate scenery, and forge social relationships. Writing in 1875, Robert Louis Stevenson called this invisible element of the picnic its "spirit."[75] Essential to the spirit of the picnic was its relationship with the natural world:

> Things fall for us into a sort of natural perspective . . . [when we] are gone before the sun is overcast, before the rain falls, before the season can steal like a dial-hand from his figure, before the lights and shadows, shifting towards nightfall, can show us the other side of things, and belie what they showed us in the morning. We expose our minds to the landscape (as we would expose the prepared plate in the camera) for the moment only during which the effect endures; and we are away before the effect can change.[76]

Across the Atlantic, the spirit of the picnic also would be among the nineteenth-century observations of American naturalist Henry David Thoreau (1817–62).

Writing in his journal, Thoreau conveyed the way in which the landscape figured in his descriptions of food and spirituality, in which "eating became a sacrament . . . sitting at the communion table of the world."[77] Scholar John Gatta has argued that this engagement in the ecology of food gathering was pivotal to Thoreau's transcendental philosophy, activating its deepest realizations of the relationships between the individual and the social environment.[78] In what would be his last manuscript, Thoreau wrote: "The fields and hills are a table constantly spread. . . . [Berries] seem offered to us not so much for food as for sociality, inviting us to a picnic with Nature."[79] The savored picnic foods were "slight and innocent" flavors, which, Thoreau claimed, "relate us to Nature, make us her guests, and entitle us to her regards and protection."[80] The place of the picnic was also quintessentially an American place.

Alexis de Tocqueville had traveled Michigan territory with his friend Gustave de Beaumont. Members of Tocqueville's family had been imprisoned and some guillotined during the French Revolution, and he traveled in the shadow of the Atlantic's revolutionary era. But it was in the upper reaches of the woods and water that he found an unsettling solitude, a harbinger of changes in the landscape yet to come under the influence of global capitalism. Tocqueville visited both Mackinac Island and Sault Ste. Marie, at the southern and northern sides of the UP region. He embarked on a journey that inspired his classic work *Democracy in America*, but one that also emphasized the remoteness of the UP and its symbolism for the course of American "progress," described by the famous author as "the triumphant march of civilization" pitted against its "natural and wild grandeur." Traveling north, Tocqueville believed that he was on the farthest edge of European civilization, where, "if we had indeed only wanted to see forests, our hosts in Detroit would have been right in telling us that we need not go very far, for, a mile out of the town, the road goes into the forest and never comes out of it."[81] That this ocean of trees might cease one day to be vast was unimaginable. Yet within two decades of Tocqueville's visit, another observer would call Mackinac Island "one of the busiest little places in the world."[82]

The transcendental movement was born in the North American wilderness, but the transcendent practice of eating outdoors in fact originated in many cultural settings around the globe, including in Europe, Asia, Africa, and the Americas. This meant that most of the immigrants to the UP already were picnickers when they arrived. They came together bringing their recipes and picnic traditions from all these places. By the nineteenth century, the Western picnic was a widely recognized social event in which guests contributed food and ate it together outdoors. There was no host, excepting Nature. However, there were picnics that were attended by unseen guests. In some cultures, picnic-type meals connected the living to their ancestors, when held at gravesites. Chinese immigrants and African Americans were among those who continued cultural traditions of bringing food for the ancestors to gravesites. Before the advent of public parks, cemeteries might offer the gatherings a welcome respite from the lack of urban greenery and shade trees. In this way, the family memorialized the dead and acknowledged their family ties in a pleasing landscape. Picnickers also commemorated more distant social and political relationships, as the picnic at a British fort in Michigan Territory on King George's birthday intended long ago. They marked the seasonal repetition of harvests and other communal celebrations. All picnics connected diners to a place in the landscape. Like any culinary event, the picnic embraced all the senses, from taste and smell to sight, touch, and even sound. A unique social meal, the modern picnic's ingredients, seen and unseen, consistently reflected one key aspect of its definition: forging a relationship with a place in the landscape. The ecologies of food and social gatherings were pivotal in cementing the region's identity, and they also shaped an individual's memory palace among the porcupines.

THE PORCUPINE'S PICNIC

It doesn't seem right to serve "porcupine stew" at the Porcupine's Picnic, although dozens of recipes exist in turn-of-the-century and later cookbooks. One reluctant version appears below. Traveling to the edge of the woods for a picnic before the age of automobiles often required a day-long expedition, at least one cast-iron frying pan, a kettle for boiling water, tin or china plates, cups, and utensils, and the ingredients for more than one meal.

The original relationships with lands and waters became the basis for transforming the multiplicity of ethnic culinary traditions into a singular regional cuisine in Michigan's Upper Peninsula. One might call these annual gatherings outdoors "original" or "First Picnics." Powwows still include drumming, dancing, and an outdoor feast. Although in the early part of the twentieth century, some individuals were compelled to dance for money, today's powwow once again has regained more meaningful cultural currency. Early settlers borrowed recipes and techniques for making maple syrup, and First Nations people adapted their own cuisines for the cast-iron skillets and imported foodstuffs they transmitted across new generations.

Fry Bread[83]

Ingredients

½ teaspoon salt	1 cup milk
2 teaspoons sugar	2 tablespoons cooking oil
1 tablespoon baking powder	Optional: Add ½ cup blueberries
2 cups flour	to the dough.

Instructions

Stir dry ingredients together thoroughly. Make a "lake" in the flour and pour the milk in your "lake." Mix gently with hands or a fork until nice and sticky dough is formed. Adjust stickiness with additional flour or milk. Let rest for at least one hour. Pull dough into small pieces, the size of small, flattened biscuits, about ¾ inch thick. Fry in oil, turning when one side has browned to a golden color. Serve warm.

(Not) Fry Bread

Not all Native Americans are fans of fry bread, pointing out its deficient nutritive value compared with the use of more traditional grains, including maize, quinoa, acorn flour, and amaranth. Sherman Alexie has called fry bread a symbol of survival, but award-winning Sioux chef Sean Sherman points to fry bread's implications in a history of displacement and government controls over Indigenous diets. He steadfastly refuses to serve it on his menus.[84]

Gertie Hamel sits atop what might be the reassembled ruins of the cabin of Chief Chabowaywa, known locally as "Chief Shabaway," at Chimney Point, a popular picnic site in Cedarville, c. 1915. Collection of the author.

Instructions

For a healthier version, the "fry bread" in the previous recipe may also be baked as follows: Preheat oven to 350 degrees. Grease a 9 × 12 (rectangle) cake pan. Bake until brown and firm to the touch—about 50 minutes. Remove from pan and place the bread on a towel, leaned up on its side against a pot, to cool.

Mrs. Joslin's Sweet Johnny Cake[85]

An early recipe for Johnny Cake first appears in the 1890s. There were many versions of this ubiquitous traveling bread. Paul Bunyan stories claimed that "there are two kinds of lumber camp cooks, the Baking Powder Buns and the Sour-Dough Stiffs. Sour-Dough Sam belonged to the latter school. He made everything but coffee out of sour-dough."[86] Sourdough "starters" were the quick-acting leavening agents used for a pancake batter, comprised of a slightly sour, fermented mixture. Sourdough starters were kept near the shanty door to receive the leftover batter and scraps of dough or cake indispensable as answers to the next morning's appetites. Mrs. Joslin may have felt the same way. She gives two versions of the Johnny Cake, with either sweet or sour milk.

Two eggs, ¾ cup sugar, 1½ cups sweet milk, 1½ cups flour, 1½ cups corn meal, 1 tablespoon melted butter, 1 teaspoon ginger, a little salt, 3 teaspoons baking powder. Can use sour milk and soda.

Les Cheneaux Smoked Whitefish Picnic Spread

Not only porcupines enjoyed a diet of salt. Early human populations paired their breads with the memory of maritime foods, including Atlantic codfish that was heavily salted to withstand the long voyages. This modern recipe is inspired by the Les Cheneaux Culinary School, devoted to twenty-first-century explorations of food and sustainability in the village of Hessel.

Ingredients

½ pound smoked whitefish
1 cup cream cheese, whipped
¼ cup sour cream
2 tablespoons mayonnaise
½ cup finely chopped dried cherries
3 tablespoons chopped herbs
    (chives, thyme, parsley)

1 small shallot, finely minced
½ teaspoon Creole seasoning
Edible wildflowers, such as Johnny
    Jump-ups (wild violets),
    nasturtiums, or runner bean
    blooms

Instructions

Carefully pull the smoked whitefish from the skin and remove bones. Flake into small pieces and set aside. Mix remaining ingredients thoroughly in a small bowl. Add whitefish. Season to taste with salt and pepper. Refrigerate and let stand for at least an hour. Serve with crackers and a scattering of edible wildflowers.

Reluctant Recipe for Porcupine Stew[87]

Porkies are easiest to get. They're so sure of themselves, they don't run off, and a knock over the head with a club does the business.
—Archie La Rue, quoted in *The Cooking Pots of Grand Marais*[88]

Ojibwe often enjoyed one-pot meals. Meals were considered to be cooked well when they were not too mushy, neither overcooked nor undercooked. Wild game was roasted on spits or boiled in water. Saltiness was not a favored cultural taste for Ojibwe palates as it was for the porcupine. Neither was porcupine meat a beloved flavor, although an early winter capture of the animal in its den could be accomplished by an unarmed hunter and help stave off starvation. Hunting would remain an outdoor activity that attracted many visitors to the Upper Peninsula, and nearly every household knew how to prepare and cook venison well into the twenty-first century. Small game also was abundant in the UP visited by early travelers, but a lot less familiar to early cooks in settlements and towns. Across the twentieth century, cookbooks commonly continued to provide recipes for preparing such wild meats as bear, porcupine, muskrat, and beaver. By the 1950s, porcupines had disappeared from the landscape, and most recipes for faux porcupine used beef and added rice to mimic the porky quills of the past.[89]

Ingredients

4 to 6 pounds porcupine meat, trimmed of excess fat and cut in serving size pieces (Note: Any wild game or strongly flavored red meat such as goat can be substituted for the porky)

1 cup flour, seasoned with 1 tablespoon Creole seasoning or 1 teaspoon each of salt and pepper, ¼ teaspoon cayenne, and ¼ teaspoon paprika

¼ bacon slab, finely chopped and rendered

2 tablespoons cooking oil

2 cups water

1 cup tomatoes

¼ cup vinegar

1 garlic clove

1 teaspoon salt

1 teaspoon pepper

¼ teaspoon ground cloves

¼ teaspoon nutmeg

¼ teaspoon allspice

¼ teaspoon cumin

2 bay leaves

4 potatoes, diced

4 small onions, diced

4 stalks celery, diced

4 carrots, diced

Instructions

Render bacon fat in oil. Dredge the meat in seasoned flour. Brown porky meat on all sides in the hot oil in a Dutch oven or cast-iron kettle set over a fire or in the oven at 325 degrees. Add wet ingredients, then seasonings and spices. Cover and simmer for about 1½ hours or until the meat is tender. Add remaining vegetables and simmer another 20 minutes or until done.

AN ENVIRONMENTALIST'S PICNIC (1909-31)

Of a Sunday we will go a-picnicking and very often we
shall find delight in the reaches of our river.
—Aldo Leopold, Letter to his brother Frederik (1906)

When the logic of history hungers for bread and we hand out a stone,
we are at pains to explain how much the stone resembles bread.
—Aldo Leopold, *A Sand County Almanac, and Sketches Here and There*[90]

Hunting for fern fronds, collecting mushrooms, and tapping maple syrup are still treasured family activities across the Upper Peninsula. The environmentalist Aldo Leopold notes of the lowly mushroom, "It is an object lesson. One need not doubt the unseen."[91] Other early travelers, such as Louis Agassiz, had enjoyed foraging for the hidden treasures. Taking Agassiz's culinary advice, the nearly inedible "Parisian" bread from his meal has been omitted and replaced with native wild rice in the recipe below.

Hedgehogs and Fiddlehead Ferns with Wild Rice

Out here, the pine and birch are thick. Beneath the thin, sandy surface
of the Upper Peninsula beneath the path, the trees' roots reach out

like hands linking and twirling. Water penetrates the soil and when it can't go down any further, the soil perspires, and the mushrooms emerge. . . . Hedgehog mushrooms would be here any day now. The hedgehogs have little toothlike filaments beneath their small caps. . . . [The mushrooms were] growing up as if they were in a body of water. As it was, perhaps millions of years ago, this place was covered in water so when you thought about it, it made sense.[92]

—Iliana Regan, *Fieldwork, a Forager's Memoir*

Wild rice and mushrooms were harvested by First Nations people on land and from canoes on the water. Harvesting wild rice required a relationship with the landscape:

Nanaboozhoo, the cultural hero of the Anishinaabek was introduced to rice by fortune, and by a duck. One evening Nanaboozhoo returned from hunting, but he had no game. As he came towards his fire, there was a duck sitting on the edge of his kettle of boiling water. After the duck flew away, Nanaboozhoo, looked into the kettle and found wild rice floating upon the water, but he did not know what it was. He ate his supper from the kettle, and it was the best soup he had ever tasted. Later, he followed in the direction that the duck had taken and came to a lake full of Manoomin. He saw all kinds of duck and geese and mud hens, and all the other water birds eating the grain. After that, when Nanaboozhoo did not kill a deer, he knew where to find food to eat.[93]

The rice darkens during processing and cooking. Its rich, nutty flavor is unique in evoking the landscape. Fiddlehead ferns (*Matteuccia struthiopteris* (L.) Todaro), wild hedgehog mushrooms (*Hydnum repandum*), a mycorrhizal fungus with teethlike spines that lives in a symbiotic relationship with trees, and morel mushrooms (*Morchella americana*) traditionally are gathered wild in the mid- to late summer and fall (hedgehogs) or early spring (morels and fiddleheads), one long parade of foods giving way to another next year. Sautéed in butter and then steamed until tender, the ferns and mushrooms make a delicious accompaniment to wild rice and can be stirred into the rice, once both components are cooked.

Ingredients

1 cup wild rice, washed

4 cups salted water

2 tablespoons butter

½ pound hedgehogs, morels, or other wild mushrooms

12 fiddlehead ferns

Instructions

After rinsing, then draining the rice, add wet rice to the salted water. Bring to a boil, then cover and simmer for about 45 minutes, until the water is absorbed and the rice has darkened but is not mushy. While the rice is cooking, prepare the mushrooms and fiddlehead ferns by sautéing them in butter. Cover and steam slightly. Season with salt and pepper and set aside. Add to the cooked rice and fluff with a fork.

Purist's Trout

This recipe pays homage to conservationist Aldo Leopold, whose experience of UP picnics spanned decades. The title (but not the recipe) is borrowed from *The Ford Times Traveler's Cookbook*.[94] In that book, Kennedy and Rodgers define the purist's claim "that the flavor of the trout is enhanced when it is eaten with the fingers." The recipe itself is my mother's. Since her mother Gertie died when she was a small child, she must have learned it from her older siblings (likely either Elda or Arlo) or from her father, all of whom were among the great fishing and cooking folk in the UP. Much later, the 1947 list of Aldo's camp provisions included both packaged foods (spaghetti and tinned food) and ingredients for picnics (fresh perch), all employed for cooking inside and outside of his Les Cheneaux field shack. Among the basics were blue cornmeal, Crisco (shortening), and flour.[95]

Ingredients

1 pound fresh lake trout or other small fish filets, cleaned but not dried off

1 cup flour

½ cup corn meal or blue corn flour

1 teaspoon salt

½ teaspoon black pepper

1 teaspoon cayenne or creole spice mixture (optional)

1 tablespoon cooking oil, Crisco, leftover bacon grease, or lard

Instructions

Put a mixture of flour and cornmeal, seasoned and stirred together with salt, pepper, and creole spice mixture (or simply cayenne), in a brown paper bag. Add the cleaned filets of perch, walleye, or trout and shake until lightly covered. Fry in a skillet in medium-hot oil until cooked, about 10 minutes, turning sides when the coating turns golden brown.

Lumberjack Blues with Maple Syrup

Blue cornmeal was a ubiquitous ingredient across the UP, interchangeable with buckwheat and other hearty grains. It was among the ingredients stored by Aldo Leopold in his summer cabin's pantry. Techniques of boiling the sap from maple trees were learned from First Nations peoples in early encounters. The sap of trees other than maples was also consumed. One of my own earliest childhood memories is tapping the maple trees off Lakeside Road in Cedarville with my grandfather, Gertie's husband. The maple syrup we collected in wooden buckets to boil in the spring lasted all winter long. It is the perfect complement to the nutty flavor of the Blue Corn Cake.[96]

Ingredients

¾ cup blue cornmeal
1 teaspoon salt
1 tablespoon sugar
1 cup boiling water
1 large egg, beaten

½ cup milk
2 tablespoons butter, melted
¾ cup all-purpose flour
2 teaspoons baking powder
1 cup blueberries (optional)

Instructions

In a medium bowl, mix the blue cornmeal, salt, and sugar. Stir in the boiling water until all the ingredients are wet. Cover, and let stand for a few minutes.

In a measuring cup, combine the milk, egg, and melted butter. Stir the milk mixture into the cornmeal mixture.

Combine the flour and the baking powder. Stir into the cornmeal mixture until just incorporated. The batter will be blue. Add blueberries, if desired.

Heat a large skillet over medium heat and grease it with a dab of butter.

Spoon batter onto hot skillet, and when the entire surface of the pancakes is covered with bubbles, flip them over and cook the other side until golden. Serve immediately for a savory side dish or with pure maple syrup and fresh berries as dessert.

3

THE FLOATING PICNIC

Here, history surfaces as not some smooth and linear passage of time,
but a messy mix of conflicts, upheavals, resistance, wars, drawing of
borders, and transformations of collective and individual identities.
—Anand Yang[1]

At sea at least a traveler contemplates a vast horizon at which he always
looks with hope. But in this ocean of trees, who can show you the way?
—Alexis de Tocqueville, *A Fortnight in the Wilderness*, August 1, 1831[2]

From a distance, the large party of gentlemen-scientists paddling in four canoes along the shores of Lake Superior in the summer of 1848 might have looked like their Ojibwe-speaking counterparts. Their meals would have suggested that they were nothing of the sort. On closer examination, there were the cooking utensils stored in the bow, and the canoe's makeshift masthead was a cast-iron skillet, an intentional symbol of the distinctive cuisine with which they proudly traveled. Boasted one of the travelers, "Our canoe was distinguished by a frying-pan, rising erect over the prow as figure-head, an importance very justly conferred on the culinary art in this wilderness, where nature provides nothing that can be eaten raw except blueberries."[3]

The canoe party was the scientific trip led by the famous Harvard scientist Louis Agassiz, who also carried along the bulk of their own global provisions, including salt pork, sea biscuits, wheat flour, salt, tea, and coffee. Instead of indulging in the flavors of native wild rice, they ate potatoes. When provisions of pork and biscuit dwindled and local foods seemed scarce, only then would the visitors contemplate eating *tripe de roche* (an edible lichen, when boiled). In fact, the global sojourners also found plenty of local wild birds, rabbit, and fish, lots of fish, even fish for breakfast. Lacking yeast, the men pressed a dough of flour, water, and salt into the iron and baked a fine bread to accompany their fire-roasted pigeons and duck. They had brought with them coffee and tea, both of which were shipped in from the tropics, halfway around the world, but they sweetened these global drinks with the sugar made from locally tapped maple syrup. During daylight meals, the men picnicked in clearings along the lakeshore. They are depicted with their food spread across a blanket, where they sat on the ground near the "Island of St. Ignace" in midsummer.[4] At night they listened to lectures and observations by Professor Agassiz. They discussed and debated his ideas on the edge of a wilderness, home to a separate species of humans whose habitat had shaped the outcome of nature and culture.

Agassiz and Cabot "picnicking" near St. Ignace, 1848. The group arrived by boat and first glimpsed the distinctive shorelines and the edge of the woods from the vantage point of the water. Source: Agassiz and Cabot, *Lake Superior*, facing page 78.

The Upper Peninsula was what one scholar has called "a space of flows," in part because it was connected to the world via networks of waterways and commerce.[5] Thus began an era of sourcing the ingredients of meals from an array of local culinary traditions and the global marketplace of ideas and goods. While held outdoors, their nineteenth-century campsite meals perhaps cannot be called true picnics, but the golden era of the picnic was not far behind. And the so-called classic picnic would arrive at its destinations in boats.

FROM CANOES TO STEAMSHIPS

The practice of glimpsing the landscape from one's vantage point on the water continued well into the second half of the twentieth century, when even train and automobile travel often concluded with a boat ride. Many parts of the Upper Peninsula region remain reachable only by boat and thus some are not always accessible year-round. Yet no view of the Upper Peninsula's landscape would be complete without consideration of its waters. Louis Agassiz, with his fleet of four canoes, had observed this dialectic when he offered his observation of Lake Superior:

> In geographical position the lake would seem naturally to lie within the zone of civilization. . . . But on the north shore we find we have already got into the Northern Regions. . . . The lake shows in all its features a continental uniqueness and uniformity, appropriate to the largest body of fresh water on the globe. The woods and rocks are everywhere the same, or similar. The rivers and the islands are counterparts of each other.[6]

The corresponding purpose of rivers and islands appeared to demonstrate the unity of their belonging to a singular system of land and water carved from the region's natural history and reachable by boat.

Not only the early voyageurs and curious scientists traveled in birch canoes. For generations before, Anishinaabeg (including Ojibwe) identity and culture relied on the connections that canoes could trace in the landscape. The canoe (*wigwaas jiimaan*) was well suited for the UP landscapes. Constructed from

A large party of canoes arrives at the confluence of the St. Mary's River and Lake Superior, c. 1900s–1910s. Photograph courtesy of the US National Archives and Records Administration (77-SOO-u-019).

the bark of local birch trees, canoes were used for transportation, harvesting wild rice, fishing, and trapping. The realms of water were equally the counterparts of what was and would be the wilderness and its woods.

From earliest times new settlers arrived by boat to the peninsula and its many islands, until the winter's lake ice prevented most travel. Maritime culture included hours spent on the water, listening to familiar sea shanties, feeling the lake breezes, and accumulating a knowledge of place as not defined by overland transfers but gained from mobility between ports. The maritime traditions also shaped the shared culinary roots in port cities. In time, there were new and innovative cultural interconnections made possible by the global mapping of rivers, lakes, and oceans.

Global technologies also made possible improvements in transportation. The steam engine, an essential component of manufacturing during the Industrial Revolution in Great Britain, was applied to the demands of distance in North America. In August 1807, the precursor of the *Clermont* made the voyage between New York and Albany on the Hudson River. Described by one observer as "a monster moving on the water, defying the winds and tides, and breathing fire and smoke," Robert Fulton's steamship successfully replaced horse ferries and windsails.[7] Steamships reduced shipping time and expense for the movement of passengers and commercial cargo in the long nineteenth century. From the Hudson, Thames, Mississippi, and Congo Rivers to the subsequent oceanic and lake voyages, steamboats expanded populations, enhanced mobility, and drove commercial growth. Their speed and mobility came at a high environmental cost, however. Steamships had delivered cheaper and faster travel but required stands of oak and pine (and later coal) to fuel their engines.

The new oceanic crossings by steamships provided all travelers with a common diet of salted and dried fish and meats, plus foods frequently pickled and preserved in vinegar. Maritime traditions added new flavors to the local diets of early settlers over the centuries, regardless of where they had originated. Lake crossings became a mainstay of the flow of residents and tourists alike. Arriving by boat remained the common thread of experience for most inhabitants and their picnics; from canoe to steamship traffic, populations of sojourners reached turbulent waters.

THE CULINARY WATERS

The Upper Peninsula's natural history coincided with a turning point in the region's culinary history. The creolization of Euro-American and native flavors was underway as the forces of globalization were opening the wilderness to the dramatic century and a half of change ahead. The modern-day enterprises had relied on the scientific adventures of men like Louis Agassiz and Douglass Houghton, Michigan state geologist from 1837 to 1845, who described his own "wading the streams by day, tortured by swarms of mosquitoes at night—often short of provisions, and often drenched by rain—were it not that courage is uplifted by the love of science, both for its own sake and the good it is to accomplish. . . ."[8] While the devastating consequences of the European invasion are undeniable, some of its most enduring legacies also resided in the cooking pots and culinary tales of the region's history, a history written by both people and provisions arriving by boat.

For the earliest French voyageurs who arrived by canoe, the traveling diet differed little from that of their later British counterparts. Their meals were comprised of twice-baked sea biscuit, smoked pork, and peas, carried on canoes in canvas sacks and eaten with individual spoons in communal fashion. One voyageur traveling by canoe around 1800 between Lachine (Montreal) and

Mackinac Island in Lake Huron was personally outfitted with something akin to a picnic basket. He took along this "traveling basket, containing a boiled ham, some sea biscuit, salt, tea, sugar, and pepper, with a tea-pot, a small time kettle in which to boil tea water, a tin cup for tea drinking, two tin plates, two knives and forks, two iron spoons, and a small canvas tent for fair weather."[9] As global goods were gathered and sold in exchange for pelts, Indigenous communities were drawn increasingly into their orbit as trading partners and sometimes as wives. Multiple foodways, altered by place and provisions, coexisted. The European permanent settlements and forts remained relatively unobtrusive, the numbers of inhabitants small, claiming a minimal environmental impact on what it meant to be in the Ojibwe wilderness (*bagwaj*)—that is, until the 1840s.

Mining and logging brought thousands of new settlers from around the globe. The science of the wilderness had acquired a new value in its ability to create wealth and shift resources and populations. Not everyone would share equally in the bargains that were made. The new immigrants brought their own recipes and lists of ingredients that were truly global. Arriving on passenger and cargo ships, the immigrants together would shape an American cuisine. The copper industry attracted immigrants from around the world, including Cornish, Finnish, Prussian, German, Swedish, Danish, and Italian settlers, who labored in the mines. So, too, did the mining of iron ore. As the sea shanty called out: "Come all ye bold sailors that follow the Lakes / On an iron ore vessel, your living to make!"[10] And come they did from foreign realms: miners, blacksmiths, tanners, saddle makers, grocery store owners, brewers, clergy, engineers, firemen, historians of mining, and cooks.

These encounters provide historians with a recipe for understanding how a truly global community in the far reaches of the Michigan Great Lakes eventually created a distinctly American regional cuisine and unique food traditions centered around the picnic. The portable foods like the pasties spread beyond ethnic groups engaged in mining and became recognizably an Upper Peninsula cuisine. The everyday diet and shared picnic fare clung to the relative predictability of abundant wildlife, including fish and small game that were salted and smoked. Here in the Upper Peninsula, hunting, fishing, and trapping remained important. There were few farmers. The growing season for agricultural pursuits was extremely short in the Upper Peninsula. Some crops failed even to yield a harvest. Potatoes could be grown with decent results, but they and other vegetables struggled to come to fruition before the snows arrived. Even the wild strawberries at St. Ignace, it was noted, had not ripened by the first of August in 1841.[11] But the fishing seemed endless in the nineteenth century, and whitefish and walleye were caught easily by scooping them up in nets. Without much effort, thousands of barrels of fish could be had. Hunting seemed not to diminish the abundance of foods. Certain species of birds and animals even increased around human settlements. Accordingly, quail and even deer were more abundant on the edges of the forest than in its interior, where "the most striking feature of these woods is their stillness and loneliness."[12]

Rough Seas Ahead

While deep, the waters were anything but still. The Great Lakes proved to be a vast, watery graveyard for many over the next century. The particularly dangerous Lake Superior would become home to numerous shipwrecks, with more than 3,700 identified to date. Despite the area around Isle Royale being known for its frigid waters and sudden storms, it hosted a large fishery throughout the nineteenth century. Between the 1880s and about 1920, commercial fisheries created another boon in lake fishing that sent thousands of barrels of salted whitefish, lake trout, and sturgeon south to city markets. In return, provisions like lard, wheat flour, corn, and cheese made the return journey in schooners and steamships. For example, the SS *America*, built in 1898, was at first an excursion vessel between Chicago and Michigan ports. When it sank in 1928 off Isle Royale, it had been repurposed for freight and passengers. Five lifeboats were launched to save the few passengers and crew. One island resident remembered locals eating the ship's cargo of fruit all summer as it slowly resurfaced and was washed ashore.[13] History had, indeed, surfaced.

History also has surfaced through the systematic archaeological excavation and recovery of artifacts from many shipwrecks. The remains of ships reveal not only the messy attempts to establish national boundaries on land and water (shipwrecks are owned by the many nation-states, under whose flags the vessels sailed) but also the nature of daily life and common maritime cuisine served onboard. Using autonomous underwater vehicles mounted with sonar equipment, scientists have identified wrecks up to depths of three hundred feet under the waters of Lake Huron.[14] The steamship era ended when the ship SS *Noronic* (known as the "Queen of the Great Lakes") was destroyed by fire, resulting in more than one hundred lives lost in 1949. On Lake Superior, where more than 240 ships are known to have been lost off Whitefish Point, the most famous shipwreck was the SS *Edmund Fitzgerald*, a freighter that sank in 1975, long after the golden age of steamships. The technology and the dangers of the Great Lakes were persistent actors in the lives of locals, who routinely sailed four of the Great Lakes, which had been declared international waters following treaty agreements by Canada and the United States in 1909.

CEDARVILLE BOATWORKS

Gertie's husband, Robert Hamel (1888–1973), is best remembered as an expert boatbuilder. His *Chippewa* rowboat, a fourteen-foot-long Whitehall-style lapstrake vessel with a "very low freeboard, plumb stem, and wineglass transom," rests in the local Les Cheneaux Maritime Museum.[15] He and older brother Harrison formally started up their boat construction enterprise in 1907. When Harrison moved away for some time, Robert continued boatbuilding on his own. Robert was one of five brothers, the sons of Michigan pioneer Anthony Hamel and Ida Mae Truscott.

Born on Mackinac Island in 1854, Anthony boarded at the Truscott family home, where he met and married the daughter of George Truscott. Anthony and Ida then moved to the Les Cheneaux Islands, where Anthony was a commercial fisherman in the summers and harvested ice in the winters. His efforts on the lake were more successful than those on land. The first attempt at proving the lands he had settled failed because they had been inadvertently omitted from the early government surveys in 1840 and 1845. He finally succeeded in homesteading in 1893, during the administration of President Benjamin Harrison. Anthony eventually built their log home on Lakeside Road, near Cedarville, and he towed a barge carrying Ida's beloved piano from Mackinac Island to the new home in the Les Cheneaux Islands.[16] Anthony's son Robert also fished commercially, as would two of Robert's sons, Arlo and James.

Truscott family home on Market Street under construction on Mackinac Island, 1900. Wood for construction on Mackinac mostly originated on Bois Blanc Island, a site of later picnics. Photo courtesy of Mackinac State Historic Parks Collection.

The Cedarville Boatworks' operations were responsible for handcrafting vessels of many sizes and types. The *Ferro*, built by Robert in 1912, was an early commercial steam tug used in the family fishing business. It hauled and delivered catches of whitefish and lake trout by the ton load. Other prized boats included the launch *Peerless* and the fifty-two-foot *Alice B*. The *Peerless* caught fire two minutes off Mackinac Island in November 1920, when its gasoline

Gertie's youngest daughter, Hyla Hamel Goucher, poses by the replica of the *Chippewa*, originally built by her father, Robert Hamel, around 1910 and reproduced by Cedarville's Great Lakes Boat Building School a century later. Photograph by the author, c. 2013.

engine backfired and sparks exploded the cargo of $1,200 worth of hams, bacon, salt pork, and lard destined for H. P. Hossack's general store in Cedarville.[17] Earlier, Anthony himself had reconditioned a schooner into a steam-powered fishing tug called the *Joker*. That vessel had the last laugh and ended up sinking in the icy waters near Moscoe Channel one winter. The piece of land at the end of Strongs Island is still known locally as Joker's Point. Like many locals, the Hamel family transported visitors, sold fish and ice to the local hotels, and carried on their seasonal businesses in a cycle of commercial activities linked to the water. In the summer, the *Peerless* and the *Ferro* carried fish and transported passengers across the Great Lakes, including to Cheboygan and Rogers City, where Robert must have first met Gertie sometime after 1912. By 1914, R. P. Hamel's company was reported in the local newspaper as having enjoyed a prosperous summer season and the business was described as a "growing enterprise" before the November 1920 disaster.[18]

Building boats was a lucrative venture throughout the history of the Upper Peninsula. Everyone, from residents to visitors, relied on boats for transportation and supplies. Smaller rowboats like the *Chippewa* required one or two oarsmen, they were quick, and they performed well in the choppy waters of

The E. J. Mertaugh Boat Works of Hessel went into business in 1925, becoming the first franchisee for Chris-Craft wooden boats with marine combustion engines in Northern Michigan and Canada. Photo courtesy Jack Deo/Superior View.

the Great Lakes. Lapstrake rowboats also served less experienced sailors. Most of the homes and cottages near the lake had several rowboats and sometimes a canoe. The demands for well-crafted vessels kept Robert Hamel and several other boatbuilders busy, including E. J. ("Gene") Mertaugh and sons, beginning in 1925. The small vessels were commonplace, used for visiting family and friends, fishing for meals, and wooing a sweetheart. Locals never tired of being on the water, and visitors soon learned to keep their conversations to a hush since the calls of loons and human conversations were amplified by the cooling of the air above the lake surface and the slowing of refracted sound waves.

STEAMSHIPS OF THE GREAT LAKES

Larger iron vessels were built Down Below. The steam engines and coal-fired boilers for the passenger steamships operated by the Detroit & Cleveland Steam Navigation Company were built by the Dry Dock Engine Works at Wyandotte and sold to the Detroit Dry Dock Company, which constructed the rest of the wooden and steel ship. Designs included the sidewheeler and passenger steamers with steel hulls. The extensive Detroit shipbuilding operations relied on a machine shop, sawmill, carpenter shop, boiler shop, smith shop, forge, paint shop, and dual dry docks before lifting the vessels into the water. The *City of Alpena* passenger steamer built there remained in operation from its year of build in 1893 (with a refit in 1912) until 1957. The *City of Mackinac* seen in Gertie's album was launched in 1893, the same year as the *City of Cleveland*. Like the *City of Cleveland*, the *City of Mackinac* was an overnight passenger vessel that had side paddlewheels churned by its steam engine. It sailed as the *City of Mackinac II* between 1912 until 1920, then as the *City of Holland* in 1922 until it was towed to Sturgeon Bay, Wisconsin, to be scrapped after 1936. After a disastrous fire necessitated an entire rebuild, the *City of Cleveland* was launched again in 1908 for her maiden voyage from Wyandotte to Sault Ste. Marie. With a capacity of 4,500 passengers, the *City of Cleveland* and similar steamships propelled the future of tourism in the Great Lakes for nearly half a century.

Regular passenger service had begun in 1817. Ever since the Sault Ste. Marie Canal was completed in 1855, larger and larger vessels had been able to navigate the confluence of the St. Mary's River and the northern lakes region. The "*saut*" (seventeenth-century French word for "jump," meaning a cataract, waterfall, or rapids that required traversing around) became "Sault" or "Soo" in colloquial English. Journeys that had once taken seven weeks now took minutes.[19] Enormous ships carried passengers and freight. Other regular voyages transported tons of iron, copper, ice, and timber to Chicago, Cleveland, Detroit, Buffalo, Toronto, and beyond. The tourist-packed steamships offered accommodations: room and board. About a third of the passengers chose to purchase sleeping berths. Of course, those passengers "who prefer to bring a well filled lunch basket" would pay far less for their passage alone.[20] A steady flow of curious passengers arrived daily for transport in the busy summer months of the late nineteenth and early twentieth centuries.

The great steamships also catered to the rapidly growing urban populations of Midwest cities. By the end of the nineteenth century, the Upper Peninsula became more than the occasional playground of the wealthy urban industrialists. Easily accessible tourism afforded some Americans the newfound ability to access the wilderness that urban expansion and global industrialization were rapidly destroying. Well-to-do Americans from Cincinnati, Detroit, and Chicago became these "Summer People," families ensconced for the summer and fathers often visiting at weekends. Some of them, after repeatedly visiting with their families, eventually built their own lake cottages. Other visitors frequented a burgeoning market of hotels for restorative

Advertisement for Detroit & Cleveland Navigation Company with steamship lines between Detroit, Mackinac Island, St. Ignace, and Chicago, 1925. Courtesy of Detroit Historical Society, 2011.062.011.

sojourns and annual family vacations in the summertime. Once the hotels and boardinghouses of the UP housed temporary guests, visiting members of local families, or seasonal workers. The new wave of tourism now promoted a distinctive view of the region as a water world, guaranteeing guests the opportunity to "play and rest where health and happiness abound."[21] For the summer people, the UP was perceived to be a static and comforting landscape, unlike the chaotic urban streets they had left behind when they climbed aboard the steamship.

The picnic season was intertwined with the schedule of the steamships. By 1925, the popular Detroit & Cleveland Navigation Company advertised the season's duration, beginning in June and ending in September. Navigation between Detroit, Mackinac Island, St. Ignace, and Chicago would open Thursday, June 25, from Detroit, and Saturday, June 27, from Chicago. Liners left Detroit three days a week: Tuesdays, Thursdays, and Saturdays; and they departed from Chicago on Mondays, Thursdays, and Saturdays, with the last liners leaving Detroit on September 5 and Chicago on September 7. One advertisement's images included iconic tourist scenes of interest to would-be passengers: the steamship connected Chicago's palatial Municipal Pier on the Lake Michigan waterfront to Arch Rock on Mackinac Island, while the classical goddess-figure clad for battle (a symbol of the city of Chicago after the Great Fire) and a forest gnome, a buffalo, and a frog look on.[22] The Chicago Municipal Pier stretched more than a half mile out into the lake. Its construction was a symbol of technological "progress" through modern engineering. Its completion on the lake's waterfront in 1916 had been celebrated by crowds of more than seventy-five thousand in a single evening and was well worthy of boasting rights.[23] In 1921, the city was still applauding this technological feat by holding the first Pageant of Progress, an industrial and business exposition attended by more than one million visitors. One observer noted how the pier uniquely combined "the business of shipping with the pleasure of public entertainment."[24] Among the exhibits was the portrayal of Chicago as "the greatest lumber yard in America," by bringing "the lumber jacks and log rollers from the northern woods, and demonstrations of how logs are rafted down a river."[25] The steam company's 1925 advertisement succinctly emphasized the essential differences between the two lakefront landscapes, one profoundly urban and the other still occupying wilderness. Detroit & Cleveland Navigation Company also successfully exploited

Tug *James W. Croze* and picnic scow at Cook's Bay, east of Arnes dock, West Hancock, filled to capacity by the picnickers. Courtesy Michigan Technological University Archives and Copper Country Historical Collections, Earl Gagnon Photograph Collection.

the city's new motto: "I Will" (written on the warrior's breastplate) unofficially had replaced the original motto, "Urbs in Horto" (City in a Garden), around the time of the 1893 World's Fair. Now the phrase was used to beckon the former garden dwellers to the wilderness of the Upper Peninsula.

FROM CAMPING TO PICNICKING

The steamships, together with smaller passenger boats and local vessels, also connected the regional towns and cities to the growing tourist industry beyond the pier on Mackinac Island. Across the Great Lakes, businesses emerged to carry picnickers to their destinations. By 1911, the Arnold Transit Company owned several smaller steamers that were able to navigate the region's narrower channels and deliver goods and passengers to a wider circuit. Frank Kramen remembered the days of the early hotels, whose appearance kept pace with the swelling population of tourists in the Les Cheneaux Islands:

The arrival of the island steamer was always an event everyone looked forward to. It carried passengers, mail, and freight. If you had free time, you would hurry to the dock to see who and what was arriving. Porter Johnson always met the boats to sell his little white bags of popcorn for ten cents. He would throw the bag up to the customer and they would throw the dime down.[26]

One of the earliest Cedarville hotels was owned by the McBain family. They first arrived in the area as summer visitors in the 1880s. Departing Mackinaw City for Mackinac Island by steamer, three generations of the McBain family and their luggage then traveled the rest of the way to Boot Island in Anthony Hamel's sailboat. Each summer afterward, they camped out in tents whose center poles were living trees, until finally they built their own cottage. Anthony continued to supply the family with whitefish and perch, but many of their provisions had been brought from their home in Grand Rapids. Most travel was by rowboat that connected Boot Island with the lumber camp's general store in Prentiss Bay. By 1896, the family's summer colony had a permanent headquarters, and eventually they operated the Lakeside Hotel.[27]

At the turn of the century, sturdy wooden planks were often used to construct summer picnic tables and benches. An account of a 1900 picnic at McGulpin's Channel displayed the appeal of an outing with "well filled picnic baskets" that served a gathering from Coryell Island. Several large cakes, hot coffee or tea, and perch cooked over a campfire were served to the picnic group.[28] The Hamels and other locals provided a steady supply of fish to visitors. Many visitors longed to catch their own fish. Local hotels also employed fishing guides to take tourists fishing. In 1897, the Islington Hotel alone engaged thirteen guides, who were expected to be able to "row a boat all day when called upon."[29] Visitors shot ducks, hunted deer, and went sport fishing. Even women rowed boats when called upon.

PIRATES AND PICNICS

A row of cottages along Big LaSalle Island in the Les Cheneaux area had its start in 1908, with the summer home built by Hubert Heuck, who also had been coming to the area since the late 1890s to escape the Cincinnati summer, enjoy

McBain family picnic, Cedarville. Courtesy Les Cheneaux Historical Association, Andrew Tanner Collection.

Fish fry, August 1903. Courtesy Les Cheneaux Historical Association, Andrew Tanner Collection.

the curative air, and fish in the lake waters. The spot was selected because it was rowing distance from Cedarville. Other Ohio family members and friends soon followed suit, and their cottages became known to locals as "Cincinnati Row." Hubert Heuck had picnic tables and benches built for picnic spots on Government Island, at Peck Bay, and at Sand Cove, promoting picnicking and ferrying picnickers in the Heuck family's luxury gas-powered motorboat, a Truscott motor launch built in St. Joseph on the shores of Lake Michigan.[30] The next generation of Heuck picnickers bought a World War I surplus steel lifeboat they playfully named *Captain Bing*, after the popular nursery rhyme and folksong:

Captain Bing was a Pirate King
And sailed the broad seas o'er;
Where none had sailed his bark
Where none had sailed before,
And filled his hold so full of gold
That it would hold no more.[31]

The Cincinnati families continued to gather annually for the summer picnic for the next hundred years. They are still going strong into the twenty-first century.

An extraordinary silent, black-and-white 16 mm film records the 1926 antics of the Heucks and members of other early families enjoying a summer picnic and acting out an original, scripted play titled *Buttercup and the Pirates* (1926).[32] The home movie was shot at Bush Bay and likely had been inspired by that summer's popular Hollywood silent adventure film *The Black Pirate* (1926), which starred Douglas Fairbanks. Buttercup was the name of the newspaper comic strip character, the son in *Toots and Casper* (1920–56), a comic about a family and their friends and neighbors, as well as the name of an earlier character in the Gilbert and Sullivan comic opera *H.M.S. Pinafore* (1878). Filmed during Prohibition, the home movie scenes included a beachfront campfire and kettle, the treasure chest carried from the beach, the abduction of Buttercup, a pirate ship, and pirates hoisting a bottle of "rum" (although actual drinking on camera was prohibited by Hollywood studios at the time). As the "Pirates" battled the "Settlers," family members brandished weapons and dressed themselves in earrings and scarves, while their children donned fake

Movie poster from the silent film *The Black Pirate* (1926). Courtesy of United Artists.

Indian headdresses for a colorful reenactment of the classic pirate tale of rescue and revenge in the Les Cheneaux Islands.

BOATS AND BOOTLEGGERS

Prohibition, a nationwide constitutional ban on the production, importation, transportation, and sale of alcohol (in the period between about 1920 and 1933), itself ushered in a real era of piracy and bootlegging across the UP. There was already a long tradition of local distilling and brewing, using everything from spruce and hops for brewing to grapes and other fruits successfully grown by nineteenth-century Italian immigrants for winemaking and grappa. During the Prohibition era, the Northwoods proved fertile ground for the illicit distillation of barrels of spirits and moonshine, especially when the harsh winters helped isolate the inhabitants. Moreover, their knowledge of lake currents, swamps, local trails, and wilderness hideouts allowed transporters of whiskey and rum from Canada to easily pass through the region. Beginning in 1910, wooden speedboats were manufactured by the Smith Ryan Boat Company (and later as the Chris-Craft vessels after 1924). The speedboats handled the tourist trade during daylight hours and made rum-running a nighttime occupation. Based on local accounts, both men and women continued to imbibe at dances, picnics in the woods, and other social gatherings.

Prohibition was a controversial political movement that gathered steam in the twentieth century, but it had much deeper roots. The Women's Christian Temperance Union's *Howell Cook Book* suggests the coded racist connections between anti-immigrant, anti-black sentiment and temperance "dry" views, when they exhorted readers to come and join the "White Ribboners," who believed in "whiteness for heart, soul and body."[33] The UP had its share of white supremacists and KKK organizers for temperance (and racist and xenophobic activities) but also had plenty of "wet" supporters from the German, Italian, French, Catholic, and other cultural communities. The proximity of the UP to Canada and the Great Lakes' maritime traffic was a natural boon to widespread disregard of Prohibition and the illegal trafficking of spirits. Not surprisingly,

Beach picnic near Cedarville, Fourth of July 1908, with picnickers posed with fish and bottled drinks by their rowboat. Photo postcard, Hamel family album.

Michigan was the first state to ratify the Twenty-First Amendment repealing Prohibition in 1933.

Drinking at picnics was commonplace, even throughout the era of prohibition, and added to the revelry expected. At picnic sites that were often remote spaces in the landscape, picnickers felt emboldened to partake in beverages that were brought in bottles and glass canning jars. Spirits were distilled and beers were brewed locally. The flavors of the home-brewed spruce beer were among the most enticing.

EATING AND DRINKING THE FOREST

Although at the end of the nineteenth century it was still possible to see "in every direction the woods," differentiating its many parts was a matter of experiencing something imagined to be both eternal and ephemeral. The wilderness had a visceral impact noted by many who worked and lived there. Some even humanized its force. Stewart Edward White (1902) described the picnic's place with nostalgia for its scented mysteries:

Not an opening of any kind offered the mind a breathing place under the tree sky. Sometimes the pine groves,—vast, solemn, grand, with the patrician aloofness of the truly great; sometimes the hardwood,—bright, mysterious, full of life; sometimes the swamp,—dark, dank, speaking with the voices of the shyer creatures; sometimes the spruce and balsam thickets,—aromatic, enticing.[34]

The picnickers consumed the forest with all their senses, not simply with the meal's food and drink. Consuming maple syrup had been described as literally "drinking the forest."[35] The tree's sap, or water, was collected, and it became a syrup when boiled down. Maple syrup producers were mere "enablers," since it was not augmented with other ingredients, while the syrup's consumers were literally "drinking" the pure, unadulterated wilderness (tree sap minus a little water content).

Spruce provided another way to drink the forest. Its scent was remarkably floral and woodsy, and it made the memory of the wilderness last beyond the edge of the forest. Best of all, spruce could be brewed into beer. Spruce boughs were believed to have medicinal qualities and so were used in cooking. Green spruce logs were used for construction or in cooking fires to support the pot or kettle. When boiled, the fresh shoots provided vitamin C. For this reason, spruce beer had become an early favored beverage for sailors prone to scurvy on long voyages and thus the drink spread around the world with European maritime culture. Similarly, the oily foliage of northern white cedar called by Ojibwe-speakers *nookomis giizhik* (*Thuja occidentalis*) was rumored to have cured the scurvy of Jacques Cartier in the sixteenth century, when consumed medicinally, and a soup was even made from the inner bark.[36] Bottled spruce beer was popular in colonial societies of the Americas, including in the Caribbean, where it was marketed commercially. Amelia Simmons's recipe "For brewing Spruce Beer" at home appears in the first American cookbook, *American Cookery* (1796):

> Take four ounces of hops, let them boil half an hour in one gallon of water, strain the hop water then add sixteen gallons of warm water, two gallons of molasses, eight ounces of essence of spruce, dissolved in one quart of water, put it in a clean cask, then shake it well together, add half a pint

of emptins [a liquid leavening made from hops or potatoes], then let it stand and work one week, if very warm weather less time will do, when it is drawn off to bottle, add one spoonful of molasses to every bottle.[37]

The beer was known on both sides of the maritime Atlantic, and it had been recommended by James Lind in his *Treatise on the Scurvy* (1753), among others, as a medicinal curative. Spruce beer recipes also appeared in the appendix of the 1803 edition of Carter's *Frugal Housewife*.[38]

Although Simmons was writing from her home in Connecticut, it is quite possible that bundles of spruce boughs and the brewed drink were traded locally from the UP during colonial times. Spruce beer was made and drunk at Fort Michilimackinac, catching the attention of one trader, who noted, "Here are three or four kinds of Spruce pine, one of which is the best for making beer of any on ye Continent."[39] The recipe's addition of molasses to the concoction was quintessentially American and a consequence of the combined growth of the slave trade and Caribbean sugar production in the Atlantic. The popularity of spruce beer rivaled that of wine, which was much more expensive to acquire. Spruce also could be infused and drunk as nonalcoholic tea. While the spruce tree might grow to twenty feet in circumference, the spruce (and balsam) of the UP mostly were associated with the shrubs that appeared in the expanding areas of secondary growth at the forest's edge.

Picnics and Ice

Alcoholic beverages were clandestine guests at the picnic. In the nineteenth century, alcohol commonly was added to hot drinks, which do appear in most early photographs of UP picnics. Mugs and kettles also can be seen at sites of campfires. Summertime brought a greater desire for cooled drinks, with and without spirits. Ice was only one way to achieve a refreshing, "chilled" beverage. Long before refrigeration, watermelons were buried in the beach sand and glass bottles were placed in the cool lake waters. Ice was purchased as well by households and businesses. Bostonian businessman Frederic Tudor, known as the "Ice King of the World," was the first to sell ice globally. In the early nineteenth century, he began to ship North American ice to faraway places, such as the Caribbean and India. Stored in local icehouses, ice was available year-round in the UP.

Thanks to the long and unrelenting winters, the UP ice was not only abundant but also special. Hotels had their own icehouses to save the big blocks of ice harvested from the winter lake. Freighters purchased these ice blocks for use in transporting perishables all the way back to the tropical Caribbean.[40] If Peter White's 1905 Marquette, Michigan, recipe for rum punch is any indication, locals in the UP combined the best of both worlds by adding imported Jamaican and Cruzan rums to other ingredients (including strong tea) and an eight-inch-square block of ice that was waiting in the punch bowl.[41] White (1830–1908) had successfully moved on from more humble beginnings sailing on commercial schooners to become the Commissioner of Parks and Cemetery and a civic leader in Marquette.

Commercial fishermen, like Grandpa Bob Hamel, had a more practical use for the ice. They used the harvested ice blocks to store their large catches of fresh fish prior to transport. Robert Hamel, like his father before him, harvested the ice in the winters. The special lake ice also held a beautiful, clear blue

Harvesting ice on the Lake Huron Dam. Photo courtesy of Michigan Technological University Archives and Copper Country Historical Collections.

luster. According to John Griffin of Cedarville, this color was believed to be due to the repeated blowing away of snow, followed by the freezing over of new layers of moisture on the lake, a common phenomenon in the unrelentingly long UP winters. This process of gradual compression of the water in snow reduced its air bubbles. Similarly, the same processes had increased the density of the ice of glaciers, which gained their tint by reflecting the blue color of the light spectrum.

Ice harvesting was an annual season across the UP. In the time of Harold Dunbar Corbusier on Mackinac Island (c. 1883), ice harvesting was a community activity in view of everyone.[42] Once the lake ice was thick enough (about a foot and a half), it was possible to travel across it on dog sleds or horse-drawn sleighs. Year-round residents made expeditions across the ice to Bois Blanc Island or Round Island, whose larger stands of woods yielded firewood for cooking and heating houses during the cold and snowy winter. In the harbor, horses dragged a rake-like ice plow across the ice, scoring and marking the lines of the blocks for cutting. It was difficult and dangerous work to create a canal through the thick ice. Harvesters then moved the blocks to a nearby place on the lake that had been cleared of snow. There the blocks of ice could be drawn up onto sleds to be transported to an icehouse. By the time of summer picnics, the winter's ice was a distant, stored memory, yet able to be retrieved for special occasions, for drinking lemonade or rum punch cocktails, and for making ice cream. Until electricity and refrigeration became widespread innovations in the 1930s, ice harvesting was still commonplace. Permanent residents had underground cellars lined with sawdust for the great blocks of ice, and their ice boxes in the kitchen stored smaller chunks. In summertime, the ice became the memory of the monochrome winter. It wasn't the only suggestive element in long-forgotten picnics.

SOUVENIR OF A PICNIC

I returned once again to Grandma Gertie's album and the set of photographs taken that day in July 1911. There was something nagging me about the one and only building slightly visible in the background edge of one of the five picnic photos I had spent so many years thinking about. I searched for other old photographs of Boblo, the dock at Pointe aux Pins, and its old Hotel Pines. This limestone building, with its distinctive arches, was not visible in any of them. Then, unexpectedly, I found the architecture across the lake. The building was part of the Bob-Lo Island Amusement Park, in operation between 1898 and 1993. My grandmother's picnic had taken place on the *other* "Bob-Lo" island, Down Below at the mouth of the Detroit River, on the Canadian side of the Great Lakes.

Because Bob-Lo was reached only by steamship and ferry boat, Gertie's outing suggested something else about Great Lakes steamship travel. Now more aware of her travels by boat, I noticed her album was filled with scenes of the *City of Mackinac* steamboat, of women on smaller boats and barges and docks, and often posing on the deck of a steamship or ferry. Friends and family cavorted in front of the Anchor Monument, the remnants of the SS *City of Cleveland*, erected at Bob-Lo in 1909 as a tribute to the lake sailor and the inland maritime activities on the Great Lakes. Residents of the far north were not only the recipients of tourists and guests, whom they welcomed to the UP. They, too, were travelers to special picnics held afar. The Detroit and Cleveland Steamship Company had included one stop in Rogers City on Mondays and Wednesdays, plus stops in Cheboygan, Alpena, Ste. Ignace, and Mackinac, for its destination voyages going south to Detroit, a route unavailable in 1889.[43] Other excursion steamers like the SS *Ste. Claire*, built in 1910, could disembark more than two thousand passengers in a single trip to Bob-Lo. The Ferry Company owned the island and the dedicated ships that sailed there for the next eighty years. The owners tried to keep careful control over guests and their behavior by outlawing alcohol and rowdiness, African Americans and "Zoot-suiters." At first, the island guests enjoyed Bob-Lo picnics in a manicured recreation area, alongside a dance hall, and a small amusement park around the turn of the century. In 1908, improvements included baseball diamonds, a horse barn, a souvenir building, and four picnic shelters.[44] Palm trees imported from Cuba and a huge new dance pavilion were planned for 1912–13. In 1948, the US Supreme Court ruled against the racial discrimination practiced by the island's boat company and Bob-Lo operations.[45] By the 1950s, the Bob-Lo Island Park was so popular for families and company picnics that picnic reservations were required. Monster picnics with ten thousand guests were arranged by organizations, who held annual events among the island's five thousand picnic tables and benches.[46] The Bob-Lo Island Park's masthead eventually claimed its picnic prowess: "Bob-Lo, Where Most Picnics Go."[47] Eventually, Bob-Lo declined in the wake of the postwar ability of the family car to reach vacation spots far away from urban centers. The memory of Gertie's picnic had been my gateway to her life and my family's place in the Upper Peninsula. Perhaps its actual location didn't really matter as much as her own recorded memories of the gaiety of the day with watermelon and friends.

A souvenir (from the French word meaning "to remember") is a remembrance or memory. The photographs were souvenirs, imperfectly understood images, with complex, sometimes even unseen meanings embedded in their many "readings." In another of the album's photographs, Gertie again poses with friends. This time there is a box camera hanging from a leather strap around her wrist. It was likely one of the Kodak Brownies ("Operated by Any School Boy or Girl," boasted the contemporary advertisements), which initially sold for only one dollar. In this photograph, Gertie stands at the ready to make her own memories, with their own set of associations and personal significance.

The summer picnics also cannot be understood without reference to the long winters that the summer seasons had preceded and would follow. Winters isolated by the lake ice made the region culturally distinct. The return of summer restored access to the water and to the world beyond. The picnic season meant locals socialized after their workdays. The picnic season brought family members, who had migrated out of the region during economic downturns. Finns had left after the failed 1913 strike. Some locals moved away during the Great Depression or during wartime. Other family members would follow the expansion of shipbuilding and the creation of the automobile industry. From far-flung places, they returned home for the summer picnic.

Gertie's brother-in-law Guy Hamel wrote of the simplicity of the "picnic" reached by boat in his diary, dated July 18, 1913: "We lifted the outside nets today. The Girls Bachelor Club (G.B.C.) gave a marshmallow roast on Government Island tonight. It was a swell night. . . . There was a full moon on a still calm night." The intimacies of resident rowboats and canoes gave way to larger vessels, although the romance of the waters lingered. Modern steamships were romanticized as "honeymoon ships" and "floating palaces," and they would once again remind the "islanders" in the Upper Peninsula of the journeys ahead toward the century's promises of modernity. The monstrous movers of people and goods across the Great Lakes were not the only nor would they be the last technologies to transform the culture and foods of the picnic.

PICNIC WITH PIRATES

Everyone loved to go to our Round Island beach parties . . . the silverware came from the Chippewa Hotel and later the Town Crier *reported that there was buried "silver" in the sand of Round Island.*
—Thomas W. Pfeiffelmann, *Mackinac Adventures and Island Memories*[48]

Jokes and pranks were commonplace among the families that summered annually. Amidst the revelry and laughter of Summer People and Locals, who socialized together over the years, many enduring friendships were formed. Arriving at the summer cottage was a ritual performed repeatedly, with many lucky visitors and part-time residents making their way to the UP for twenty, fifty, or even sixty summers.[49]

Whitefish Walks the Plank[50]

[I was served] a whole whitefish, on a plank three feet long. . . . Here they produce both planks and fish. The fish they served me was caught the day before, and the plank at that time was in the tree.
—Ebert Hubbard, "In Copper Country," 1914

And what tastes better than a really fresh whitefish cooked to the Queen's taste over an open fire?
—Guy H. Hamel, Cedarville realtor, c. 1940

This recipe was inspired by the enormous salt-crusted fish still cooked on cedar planks at Calumet's Michigan House Café, home of Red Jacket Brewing, which is famous for their vintage beer (a flagship oatmeal brew from a 1905 recipe).[51] The Michigan House Hotel and Buffet has stood on the corner of Sixth and Oak since at least 1895. The 1906 painted mural of brew-happy picnickers still decorates the ceiling.

Recipe: Cooking fish on a cedar plank adds a smoky flavor to the mildest of fish, enhancing its moist texture and sweet taste. Soak your wooden plank in water (maple, cedar, or alder work well) for at least 1 to 2 hours. Place the cedar plank that has been soaked in water on the grill and let it start to smoke and blacken. This will allow the quick-cooking fish to absorb more flavors. Place the lightly seasoned fish on the board and reposition the plank in a region of indirect fire. Cover and cook until done.

Sailor's Duff (1909)

Duff is basically any type of steamed dough in the maritime world. Sailors would be rationed the meal's flour and hang their dough in cloth bags suspended in the copper kettles to be steamed with the day's meat rations onboard long voyages. Salt (saltwater) and perhaps a bit of sugar, and sometimes bits of pork, were typically added to this savory mainstay. Duff's fancy relative was Plum-Duff, a version with raisins or currants or other dried fruits ("plums") prepared on Sunday. Food supplies across the Upper Peninsula relied on the regular arrival of steamers in most months of the year, until the formation of winter ice made the lakes unnavigable. The economic importance of maritime shipping increased after the completion of the Soo Locks in 1855 and further linked the UP to global markets. This recipe for Sailor's Duff is a Sunday version of the English steamed pudding.[52]

Recipe: ½ cup molasses, 2 tablespoons sugar, 2 tablespoons melted butter, 1½ cups sifted flour, 1 teaspoon soda in ½ cup boiling water, 1 egg, pinch of salt. Steam 1 hour—this serves 7 persons. Sauce: ½ cup powdered sugar, 1 egg beaten thoroughly. Just before serving, add ½ pint cream whipped.

Rumrunner's Down-the-Hatch Tea[53]

Bootleggers found themselves in busy lake waters during Prohibition time. Speedboats carried tourists to and from larger ports in the UP by day and bootlegged northern alcohol to southern destinations by night. The run between Canada and the Upper Peninsula was difficult to police, and small boat owners could make a bundle on a quick journey overnight carrying distilled spirits.

Ingredients

2 tablespoons or 1 part maple syrup

1 part whiskey

1 part gin

1 part dark rum

1 part vodka

1 part sour mix (of pulverized
    berries and citrus juice)

Mint leaves

2 cups lake ice, shaved

Instructions

Mix the ingredients above with 2 cups of blue lake ice. Shake. Garnish with mint. Makes four cocktails.

PICNIC BREAKFAST ON THE DOCK WITH A BRASS BAND

The Hossack bakery has been in commission turning out good things for some little time but we have yet to see the famous "sticky buns." The tourists far and wide know these buns and when the bakery is turning them out nearly every launch that visits Cedarville takes away a consignment of these buns. It often happens that few of the items reach the home dock.
—*St. Ignace Enterprise*, June 22, 1916

Hotels offered guests everything they had dreamed about a magical vacation, from brass bands and popcorn on the arrival dock to clean lake air, rowboats, and fishing guides, once the guests had unpacked. Groceries and various picnic and household supplies were delivered by boat from local stores to cottages and cabins across the region. Among the more unusual offerings were the famously delicious sticky buns baked at the Hossack family bakery in Cedarville and sold on the docks alongside bags of popcorn to arriving passengers.

Sticky Buns[54]

Ingredients

Dough

1 package dry yeast
¼ cup sugar, divided
¾ cup warm milk
1 egg, beaten

1 teaspoon salt
3¼ cups flour
⅓ cup butter, softened

Topping

½ cup brown sugar
3 tablespoons light corn syrup
⅓ cup butter

3 tablespoons honey
½ cup walnuts or pecans

Filling

3 tablespoons melted butter
½ cup brown sugar

1½ teaspoons cinnamon

Instructions

In warm milk, dissolve yeast and 1 teaspoon sugar. Let rest for 10 minutes. Mix in sugar, egg, salt, and butter with a spoon. Add about 2½ cups flour and mix well. With clean hands, mix another ¾ cup flour to make a soft dough. Place on a floured board and knead until smooth and makes a ball. Place dough in greased bowl; grease dough. Cover and let rise in a warm place until dough is doubled, about 1½ hours. Grease a 9 × 13 pan. Prepare topping by heating ingredients over low heat, except the nuts. Sprinkle nuts in pan and pour topping over nuts. Punch down dough; place on a floured board and knead briefly. Roll dough to about 12 × 20.

Spread with butter and sprinkle on sugar and cinnamon mix. From long side, roll as a jelly roll. Cut into 1-inch slices and place in pan. Cover and let rise until doubled. Bake in a preheated oven, 350 degrees, for 30 minutes. Turn pan upside down on tray to cool.

Coffee with Chicory

Hot drinks were welcome guests at a picnic Up North, especially after a chilly boat ride. Coffee was preferable to tea at the turn of the twentieth century, but it was a relatively expensive drink that originated in the tropics. Various additives, including tree bark and sawdust, found their way into UP coffee pots. First documented in the logging camps, coffee beans were hand ground fresh each morning, with the cooks having to rise at about 2:00 a.m. for the extra hour it took to please one hundred men with their morning java. A favored combination, especially among French immigrants, was coffee with chicory. By about 1902, chicory was grown successfully along the Great Lakes at Port Huron. The Great Lakes chicory dominated 90 percent of the American chicory trade from the era of the First World War, when European supplies were embargoed.[55]

Instructions

Slowly roast the peeled and cleaned chicory root, finely sliced, cut in small pieces, and placed on a roasting pan, at 200 degrees for about 5 to 7 hours until toasty. Grind when cool. Use with ground coffee, brewing as you would brew the coffee alone, by pouring hot water over the coffee and chicory through a coffee filter or by immersion in a French press. The ratio of coffee to chicory root should be adjusted to individual taste; start with a 3:1 ratio (coffee to chicory) and two tablespoons of the coffee-chicory grounds with 6 ounces of boiling water.

Maple Popcorn

In the 1920s, bags of popcorn cost five cents at the Cedarville Dock on the wharf near the main street. As a ten-year-old boy working as a cook's assistant on the launch *Lotus*, John Sellman remembered how the man operating a popcorn machine "poured just the right amount of popcorn into the container that hung over a blue gas flame which then gently swung back and forth until the popped corn began pushing the lid open and the corn spilled onto the bottom of his glass-enclosed cart."[56]

Ingredients

8 cups of popped corn

3 tablespoons butter

3 tablespoons maple syrup

2 tablespoons brown sugar

1½ teaspoons salt, plus salt in a shaker

Instructions

Make the popcorn. Combine 3 tablespoons butter, 3 tablespoons maple syrup, 2 tablespoons brown sugar, and 1½ teaspoons salt in a glass measuring cup. Heat together until melted in the microwave or on the stovetop. Pour over the pre-made popcorn to coat the popped kernels evenly. Spread on a baking sheet and bake in a 350-degree oven for about 15 minutes, until crisp, turning occasionally. Sprinkle popcorn with finishing salt to taste.

FLOATING ISLANDS

Family lore claimed that Gertie's signature recipe was something called "Floating Island." Originally a fancy European dessert comprised of poached meringues "floating" in a sweetened or custard crème, the popular midcentury *Betty Crocker's Picture Cookbook* eventually boasted a recipe for the home cook in lean times. For outdoor picnics, the dessert's meringue could be made ahead and stored or whipped up on the spot in the way that ice cream was made at a picnic. Floating Islands were companions to the surplus of summer fruit and welcome picnic treats playfully anchored in the watery landscape.

Lafcadio Hearn's Classic Floating Island[57]

Recipe: Beat the whites of 5 eggs with a little currant jelly until they are quite thick. Sweeten a pint of cream, add a teaspoon of extract, pour it in the bowl, and then drop your whites of eggs and jelly by the spoonful on the cream. If you cannot procure cream, you may make a substitute of a custard, made of a pint of sweet milk, yolks of 2 eggs, and ½ cup of white sugar cooked together.

4

THE PICNIC TRAIN

As for the food, those summers were one long picnic.
—Nika Hazelton, *The Picnic Book* (1969)[1]

For every native of every place is a potential tourist,
and every tourist is a native of somewhere.
—Jamaica Kincaid, *A Small Place* (1988)[2]

The sensations experienced upon a return to city life and hustle
from the quietude of the wilderness are somewhat indescribable.
—William H. S. Harding (c. 1875)[3]

INTRODUCTION

The album page near the end of the book tells another story, another dimension of Gertie's picnic world. It is a story of the lake, a train, and three boats. In the first of four photographs on this page, she poses in the middle of the railroad tracks near the caboose of a train. It is the early winter in about 1914, and there is snow on the ground. Gertie is wearing boots. They are covered with snow. She wears a hat and a fashionable dark coatdress, bundled into a matching dark

Gertrude Meyer ready to board a train,
Hamel family album, c. 1914.

wool outercoat. In her right hand, Gertie holds the chain of her pocketbook and grasps the small white train ticket. The photographer casts a shadow in front of her on the snow. Clockwise, a photograph of the *City of Mackinac* with its steamboat passengers crowded on the upper deck, then another with Gertie posing alone by the autumn lakeshore, where the fallen leaves on the ground have left the branches of the trees shivering and bare. The last photograph is also on the lake, with a large wooden dock and two vessels, a rowboat—the *Mary* [O?]—and a larger, longer vessel, perhaps the *Alice B*. Like the passengers one sees or imagines in the images, these photographs take the viewer along with Gertie on a journey that relies on both the boats on the water and the trains that will wind their way across the land even in winter. These photos suggest the end of the picnic season.

In Gertie's short lifetime, the world had changed. It had been interconnected by a complex network of railroad tracks and steamers. In less than a century, the world had constructed hundreds of thousands of miles of railroad tracks that were linked to bodies of water. By 1900, the new age of railways offered unique vistas of a modern global experience. Writer Christian Wolmar put it succinctly: "Quite simply, without the railway, the United States would not be the United States of America."[4] To paraphrase Wolmar, the Upper Peninsula would not have been the Upper Peninsula without the shipping and rail connections that delivered its ores and forests to the world and welcomed the world back to the wilderness that remained. Even the seasons of the picnic had been transformed.

THE IRON ROADS

Iron roads were train tracks that eventually ran through much of the Upper Peninsula. The railroad greatly impacted many facets of life, providing a key transportation link prior to the days of the automobile. Trains not only carried iron and copper ores and hewn logs from the region across the nation. The railroad was also an essential node of the transport network for provisions and manufactured goods needing to be shipped regularly into the UP. The railroad connected the rest of the world to the steamers of the Great Lakes. We need only follow the iron roads to find more picnics.

The railroad was a global phenomenon. The first railroad to link two towns on double tracks with a steam engine was the Liverpool & Manchester Railway, opening in Britain in 1830. Three years later the first tracks were laid in Michigan. By the twentieth century, there were more than six hundred thousand miles of railway built around the world. The first trains in most places were horse-powered, and only later were steam-powered locomotives placed into service. In North America, the transcontinental railway was renowned for its excellent meals served by waitresses known in the 1890s as "Harvey Girls."[5] By 1900, in most parts of North America, trains had already surpassed steamboats as the dominant form of transportation, but in the UP the two forms of transport seemed irretrievably linked.

In the far northwest of the Upper Peninsula, the first railway, the Iron Mountain Railroad, was chartered in 1855, replacing the original horse-driven tramway with steam. After a wait of nearly two years, the steam locomotive arrived by ship at Marquette. Not all of the early tracks were made of iron rails. A wooden track served the steam-powered trains of some of the early lumber mills. At the state's farthest point north, the Keweenaw Peninsula saw iron roads in the Copper Country constructed by private companies to transport goods to harbors. Although the movement of freight was uppermost in the desire to extend tracks, passenger trains were not far behind. In the 1880s, the cities of the UP were connected by railway tracks, and lines contracted with steamship companies to carry the railway cars across the lakes, ending the long centuries of relative isolation for many parts of the UP. If a transcontinental railroad could link two oceans, the technology also could find a way to connect the two peninsulas of Michigan.

The *St. Ignace*, a wooden ferry, did just that. That it was equipped with ice-breaking technology allowing operation outside of the summer season spoke to the expansion of possibilities for the UP region's growing population. A few entrepreneurs were willing to embrace that vision. The upscale vacation retreat on Mackinac Island, the Grand Hotel, was built in 1886–87 by two railroad companies and a steamship company working together to develop their lucrative passenger markets in North America. Luxury train service was also available by train on the Soo Line connecting Minneapolis and Montreal across the UP via Sault Ste. Marie ("Soo" being the phonetic spelling for Sault, the eastern terminus). Luxury service meant meals were served onboard and the leather seats and sleeping berths provided greater comfort. The St. Paul Railroad sought to capture the Lake Superior market for travel, linking Chicago and Milwaukee with its "Lake Superior Division." The railroad extended into Michigan towns, reaching Hancock and Marquette in the north. Their trains were advertised in the *Calumet News* as "Solid Trains, Fast Time . . . [with] Pullman Buffet Sleeping Cars" for would-be passengers traveling in 1897.[6]

For travelers at the other end of the Upper Peninsula, travel by rail became more common during Gertie's lifetime. Construction of the state's iron roads peaked in about 1911, when more than nine thousand route miles were operating in all of Michigan.[7] These trains reached Mackinaw City, Cheboygan, and Rogers City on the shores of Lake Huron, connecting the Lakes by trains traveling to Detroit, Chicago, and Cleveland, and competing with the routes of steamships until they reached the northern waters. Trains worked their way through the interior of the region, providing fast connections to the lakeshores and becoming part of the everyday reality of modern transport. In 1913, the world's tallest railroad terminal was built in Detroit, drawing even more attention to rail travel as stylish and modern. The ease and availability of relatively economical transport via trains cut travel times and made it possible to travel longer distances more frequently. Moreover, the trains tried to seize the commercial potential of the UP's picnic destinations.

The building of railroads also accelerated the movement of the region's natural resources. The plunder of centuries-old pine and hardwood forests of the Upper Peninsula continued to reap huge profits, leaving behind clear-cut fields of stumps and only a few remnants of old-growth stands, for example, in the Porcupine Mountains and the Keweenaw Peninsula. Appropriation of land and wealth were not the only inequities that emerged in the UP, although the loss of biodiversity was inseparable from the cultural losses of Indigenous peoples. The rise of the modern mining industries brought forth its own set of clashing interests. Mine owners and labor fought battles as the landscape was ravaged and exploited by new technologies. Deforestation, toxic debris from mining and smelting, and the diversion of lakes and rivers by damming, digging, and the construction of the Soo Locks all led to vastly diminished and permanently altered landscapes. Opening the lakes to ocean waters eventually introduced new, destructive species of fish, like lampreys, river herring, and voracious trout, into fresh lake water habitats, upsetting local ecologies.[8] The lampreys arrived in Lake Ontario in the 1830s and took a long century to reach the other Great Lakes. In England, lampreys had been baked into sea pies since the Middle Ages.[9] In the Upper Peninsula waterways, this foreign fish devoured the local fishing industries.

The lived experience of iron roads and forest loss skewed palates immediately toward a more globally dependent cuisine. Trains were significant in altering the food chain. They transported passengers and freight, enhancing the mobility of immigrants and enabling the distribution of foods across the nation and the globe. At the time of the first official American government census in the nineteenth century, most of the UP's population was foreign born, and communities were far from achieving a homogenous cultural or regional identity. Added to significant ethnic differences were socioeconomic, racial, and gender divides that intensified throughout the nineteenth century. These disparities were reflected in the foods people ate.

The Migrants Arrived in Pittsburgh, One of the Great Industrial Centers of the North in The Migration Series, Panel 45 (1941) by Jacob Lawrence. © 2023 The Jacob and Gwendolyn Knight Lawrence Foundation, Seattle / Artists Rights Society (ARS), New York. African American travelers were compelled to carry picnics on their train journeys.

Less than a century after slavery, the image of the picnic basket itself symbolized freedom, as the painting by African American artist Jacob Lawrence *The Migrants Arrived in Pittsburgh* in *The Migration Series*, Panel 45 (1941) suggested visually. Since the end of Reconstruction (1865–77), tens of thousands of blacks had fled the South for northern cities. Trains were a vital link for the Great Migration, an era that witnessed more than half a million African Americans moving from the South to the North and Midwest between 1916 and 1919. Lawrence's painting depicted one of these historic train journeys, with a black family of travelers seated around a picnic basket. The visual irony of Lawrence's picnic was emphasized by the fact that the picnic took place in front of Pittsburgh factory smokestacks seen through the train window. Was the satisfaction not to be found in the food (merely imagined in the unopened basket) but perhaps rather in the journey itself? Likely, for the African American travelers during the Great Migration or for any person of color escaping the South in the Jim Crow era, the picnic basket was a more complex symbol. It also might substitute for the roadside restaurant foods off bounds to people of color in a still-segregated America. The ravenous bounty of the ideal American picnic remained mostly unreachable for many Americans, especially during the interwar years leaning into the Great Depression.

Building the railroad brought new arrivals everywhere, including to the Upper Peninsula. Racial minorities sometimes arrived by train or on foot, as the African American experience demonstrated. The train tracks themselves had long been a symbol of freedom, sentiments that echoed in the popular abolitionist words of "Get Off the Track," sung by the Hutchinson Family Singers in the nineteenth century:

Ho! the car Emancipation
Rides majestic thro' our nation,
Bearing on its train the story,
Liberty! a nation's glory.
Roll it along, thro' the nation,
Freedom's car, Emancipation![10]

Many made "haste to Freedom's railroad station" when they traveled to the Northwoods.

Like the African American presence, the UP's Chinese community was similarly small and likely also connected to the extension of the railroad across the West and the expansion of mining. Asian laborers were essential to the construction of railroads in Cuba, in the American West, and in the South. As the iron roads plunged into the Midwest seeking profits off transporting Nature, including the UP wilderness, the trains also carried laborers. African Americans were employed on trains as porters and cooks. A cadre of African Americans worked for the tourists and summer guests, as guides, housecleaners, and cooks, or by delivering groceries and supplies. Their presence was mostly seasonal.

The first arrival of an African American population was a generation before the age of trains, but a small community was persistently scattered across the region. The first recorded African American presence was in 1782 on Mackinac Island, where the new fort commander Daniel Robertson brought two enslaved Africans captured in Spanish Missouri. Jean and Marie-Jeanne Bonga were married and then freed, and they ran the first hotel on the island. Mr. Bonga and the Bonga descendants worked in the fur trade, some married Ojibwe women, and some became interpreters and guides. Some African Americans no doubt reached the UP as runaways, escaping slavery and discrimination in the South during the nineteenth and twentieth centuries. Census records for 1900 show only two African American farmers out of 1,350 residents in Chippewa County. Other African Americans came primarily as cooks and porters on the railroad. One elderly African American known only as "Snowflake" was a prominent citizen of the Keweenaw Peninsula. Not all communities welcomed racial diversity; the Ku Klux Klan racial purification movement formed in the South in the 1860s and promoted an anti-immigration stance among members. Recruitment efforts of the racist KKK eventually reached across the UP, especially after 1915. Despite the presence of hate organizations, many African Americans worked continuously in the UP. On Mackinac Island, African Americans lived in segregated housing there, or sometimes on the Upper Peninsula mainland, from the 1890s on into the twentieth century. These hotel men, mostly porters, waiters, and other hotel employees, were occasionally photographed enjoying their own group picnics during summers on the island, drinking and smoking cigars. African American women followed later in the century as maids, waitresses, and hotel kitchen staff.

In the Copper Country, African Americans and Asians arrived by train. Many Chinese immigrants and their families were laundry workers, who sometimes owned their own laundries and other small businesses, but more often they worked for others. Their presence is perhaps not surprising since more than seven thousand Chinese were building nearly three thousand miles of the Canadian Pacific Railway to the north of the Great Lakes during the last quarter of the nineteenth century.[11] Some Asians arrived in the UP before or around the time of the Chinese Exclusion Act (1892), but relatively few families stayed for very long because they considered Canadian cities to be much friendlier places. In the UP, they clustered in the mining areas of Calumet, Marquette, and Sault Ste. Marie, where the trains were plentiful and Canada was accessible across the lake.

The Asian American and African American cooks, whose culinary traditions were appropriated by others, largely failed to leave behind their own legacy of printed recipes in the UP before they moved on. However, their culinary shadows can be glimpsed in community cookbooks, for example, in "local"

Hotels on Mackinac Island supported a large service community of African American waiters, porters, and maids, who lived and socialized in segregated communities in the 1880s. Photograph by William H. Gardiner. Courtesy of Mackinac State Historic Parks Collection.

recipes for Southern foods. The taste for these foods appeared to push its way to the Northwoods from Southern fields and kitchens. The *Superior Cook Book* (1905) had recipes for "Chicken Southern Style," and "Southern Sweet Potatoes," "Southern Corn Cakes," and "South Carolina Biscuits."[12] There were no recipes for Chinese food, a cuisine that would be interpreted through Orientalist palates for an American audience in North America's big-city restaurants, like those in New York and San Francisco.[13] The same 1905 local cookbook does offer a recipe for "Oriental Delight," a popular, sweet concoction made with ground figs, dates, and raisins, mixed with sugar, well known in Turkey, Syria, and other West and Central Asian cuisines.

Traveling on trains often *required* a picnic of sorts. City train depots sold food at lunch counters, and food vendors offered up chestnuts, sandwiches, tea, and other snacks. Restaurants were typically located adjacent to the larger train stations, serving arriving and departing passengers and people awaiting family and friends. Historian of picnics Walter Levy places the railway meals taken on the train in a special category of indoor picnic, claiming that they "do not fit into a standard picnic repertoire."[14] The custom of eating onboard the train likely was a holdover from travel on steamships, recognizing that the cost-saving effort of bringing food would appeal to some passengers. Travelers sometimes chose to bring along their own food, equipment, and supplies in luncheon carrying cases that were personalized and condensed versions of larger picnic baskets equipped with cups or glasses, plates, and cutlery. The meals brought from home or purchased en route for destinations afar could not match the anticipation and delight of the picnic sites reached via the Sunday Picnic Train.

THE SUNDAY PICNIC TRAIN

Among the most popular social activities in the UP's Copper Country was the Sunday Picnic Train, a special train of the Copper Range Railroad. A successor to the Northern Michigan Railroad, the Copper Range operated from 1899 to 1972. It was named for its corporate owner, a company that also mined and processed the ores of copper. In fact, as archaeologist Richard Fields has pointed out, the "Copper Range grew from a vision for a regional railroad to a multifaceted mining company."[15] The cofounder of the Copper Range Company (and the stock brokerage firm of Paine, Webber, and Company) was William Alfred Paine (1855–1929), a rich Boston entrepreneur who sold shares in the company and proceeded to construct the railroad through the heavy forests south of Houghton. It was difficult terrain, through wilderness and up and down hillsides, crossing many streams, ravines, swamps, and bluffs between May and December 1899. Building the tracks required cutting large tracts of trees from the forests too remote to profit from transporting and selling their timber, so the wood was burned.[16] When the Copper Range Railroad was completed, the trains carried fifty-ton loads of copper ores from the South Range, passengers in Pullman cars, and various freight, including lumber from new sawmills.

The Copper Range included the Baltic lode, six miles south of Houghton. The Baltic Mine formed the basis of the Champion Mining Company, co-owned by the Copper Range Company. The Trimountain Mine followed in 1899, eventually giving birth to the Copper Range Consolidated Copper Company between 1901 and 1903. During this same period, Copper Range began to explore the possibility of developing the processes of milling and smelting that followed mining of the ore-bearing rocks. In this way, the Freda stamping mill came into being along the Lake Superior shoreline in 1902. Because of the relative purity of the area's native copper (as much as 99 percent), the job required of the company's Michigan Smelter was sometimes limited to skimming the silver impurities off the top of the heated copper in reverberatory furnaces and fashioning ingots, techniques in full operation by 1905.[17]

The consolidated operations began to employ large numbers of skilled and unskilled laborers. Miners lived in company-owned communities, in which services and activities were dictated by company policies. In addition to providing boardinghouses, family housing, hospitals, schools reached by a special company train, municipal water systems, libraries, insurance schemes, banking services, and company stores, Copper Range also provided leisure and recreational activities to build community among the workers. There were bowling alleys and baseball teams, as well as football, skating, and hockey. Land was offered to churches, and there was auditorium space for meetings, musical performances, and dances. There were also exclusive employee excursion trains to Freda Park.

Beginning in 1905 and continuing through Labor Day of 1917, the railway's special Picnic Train delivered picnickers to their destination picnics. As picnic fever swept the region, more than fifteen Picnic Train coaches, twice on Sundays and holidays (between 9:00 a.m. and 9:00 p.m.), ran from Calumet to Hancock to Houghton and then another seventeen miles west to Freda Park, a Keweenaw Peninsula picnic park well groomed by the railway company, with beer and food vendors. There, in the shadow of the nearby stamp mill owned by Champion Copper Company, hundreds of picnickers gathered on their days off. They enjoyed swings, horseshoes, tennis, dancing, and strolling along paths in the woods and on the rocky shore of Lake Superior. A horse-drawn beer wagon appeared in the afternoon. Foods could be purchased at the pavilion's lunch counter or grilled on the spot in barbecue pits. Picnickers emptied the train with their woven picnic baskets in tow or repurposed metal dinner buckets in hand, ready to enjoy the day's outing.

The Freda Park picnic train, 1908. Courtesy Jack Deo/Superior View.

Private excursion trains destined for picnics ran along other railway routes in the United States as well, including one between Fort Washington and Camp Hill, about fourteen miles from Philadelphia, Pennsylvania. A Northern Pennsylvania Railroad train with ten cars was involved in a deadly head-on accident with another train in July 1856. It was carrying between five hundred and six hundred passengers for a church picnic. Noted one observer of the collision, "Fortunately, there was a quantity of ice and ice cream on the train; this was given to the wounded; it refreshed them greatly."[18] Another picnic train tragedy occurred in Broken Hill, Australia, in the context of the First World War and heightened interethnic tensions. An ore train, belonging to a private tramway, had been refitted to carry 1,200 picnickers to their annual fraternal organization picnic. Members of the Manchester Unity of Odd Fellows were traveling to their gathering, a picnic held each year on New Year's Day. The forty open carriages in which the families traveled in 1915 were shot upon by "Turks" (one of them an ice cream vendor from Afghanistan). These rare and tragic incidents profoundly contradicted the purpose and image of the picnic as "pleasure seeking."

Whereas the picnic trains of the Copper Country repurposed the industrial railcars from mining for recreation purposes on weekends and holidays, other picnic trains closer to home were commercial efforts to create picnic parks. The Antlers Picnic and Amusement Park opened on Prairie Lake (now Lake Marion) in 1910. The park, located in Lakeville, Minnesota, near Minneapolis, used gas-electric cars run by the Dan Patch Electric Line to ferry visitors from the city to the lakeshore. The park's name was an intentional "allusion to the former abundance of deer in this region."[19] Photographs between 1911 and 1925 show crowds of visitors, many of them families with children, carrying picnic baskets and lunch boxes as they exit the train. The picnickers could enjoy swimming in the lake's waters, music and dancing, golf, and games.

The Antlers Park Picnic Train was part of an ambitious scheme to gain ridership for the Dan Patch Electric Line Railroad. As the building of railways spread around the globe, rail travel was limited to those who could afford to purchase a ticket. From its earliest days, excursion journeys on special trains like the "picnic trains" offered many people their first opportunities to be rail passengers. The novelty and thrill of the picnic excursion extended beyond the charm of the picnic foods or the offerings of the picnic site. The prospect of the train ride was met with great excitement as new passengers joined the journey toward "progress" and "modernity" on the iron roads, sometimes for their very first train ride.

Picnic trains could be found in other mining towns. Workers and their families at the Porcupine Mine combined picnics with berry-picking in Pine Plains, scenes portrayed in the novel *Inga of Porcupine Mine* (1942) by Caroline Stone.[20] In two Montana towns, the picnic trains became vehicles for the display of ethnic solidarity. In 1885, thousands of Irish miners traveled from Butte to Anaconda, where they disembarked from fourteen train coaches for a parade to the picnic grounds across town. Joining ranks between two copper smelting towns, the four thousand picnickers were members of the United Irish Societies. The picnic's immigrant foods formed the centerpiece of the heritage celebration.[21] By 1890, the Butte Anaconda Hiberian (Irish) Picnic had become an annual event, expanding to include Helena members in contests of strength and skill. Some of the picnickers were organized into military companies, with musical bands and trained guards marching in formation along town streets to the picnic.[22] In 1911, the popular Sunday BA&P trains traveled from Anaconda to Georgetown Lake, a hydroelectric project created by damming the North Flint Creek. Their trains were designated for excursions and filled with groups of fishermen and families carrying picnic baskets on the weekends.[23]

The picnic train phenomenon was not without its critics. Local churchmen in New Zealand complained that "pleasure parties going out on Sundays were the Devil's travellers."[24] Many of the Sunday picnic trains left after the local church services were finished. Like their steamship and barge counterparts, the trains sometimes were commandeered for special excursions or church events besides weekend picnics. Some excursion trains were scheduled after peak travel hours on weekdays. In July 1897, the *Calumet News* reported:

About 100 excursionists left Houghton Wednesday evening [July 21, 1897] on the special train bound for the Shrine of Ste. Anne de Beaupre, Canada. They met the regular Duluth train at Nestoria. This excursion is the largest of the year and draws from the Lake Superior region from the head of the lake to the Soo.[25]

The special train was itself an early religious pilgrimage on the UP's iron roads, likely leaving on Wednesday to arrive in Quebec, Canada, for the Feast Day of St. Anne de Beaupré (July 26). Saint Anne, known as the "Grandmother in the Faith," was believed to be a protectress. She was not only the mother of Mary but also the patron saint of the Province of Quebec, where the basilica contained two relics of the saint at the turn of the century, one brought in 1670 and another sent from the Vatican by the Italian Pope Leo XIII in 1892.[26] St. Anne was believed to be a protectress resident in the basilica. Since the first miracles at the basilica were recorded in the seventeenth century, devoted Catholics beseeched the chapel's saint with their prayers for intercessions in the form of cures and safe passage for sailors in storms on the lakes. The chance to visit the lakeshore, parks, and other scenic vistas on picnics and social outings won over any hesitation owing to the danger or cost of crossing international borders. Picnickers were enthusiastically ushering in the birth of rail tourism.

The picnic trains to Freda Park used the long summer days and the vacant mining train cars on weekends and holidays to appeal to the growing audience of picnic lovers. It is not difficult to see how the summer picnic schedule came about. Picnics constituted a season of their own, in contrast to the rest of the year. Photographs of a Copper Range Railroad passenger train stuck in the winter snow near Houghton were sold as postcards in 1907.[27] In addition to the Copper Range, many of the railways of the Upper Peninsula got their start in the timber trade or in pursuit of mining opportunities. After logging deforested the flat shoreline, the timber industry moved inland, making the transport of logs across increasingly longer distances to the Great Lakes critical to the success of their ventures. The Pere Marquette Railway had its beginnings in the timber trade and connected the UP with markets to the south via St. Ignace. The Soo Line reached from Minneapolis and St. Paul to Sault Ste. Marie and was formed in 1884 as a freight liner carrying the valuable loads of iron ore and with passenger service and connections to Chicago, an alternative to the route known as the Milwaukee [Iron] Road.

While admission to Freda Park was free, transportation to the park before the advent of automobiles was more challenging. Originally as an attempt to boost company revenues, the Copper Range Railroad initiated the picnic train scheme to Freda Park, when the railcars were not being employed for mining operations. One resident observed the excitement that went along with the picnic's journey:

> The train started out from Hancock, crossed the bridge, then turned west in Houghton and ran through the range towns, picking up passengers as it went by. Traffic was heavy and revenue was good. It was a sight to see the special train whizzing by at high speed with banners and flags flying from each coach. The picnic fever was evident everywhere.[28]

By 1908, the Freda Park picnic train extended to Calumet. The cost of a round-trip ticket was one dollar from Calumet and seventy-five cents from Hancock. After crossing the bridge at Hancock, the train turned west and traveled through the lakeshore range towns, where more picnickers waited to board. The journey wasn't over once the train reached the Freda Park Depot. Picnickers then had to walk one-half mile from the train station to the park itself, which was one mile west of the tiny town of Freda. Inside a park that was groomed and maintained by the railroad, there were buildings the company had constructed for concessions, a dance pavilion, swings, tennis courts, barbecue pits, romantic walking trails, bridges, playgrounds, an icehouse, a caretaker's dwelling, a picnic shelter in case of rain, a baggage house, and even an outhouse with multiple stalls. It was a steep climb down to the rocky beach and the shores of Lake Superior, where the picnic outings could lead to swimming and boating on the lake. The picnic trains to Freda Park stopped in 1917, the year that World War I gripped the nation and industrial labor was pulled from the community either to enlist and fight or to join the war effort in the automobile factories of Detroit. Subsequent picnics became more subdued and private, as the modest gathering for a 1918 Copper Range picnic at company manager William Schacht's residence revealed about what once had been the biggest holiday of the year: the Fourth of July celebration.[29]

THE IMAGE OF THE TRAIN AS AN ENGINE OF CULTURAL CHANGE

Trains were portrayed as aggressive, masculine forces forcing their way through a feminine landscape. They were harbingers of times to come. A decade before poet William Wordsworth wrote *Song of Hiawatha*, he penned a protest to the planned construction of railroad track through his beloved English Lake District. Wordsworth and other critics believed the railroad would destroy the "beautiful romance of nature."[30] In the poem, addressed to William Gladstone, the government minister who at the time was in charge of the nation's railways act, Wordsworth asked: "Is then no nook of English ground secure / From rash assault?" The access of the world to new landscapes both excited and frightened people, most of whom had little chance to protest the construction of the world's railway systems.

One of the most famous images to convey the excitement of travel by rail was the realistic portrayal of the busy train station painted by William Powell Frith in 1862. Simply titled *The Railway Station*, Frith's oil painting depicts the chaotic scene inside London's Paddington Station. The filled railway carriages, the

steam engine's ascending smoke, and people rushing and jostling on the plat-
form all indicate that departure is nigh. Hidden in the depths of the painting
are also its meanings for everywhere else in the modern world that would be
touched by the train. That countryside and city were now united in a web of
timetables and schedules. Frith's painting was viewed (for a small fee) by the
British public, who stood in long lines to see its depiction of what was becoming
commonplace. The view from the other side of the Atlantic, where the mech-
anization of transport was fully embraced, was slightly different. The wilderness of the Americas would be of no use if it were inaccessible. Nature would
not be destroyed, because its potential could be cultivated. Americans fully
believed in the potential of technology to conquer the wilderness and advance
modernity. They continued to believe in the promise of the picnic, whose social
utility was uninterrupted by the railroad. The British never had picnic trains,
largely because of the subtle differences in the style and organization of train
carriages. In England the train spaces were private and enclosed compartments.
In America, the passengers were traveling in large, open rooms reminiscent of a
convivial saloon.[31]

As the historian Wolfgang Schivelbusch astutely noted in his history of the
revolutionary impact of the railway journey, "The American railroad continued
what the steamship began."[32] There was an interplay between land and lake, just as
Agassiz had once observed on Lake Superior. Transportation was not just for the
elite sheltered into reserved and cloistered luxury accommodations. The train,
like the steamboat before it, brought together all ranks and classes. The speed
of the train meant it could traverse space and time with startling consequences.
Time zones and transportation-controlled schedules were imposed on passengers. Schivelbusch argues that remote regions were subjected to a "devaluation,"
but really, they were commoditized by mass tourism. According to Schivelbusch, the "traditional space-time continuum" of the old technology had been
"organically embedded in nature." The landscape of the train journey was panoramic, not only because it was the product of the revolutionary physical speed
of trains but also because of the "commodity character" of the journey itself.[33]
The landscape and the passenger, including the young Grandma Gertie with a
ticket in her hand, were also commodities in circulation. This spatial reorgani-
zation made it possible to transport the picnic to a larger audience, to recreate a
false narrative of a wilderness that no longer existed as it once had.

Even the most remote reaches of the Upper Peninsula could be connected to large cities, if their citizens wished to travel by train. Trains expanded the network of the steamships, just as leisure travel spread beyond elites to the working classes. In return, the new transportation's increased flow of tourists brought wealth, where the landscape of tree stumps otherwise might have led to a dimmed outlook. The birth of leisure travel was a global phenomenon reaching the Upper Peninsula during Gertie's lifetime. Her picnic day at Bob-Lo was part of the unfolding of a modern reality: the possibilities of steamships and trains leading the world to its desired scene of picnics and porcupines.

THE ENGINES OF ENVIRONMENTAL CHANGE

Trains carved paths through the forests of the UP and enabled others to consume the wilderness that remained. The appetite of the smelting furnace and the timber requirements of mining activities quickly led to the creation of lumber camps across the UP, where labor-intensive enterprises were intended to harvest the next most precious natural resource of the wilderness, the forest itself. A single furnace could consume acres of trees in a single day.

Once the mineral discoveries occurred, the government stepped in to acquire access to frontier lands for development. As Agassiz earlier described the Keweenaw Peninsula, "this region, then a primeval forest, was ceded by the Chippeway [sic] Indians to the United States in 1843."[34] Such a view mischaracterized Indigenous peoples as being of the wilderness, erasing their historical engagements with the wilderness. Even twenty-five years later, the copper mines were described as remaining lost in the forest; they were contained by nearly inaccessible wilderness. That status began to erode as lumber camps and lumberjacks, the men who lived and worked to harvest the timber, moved into place.

Perhaps the most popular of lumberjacks, Paul Bunyan was a larger-than-life folk legend, whose story may have been based in part on an actual northern woodsman, perhaps Fabian Fournier, a French Canadian. The historical Fournier moved through the Upper Peninsula's wilderness in the late 1860s before moving south to join a logging camp in the Saginaw area. He died in a brawl in 1875, but the exaggerated tales of his strength and stamina lived on. The tales of Paul Bunyan became celebrated through the writings of a Michigan journalist, James MacGillivray, beginning around 1906. And MacGillivray wasn't the only writer to romanticize the destroyers of the American forest as masculine folk heroes.

Conservationist Stewart Edward White had worked as a lumberjack in the area of White Pine (Ontonagon) in 1901, when it was still forested. He, too, idealized the man of the forests, characterizing him as "a strong man, with a strong man's virtues and a strong man's vices. In him the passions are elemental, the dramas epic, for he lives in the age when men are close to nature and draw from her their forces."[35] White's lumberjack-hero is not entirely heroic, much in the style of the later tragic figure created in Ken Kesey's *Sometimes a Great Notion* (1964), a story carved from the Pacific Northwest forests.[36] With the "unconsciously graceful swing" of his axe, the lumberjack fights the forest until he understands it.[37]

Later writing projects extended from Stewart Edward White's time in the woods—ranging from a natural history pamphlet on the birds of Mackinac Island to fictional and nostalgic accounts of the vanishing wilderness for Hollywood films. White's most famous work was *The Blazed Trail* (1902), set in a lumber camp in the Northwoods. It is the story of Harry Thorpe, a lumberman, who enters the wilderness as a stranger, unskilled and uneducated in its ways. It is the tale of "saw-gangs" and "swampers" in the disappearing forest. The trails down which the logs would be dragged were still called travoy roads (from the French *travois, travail*), recognizing the original French and native presence in the British territory and early American industry.[38]

White's logging activities in the Upper Peninsula provided more than a good story or two—they reaped timber for building early homesteads and supported the growth of the shipping and mining industries. Loggers lived in the shanties of seasonal camps, eating meals communally inside camp structures and outdoors. These camps were hardly picnic meals. They were hypermasculine environments, where food and drink were central components in lubricating social and economic relationships. The weekly provisions of the typical one hundred–man camp might include six barrels of flour, two and a half barrels each of salt beef and salt pork, eight bushels of potatoes, three bushels of onions, a barrel of pickles, twenty-five pounds of tea, sixteen pounds of coffee, a barrel of sugar, fifty pounds of butter, and forty pounds of lard.[39] Just such barrels are visible in scenes of local picnics in the first quarter of the twentieth century, suggesting that barrels supplied homes in the community. In White's story, the meals were similarly moments of peace for a lumberjack, like his protagonist, Harry Thorpe:

> At supper he learned something else—that he must not talk at table. A moment's reflection taught him the common-sense of the rule. For one thing, supper was a much briefer affair than it would have been had every man felt privileged to take his will in conversation; not to speak of the absence of noise and the presence of peace. Each man asked for what he wanted.
>
> "Please pass the beans," he said with the deliberate intonation of a man who does not expect that his request will be granted.

One of Thorpe's meals did include the beans, plus salt pork, potatoes, canned corn, mince pie, cookies, doughnuts, and "strong green tea."[40] The camp cook and his assistant (called a "cookee") could make or break the success of logging enterprises. Meals gave a rhythm to the day, just as important as the rhythm of men's work songs.

The music of our burnished ax shall make the woods resound,
And many a lofty ancient pine will tumble to the ground.
At night around our shanty fire, we'll sing while rude winds blow,
Oh!—We'll range the wild woods o'er while a-lumbering we go![41]

Eventually steam-powered saws like that of my grandfather Robert Hamel were used to cut logs for construction, mining, and other industries in the UP. Steam-ships and trains enabled their transport and the growth of the logging industry.

Within about fifty years, the heavy logging of UP forests was complete and new strategies for its exploitation were adopted. The giant, outdoor mess halls of lumber camps were remembered by place-names like "Hungry Hill," where the men had eaten.[42] Once altered, the wilderness itself required new investments, systems of forest management, and the increased reliance on long-distance connections. Eventually, the local smelting with charcoal fuel was replaced by shipping the raw ores for processing in other parts of the country, including

Chicago and Cleveland. In the twentieth century, the wilderness would be transformed into a resource to be protected and managed for multiple uses. It never lost its nostalgic appeal or its mystery. The exploitation of the wilderness, its iron, copper, and forests, enabled transnational flows of people, capital, and foods. Global culinary feasts on the edge of the wilderness were in the making.

THE NEW LANGUAGE OF THE WILDERNESS

The landscape of the picnic fought to live in images and words, from advertisements to paintings to short stories and novels. With its maritime connections and iron roads, the language of the forest also had become global. Simply by being accessible, the wilderness could acquire new meaning. In the brochures of the steamship company, the wilderness was abbreviated as a frog or gnome, both forest creatures in the modern imagination. In another brochure, a geological wonder such as the iconic Arch Rock on Mackinac Island beckoned tourists desiring to travel by rail and steamship from across the country and the world. There, in the northern reaches of the Great Lakes, they could purchase picnic baskets and photographs as mementos. The wilderness could be given a new name to resurrect it. Simply name the picnic and recreation park "Antlers" to create the impression of the lakeshore wilderness destination that was no longer a home to deer, thus no longer a wilderness. This same magic would conjure the disappearing landscape.

Memories of the landscape have no fixed or secure home. Ernest Hemingway wrote his famous story "Big Two-Hearted River," about fishing in the Upper Peninsula, while seated in a café in Paris. The story's beginnings were much earlier and took place on a different continent. The river Hemingway describes was the Fox River, the one he calls Big Two-Hearted River. Born in 1899, Ernest Hemingway had already become a wounded World War I veteran at the age of twenty when he visited the UP on a fishing trip. In September 1919, Hemingway traveled by train from his home Down Below to Mackinaw City with two of his friends. The men took the ferry across the straits and reboarded the train in St. Ignace. Heading north and west, Hemingway and the others then got off their train in the town of Seney.

By Hemingway's time, Seney was a small place adrift in a sea of stumps, having been cleared by logging decades earlier. The town once had been a meeting point of multiple railways and spurs, at least a dozen logging companies, and even more saloons. Instead of an imagined surround of old growth pines, Seney's landscape already had become an environment where the fern and the jackpine remained the irrefutable evidence of colonizers after a vast fire. It was a scarred landscape, not unlike the battlefields of Europe, where Hemingway had witnessed war. In his story, the men exited the train station and walked north of town, crossing the railroad tracks. There they fished at the place locals think could have been the east fork of the Fox River. The men fished and ate what they caught outdoors, picnic-style. It was after this definitive trip that Hemingway became a writer.

The picnic's landscapes were both real and imagined. As the twentieth century progressed, their meanings became intertwined with modern notions of recreation, leisure, and tourism. The train was a symbol of this modernity and the vehicle that greatly expanded the picnic's popularity, its scale, and its reach into the wilderness. Up North the picnic was becoming the ultimate event for consuming the landscape of Michigan's Upper Peninsula, in more ways than one.

Ernest Hemingway in Milan, 1918. His short story "Big Two-Hearted River" was about World War I and Nature's healing potential, although it made no mention of the war and took place in the Upper Peninsula. Ernest Hemingway Photograph Collection, John F. Kennedy Presidential Library and Museum, Boston.

HEMINGWAY'S TWO-HEARTED PICNIC (1919)

I sat in a corner with the afternoon light coming in over my shoulder and wrote in the notebook. . . . When I stopped writing I did not want to leave the river where I could see the trout in the pool, its surface pushing and swelling smooth against the resistance of the log-driven piles of the bridge.
—Ernest Hemingway, "Hunger Was Good Discipline," *A Moveable Feast* (1964)[43]

Much of the food Hemingway describes in his famous short story "Big Two-Hearted River" may have been the menus from an earlier trip the famous author made in 1919. Its ingredients were carried by the protagonist, Nick Adams, on the train and on foot as he traveled from the small town of Seney to his fishing spot. The story reveals the ingredients his lone character carries along to the nearby fishing camp: cans of beans, apricots, spaghetti, a lump of grease out of a can, evaporated milk, tomato ketchup, a loaf of bread and an onion for a sandwich, coffee, and buckwheat flour for pancakes with apple butter. The narrative follows the healing act of the fish being caught and cleaned. We don't know how he cooked them, but in his knapsack, Nick Adams still has the remaining half of the onion and bacon grease left for his skillet after the day's fishing has concluded. Once the train left him, disappearing along the train track, he felt everything else had been left behind. He was alone with only an "island of pine" in a scarred landscape. With him there was the steady certainty of the angry trout Nick Adams sought:

He thought of the trout somewhere on the bottom, holding himself steady over the gravel, far down below the light, under the logs, with the hook in his jaw. Nick knew the trout's teeth would cut through the snell of the hook. The hook would imbed itself in his jaw. He'd bet the trout was angry. Anything that size would be angry. That was a trout. He had been solidly hooked. Solid as a rock. He felt like a rock, too, before he started off. By God, he was a big one. By God, he was the biggest one I ever heard of.
—Excerpt from "Big Two-Hearted River" by Ernest Hemingway (1925)[44]

Recipe for an Angry Trout

Ingredients

1 tablespoon grease or lard   1 angry trout, gutted and cleaned
½ onion, thinly sliced

Instructions

Heat the grease in the skillet. Salt and pepper the fish to taste and set aside. Add onion slices to the pan and place the fish on top. Once the onion slices have caramelized, transfer them to the inner cavity of the fish. Brown the steamed fish on both sides to crisp the skin and continue cooking until done, about 6 to 10 more minutes.

Mrs. Koopikka's Nisua (Finnish Coffee Bread)[45]

Wildflowers and farms reclaimed the once-forested land that began to be traversed by trains. In the early twentieth century, many new Finnish immigrants were attracted by the agricultural land offers, and they resettled their families away from logging and mining onto farms, where they grew berries, wheat, turnips, apples, and potatoes, and established dairy farms. Recipes were shared from mother to daughter, among church groups, and within small Finnish communities, who harvested and thrashed their crops together and then shared communal picnic meals at the end of the workday. Finnish communities held group picnics throughout the twentieth century.

Ingredients

2 cups milk, scalded and cooled   1½ tablespoons salt
¼ pound butter, melted in the milk   1 cup sugar
1 to 2 yeast cakes or packets   7 cardamom seeds, peeled and crushed
2 eggs, beaten   6 to 8 cups flour

Instructions

Combine first two ingredients and then add yeast, when cooled enough. Mix the remaining ingredients to form a round dough and let rest in a bowl. Let rise to twice its bulk, kneading twice. Divide dough into 6 parts. Braid each loaf with 3 pieces. Bake at 300 degrees for 1 hour. Makes two loaves.

Red Jacket Cherry Salad[46]

The Montmorency cherry was brought to North America from Europe and first planted in the Grand Traverse region of Michigan by the Reverend Peter Dougherty in 1852.[47] Cherry orchards soon replaced the wooded hills that were being logged. An early recipe for cherry birthday cake was shared in the 1873 cookbook published by the Ladies of the Grand Rapids Congregational Church (reprinted in 1890), and a recipe for cherry pie appears in a newspaper clipping in the *Ludington Cook Book* (1891), which was around the time the early cherry industry became commercialized. Red Jacket was the earlier name for the 1864 village that included Calumet, the historic center of the copper mining district. Red Jacket also was the name given to the Seneca chief Sagoyewatha (c. 1750–1830), remembered as a great orator.

Ingredients

⅔ cup red quinoa
1 bay leaf
1⅓ cups water
½ pound red cherries (Montmorency
    or Rainier are preferred),
    pitted and halved
1 cup Persian or English cucumber,
    cut to a small dice
⅓ cup olive oil
2 garlic cloves, blanched
Zest of 1 lemon

Juice of ½ lemon
2 tablespoons red wine vinegar
½ cup parsley, very finely chopped
1 tablespoon shallot, finely chopped
Pinch of chili flakes
1 tablespoon capers
½ teaspoon salt
¼ cup pepitas, toasted (optional)
½ cup French feta, crumbled in
    small pieces (optional)

Instructions

Boil quinoa in water with bay leaf. Cook until done (it will begin to "sprout"), but not long enough to allow it to get mushy. Flake with a fork and set aside to cool. Prepare cherries and cucumber. The three main ingredients of the salad (quinoa, cucumber, and cherries) should be in roughly equal proportions.

Use the remaining ingredients (except toppings) to make a salad dressing. Use a whisk to blend the dressing before adding the capers. Season sparingly with salt, as the capers are naturally salty. Add dressing evenly to the salad, mixing it thoroughly. Sprinkle the pepitas and feta as a topping, just before serving. Serves 4 to 6.

ALL ABOARD FOR ROASTING MARSHMALLOWS

The roasting of marshmallows was a turn-of-the-century activity that was central to many picnics. The summer diversion once relied on homemade candies and nothing more than sticks and a firepit like the ones built at Freda Park for picnickers arriving on the Picnic Train. Beginning around 1917, Campfire White Marshmallows were manufactured in Milwaukee and sold in tins. By the 1930s, the company had printed a recipe book with 150 other industrialized foods to make with the confection, including many gelatin salads. The roasting marshmallows fad appears to have begun in New York in 1892, but newspapers quickly spread word of the new ritual from the Midwest to California. The instructions were simple enough:

> Each member of the party takes a sharpened stick and affixes upon the end of it a marshmallow. Simultaneously all those engaged hold their marshmallows over the embers as close as possible to avoid burning, and roast them carefully, turning the sticks around dexterously so as to brown the marshmallow nicely on all sides. This requires some skill. . . . When done they are morsels for the gods, resembling in flavor the most exquisite meringue, with a delicious nutty and crusty outside.

The astute marshmallow observer went further to describe the treats in their social context:

> They are a sort of sublimated combination of candy and cake, all in one bite, though the proper fashion is to nibble the roasted marshmallow off the end of the stick. One set consumed each person pokes the point of his wooden skewer through another marshmallow, and the performance is

Roasting marshmallows in Calumet, c. 1910. Photograph courtesy of Keweenaw National Historical Park.

repeated until everybody's appetite is satisfied. Marshmallow roasts are an excellent medium for flirtation, mutual regard between a young lady and young gentleman being appropriately exhibited by nibbling the marshmallows off each other's sticks. Accordingly, the idea is sure to grow in favor.[48]

The 1892 picnic recommendation was that the host purchase two or three pounds of marshmallows for a group of six persons, making this a very expensive picnic date. By the time of the Freda Park picnics in 1905, the confection was more widely available, sold as penny candy and no longer a "new fad."

Homemade Marshmallows[49]

Early recipes for homemade marshmallows evolved after the appearance of powdered gelatin, patented in the nineteenth century by Peter Cooper, the American industrialist who also built a steam locomotive. Cooper's train was known as the *Tom Thumb*, its little engine the size of a "kitchen boiler."[50] Besides the gelatin, the main ingredients in the marshmallow are not much more than water and simple sugar (plus sometimes corn syrup, available beginning in the mid-twentieth century).

Ingredients

2 tablespoons gelatin (2 envelopes)

1 cup (8 fluid ounces/225 milliliters) cold water, divided

2 cups (16 ounces/450 grams) granulated sugar

½ cup (1⅓ ounces/28 grams) powdered sugar, divided in parts for pan and finishing

¼ teaspoon salt

2 teaspoons vanilla essence

Instructions

Prepare a 9-inch baking pan by lining it with parchment paper that has been brushed with safflower oil and dusted with 2 or 3 tablespoons of the powdered sugar.

Stir gelatin into ½ cup of cold water in a small bowl and set aside.

In a small saucepan, mix remaining water with granulated sugar and dissolve over medium heat. Add the gelatin mixture, stirring it in until only the gelatin dissolves into the sugar water. Then slowly bring to a full simmering boil without stirring until the full mixture reaches a temperature of 240 degrees Fahrenheit (called the "soft ball" candy stage).

Carefully pour the hot mixture into a mixing bowl, add the salt and vanilla. Beat on low whisk setting for 2 minutes, then increase the speed and continue beating until the volume has doubled and almost tripled in size, about 10 to 15 minutes.

Scrape the stiff, beaten mixture into your pan, using a spatula covered with safflower oil to help transfer and smooth the top of the sticky marshmallow. Dust with half the remaining powdered sugar. Let cool and set for 3 hours, uncovered. Turn the loaf over in the pan and dust the other side with remaining powdered sugar. Let rest for another 3 hours. Cut in square cubes the dimensions of the sugar loaf's height. Store in an airtight container for up to 6 weeks.

5

VAGABOND PICNICS

To the woods and the fields or to the hills . . . there to breathe their beauty
like the very air . . . to be not a spectator of, but a participator in it.
—John Burroughs, 1918[1]

Am trying to add a little bright and bury my tired nerves
in this autoless island. Signed, Aunt Nellie.
—Postcard from Mackinac Island, August 14, 1920[2]

The remarkable arrival of the first automobile in the Les Cheneaux Islands was
recalled by an early hotel owner.[3] Onlookers made bets to see whether the 1906
Ford Model N automobile taken off a steamship could be driven from the dock
into the woods and whether its driver would be able to find his way through
the woods into town. Would he get stuck on the sandy trail to the Soo? Both
he and the car arrived back safely and in time for the return voyage, thanks to
the fast, rugged vehicle. Ever since its invention in the last quarter of the nineteenth century, the gasoline-powered automobile altered the parameters of the
mobility that is one of the key features of picnic food. Between 1896 and World
War II, the global spread of automobilism often was fast and furious in other
parts of the world.[4] The same rapid, single-generational cultural shift cannot
be claimed for the Upper Peninsula, where the region's relative inaccessibility,
remoteness, and "islandness" dictated the more cautious and tempered course

of technological diffusion. While the earliest beginnings of the new mobility were slower in the UP by comparison with those in big cities, the course of the car's impact in the UP was as explosive as the engine's pistons.

"AUTOMOBUBBLING"

Automobiles facilitated pleasurable moments for both spectators and picnic participants. Later, automobiles themselves became regular passengers onboard the Great Lakes steamers, but they often ended up being stored in town, since the most efficient travel between islands and on gravelly, windy, and narrow paths remained by boat or horse-drawn carriage. Still, locals remember hearing automobile horns, their sounds carried across the water from the Hessel Road to Marquette Island in the 1920s.[5] Paved roads from Cedarville on Lake Huron to Sault Ste. Marie on Lake Superior would not be built until the 1950s. Yet the cultural changes, if slowly realized, were inexorable, and the automobile soon became the centerpiece of the ultimate picnic experience.

Automobile with a picnic hamper in search of a picnic from the sheet music cover for a popular song by Walter Coleman Parker. The music and image depict the gaiety of the outing. 1905. Music Division, Library of Congress. Courtesy of Library of Congress. www.loc.gov/everyday -mysteries/item/who-invented-the-automobile/.

An early picnic cookbook, *One Hundred Picnic Suggestions* (1915), designed especially for the new generation of motorists, made the eloquent connection between automobiles and picnicking. Its cover showed an open motor hamper and thermos bottle, with platters of food spread next to the vehicle.[6] Mrs. C. F. Leyel's cookbook, *Picnics for Motorists* (1936), captured the moment of the automobile becoming a "regular [pleasurable] habit" and picnics accompanied by a road map.[7] Passionate about the picnic, American chef James Beard called it the "portable feast" more than a quarter of a century later.[8] Songs were composed in celebration of the touring experience as a wild adventure, during which the likes of "Down the road of life we'll fly, Automobubbling, you and I" were sung in an atmosphere of gaiety and frolic.[9] The play of adventure also was present in the symbiotic employment of the automobile to promote the American picnic and the picnic to advertise the automobile. The picnic trope not only promoted the stylish mode of transportation that was becoming more commonplace but was also a product of the spreading technology. Given agency, automobiles would become *essential* to accessing remote picnic sites and *creating* the extraordinary picnic. The edge of the wilderness was being redefined by automobiles, which were driven by picnickers to reach the far ends of new highway roads. Such were the sermons preached by the ultimate automobile picnickers, popularly known as the Four Vagabonds. In the age of automobiles, the typical picnic became more widespread and, at the same time, surprisingly smaller and more intimate than it once had been.

The Four Vagabonds Popularize
the American Picnic

Henry Ford, Thomas Edison, Harvey Firestone, and John Burroughs were each titans in their own respect—entrepreneur, inventor, manufacturer, poet-naturalist. Together they became the "Four Vagabonds," unlikely if stylish outdoorsmen who famously navigated the early byways of America by automobile between 1915 and 1924, camping and picnicking together several times each year.[10] Part publicity stunt and part social event, their travels were a series of pleasure-seeking picnics in the wilderness environments of North America.

The journeys were also part of an undisguised attempt to persuade the wider public to achieve the same level of independent travel in pursuit of the ultimate picnic. Writing for *American Magazine*, managing editor Mary Mullett less respectfully called out their series of travels as how "Four Big Men Become Boys Again."[11] These wealthy men had some fancy toys, thanks to Henry's Ford Motor Company.

Building on the excitement around the first automobiles, Ford's mass-produced Model T (known as the "Tin Lizzie") was introduced to the world in 1908. Fifteen million cars were sold in the next two decades, and Ford factories were built on every continent. Of course, the Vagabonds traveled in the latest model and were accompanied by a virtual caravan on wheels that included a Ford "kitchen" truck. In the wake of the Vagabonds, the number of automobile owners quadrupled. Sometimes the men traveled along the Eastern Seaboard and other times they roamed in the Far West. A trip in 1919 was comprised of fifty vehicles. In several of the group's trips, the Four Vagabonds headed for the Upper Peninsula, starting from Ford's nearby home base Down Below in Dearborn, Michigan. In the summer of 1923, three of the four men (absent Burroughs) were joined by E. G. Kingsford, a former logger, who was both Ford's cousin-in-law and a company employee at the time. Kingsford was an automobile enthusiast. He had brought the first Ford Model T cars to Marquette in 1909 and later supervised the Iron Mountain operations for Ford in the Upper Peninsula.

The 1923 itinerary famously took the Vagabonds across the Upper Peninsula, from Iron Mountain to Michigamme, Sidnaw, L'Anse, Calumet, Hancock, Houghton, and Sault Ste. Marie. During this trip, the men made key observations that would lead to the development of a new Ford product: the charcoal briquette. Although an earlier patent for "an improved machine for the molding and compression of blocks or briquets in the process of making artificial fuel from comminuted coal" belonged to Ellsworth Zwoyer, his invention used pulverized bituminous coal, not wood products, as Ford and Kingsford envisioned.[12] Earlier in the year, a news item had appeared in an issue of the *Ford News*, an employee publication of the company, reporting: "Experiments carried out in Seattle have developed a wood briquette that equals anthracite coal in heating value, according to reports. The new fuel is made of sawdust, bark and mill refuse now considered a waste."[13] The Iron Mountain Ford Motor Company operations eventually manufactured the first commercial "charcoal

The Vagabonds' support vehicles and service crew, L'Anse, Upper Peninsula, 1923. From the Collections of the Henry Ford. Gift of Ford Motor Company, THF 122576.

The Vagabonds dining in camp, 1923. The camping table that could seat twenty guests was outfitted with a lazy Susan turntable for serving dishes of food and condiments. Photograph courtesy Benson Ford Research Center, Henry Ford Museum, THF 10127.

briquettes." The new product would alter the course of culinary and cultural history by fueling roadside picnics and new generations of backyard cooking.

By the time of the Vagabonds' 1923 journey, the automobile already had changed the paths of American culture and cuisine in many cities. That year, of the more than 3.7 million cars that were manufactured in the United States, roughly half of them were Model Ts. Until the Model A appeared in 1927, the company showed little concern for comfort, since the ruggedness was well suited to the spirit of "roughing it," camping, and picnicking. Consequently, another potential "tin-can tourist" was born with each automobile purchase. Tourist industries everywhere began catering to the motorists who left home to wander. By the following year, A&W drive-ins began serving food and drinks to customers in cars, and other roadside conveniences soon followed. The business of "selling scenery" became the $3.59 billion American tourism industry by 1928.[14] Nations around the globe began to invest in paved roads

Advertising poster, "Use Ford Charcoal Briquets," 1938. From the Collections of the Henry Ford. Gift of Ford Motor Company, THF 114408.

and highways, making scenic byways, including those in the Upper Peninsula, accessible to the average citizen, who now could stop alongside the road and picnic while away from home. The portable grills and abundant, inexpensive briquettes manufactured by Ford's company even could fire up picnics in American backyards. They were being marketed to the increasingly average, middle-class customers who bought automobiles.[15] The bags extolled the virtues of charcoal briquettes, which were necessary to "enjoy a modern picnic."

Ford's Vagabonds caravan was far from average. The Vagabonds' motorized convoy ran on Firestone's rubber tires, and it was spearheaded by a customized Ford "kitchen" truck uniquely outfitted with a camp stove and special food compartments that amounted to a veritable grocery store on wheels. Other equipment, including the tents, chairs, and tables for the guests, were unpacked and reloaded daily by Ford's staff. In 1921, conservationist John Burroughs remarked, "It often seemed to me that we were a luxuriously equipped expedition going forth to seek discomfort—dust, rough roads, heat, cold, irregular hours, accidents. But discomfort, after all, is what the camper-out is unconsciously seeking—we react against our complex civilization and long to get back for a time to first principles."[16]

Key to the success of many of the memorable Vagabond meals outdoors was Ford's personal chef, Thomas Sato. Born in 1883 in Yokohama, Japan, Sato was initially hired by Clara Ford through the Japanese Reliable Employment Agency in 1915. His Japanese ancestry soon became an attraction of its own on the highly publicized Vagabond trips, and he was considered indispensable to their success. The 1923 journey to the UP was postponed while all awaited Sato's delayed return from his personal trip to Japan before setting out. Chef Sato knew the group's favorites, but there was also an element of unpredictability, because often he purchased meat and farm products available along the journey. Using the camp's outdoor fires, he roasted chickens, broiled lamb chops, grilled ham, and boiled potatoes and corn on the cob. He baked biscuits and pies, serving coffee and tea. Sometimes dinner guests sharpened sticks loaded with shish kebab beef, onion, and bacon, and the millionaires were invited to grill part of their meal themselves over the open fire. According to Ford employee F. W. Loskowske, "One thing the boss insisted upon, he always told Sato [the cook] to have plenty of food, plenty of good stuff!" The small group dined privately and with locals, including wealthy mine officials in Calumet and an Ojibwe reservation

Chef Thomas Sato, employed by Henry Ford.
From the Collections of the Henry Ford. Gift
of the Ford Motor Company, THF 127407.

family in Hancock. On the other hand, they turned down an invitation to eat at the elite and private Huron Mountain Club (where Henry Ford was a member, but reportedly did not like the chef there). Each morning Sato made a basketful of sandwiches for their impromptu roadside picnic lunches before the caravan moved on.[17]

For the ordinary cook, preparing for the outdoor meal was no picnic. It was time-consuming, relied on advance planning and organization, and thus was laborious for most women who found themselves preparing for a family excursion. Theirs was a mobile state of domesticity. Although middle-class women drivers would become commonplace during the family's week filled with errands and ferrying children, the weekend outing put men behind the wheels of cars as drivers. The same car that confirmed women's domesticity also asserted the masculine identity of male drivers. And the vehicles that transported people to picnics eventually increased in size to hold families and larger groups of traveling picnickers.

In 1902, the American Automobile Association (AAA) was formed to lobby for the passionate community of Midwest drivers who demanded safer vehicles and improved roads that would "get the country out of the mud."[18] The Chicago Motor Club, founded in 1906, was a fraternity of white men who became advocates for the city's automobiles that had appeared only a decade before. They saw themselves as the protectors of what the *Chicago Tribune* (1928) once called the "progress of motordom." By the 1920s, the city of Detroit was the "Automobile Capitol of the World," and its influential Detroit Automobile Club (founded in 1916) was soon focused on automobile tourism. Initially a federation of private automobile clubs that had formed around their shared social life while touring, AAA eventually offered roadside service and assistance in trip planning to the enthusiastic groups.

Vehicles themselves changed with the times. By the early 1920s, the once open touring cars became enclosed and more comfortable.[19] They encapsulated the gendered contradiction of an assertive masculinity. Picnicking meant adventurous dining at the periphery of civilization, but the typical picnic experience still relied on (mostly unpaid) feminine domestic labor to provide its fare. The picnic was on a collision course with a history of automobilism that included building paved roads through the same wilderness that the cars raced to "discover."

Picnicking next to their parked automobile at Bete Grise, across from Mendota Lighthouse, c. 1925. Eleanor Likovich Photograph Collection (Yellow Album, 144). Courtesy Keweenaw National Historical Park.

New Settlements in Stump
Towns and Logging Camps

Automobile traffic in the Upper Peninsula would also need to transcend the restrictions on earlier forms of transportation, which had relied on shoreline access and railroad routes that connected the spaces between the woods and waters, the centuries-old pathways of contact and commerce. In contrast, the new motor roads could meander across hills and through valleys that had been cleared by the timber and mining activities. With improved roads, they could reach into the woods and make the wilderness a navigable feast for the eyes. In 1923, the Vagabonds camped in a grove near the Iron Mountain lumber mill, one of many owned by Ford. The mill's wood was used for the wood-paneled bodies of Ford vehicles, the wooden steering wheels, and other car parts. An industrial plant there converted waste into chemicals and products, including the briquettes the company would later promote vigorously with their picnic kits.[20] Ford owned logging camps, sawmills, and mines in the UP, where their 313,000 acres of forestlands were considered replaceable natural resources. Early industrialists like Ford seemed not to comprehend the contradiction inherent in promoting scenic tourism while destroying the scenery. Their approach to environmental protection included the claim that as many or more trees were planted than had been cut down.[21]

The private wilderness camps from the end of the nineteenth century stood guard over some of the remaining forests. They had served a mostly elite male membership's hunting and fishing interests. The Huron Mountain Club was only one example of a larger number of UP establishments that catered to the wealthy. Henry Ford belonged to the club, which was near the summer cabin he and Clara Ford owned. In the subsequent age of increasingly affordable automobiles and public preserves, these private enclaves soon gave way to spaces devoted to family summer camps and activities associated with the more middle-class tourist-owners of cars. The two kinds of "camps" held in common their temporary and seasonal nature, sometimes inviting the use of tents, and often repurposing the older logging or hunting campsites.[22] Lake views or lake access was an important feature for the siting of vacation homes, and many early cottages and camps had boathouses or Finnish-style saunas.

Henry Ford, Clara Ford, and friends picnic at the Ford family cabin, Huron Mountain Club, c. 1935. From the Collections of the Henry Ford. Gift of Ford Motor Company, THF 97241.

Often the buildings were built from logs hewn from the very wilderness that was now endangered.

The UP's logged lands themselves were offered up for sale, but exceptions to the early elitist inroads did not end well for some of the arrivals. During the Great Depression, groups of visitors and would-be residents were lured by attractive offers for cheap farmland that had been cleared by the previous century's logging activities. More often they were swindled into becoming victims of the ruthless schemes brazenly advertised in city newspapers. One of the most infamous of these communities in the UP was the short-lived Elmwood (1926–29) in Iron County.[23] Settled by about thirty African Americans from Chicago, the community occupied the site of a former lumber camp on previously logged land now provided to the group. The right to set up farming enterprises and work the land was to have been delivered in exchange for their labor cutting pulpwood nearby. The company turned out to be fraudulent. The swindled but self-sufficient community survived only a couple of winters until racist elements in nearby towns railroaded the families out of the area.

The legacy of early twentieth-century racism lingered for subsequent generations of would-be picnickers seeking access to the wilderness. Middle- or
upper-class African Americans from Down Below may have desired a cottage
in the UP, but its purchase was often circumvented by the racist norms of the
real estate industry. This situation persisted into the middle of the twentieth
century. African American poet Melba Joyce Boyd has recounted the diffi-
culties encountered by her stepfather, Siegel Clore II, who attempted to buy a
lake cottage in the 1940s. Unable to find an agent who was willing to sell him
property, Clore eventually was forced to go to Tobermory, on the Georgian Bay,
situated on the Canadian side of Lake Huron, for his own picnic bench among
the birch trees.[24]

Women also sought refuge in Lake Huron's Georgian Islands in the early
twentieth century. Eschewing stereotypes of motherhood for careers, single
professional May Bragdon and other members of the Perfect Ladies Society
sought paradise vacation spots they could own themselves near Pointe au Baril.
The women purchased small islands and built cottages among the stands of
birch and pine, where they could picnic. Bragdon remembered the picnicking
and other activities when "we spent days and nights of unalloyed happiness."[25]

DRIVING THE PICNIC IN POPULAR CULTURE

The twentieth-century picnic epitomized the contradictions of modern life,
seeking the wilderness lost through urban development, while also employing the latest tools of empire and middle-class affluence toward the pursuit of
leisure and modernity. Popular American cultural forms, especially through
film and advertising, also reinforced the gendered, white image of an American picnic. One of the earliest Disney cartoon films was *The Picnic* (1930),
a seven-minute film in which Mickey and Minnie Mouse motor off to the
countryside for a bucolic and gay time with a picnic basket filled by Minnie and
a phonograph player carried by Mickey. The natural world quickly turns against
the pair, first with a front-on assault by black birds, then successive adventures
with black flies, an army of black ants, and, finally, black rain clouds. This could
have been a classic UP picnic. Picnic foods were worth fighting for: loaves of

bread, prepared sandwiches, pickles, olives, swiss cheese, honey, sugar cubes, cookies, cakes, and hard-boiled eggs. The cartoon's lesson was to forget the games and keep the focus on the picnic food.

The racist theme of Nature vs. Culture was continued when the black ants, more vilified and even Africanized in their warfare against Donald Duck, appeared in another animated short, *Tea for Two Hundred* (1948). By the time of this postwar Technicolor cartoon film, the army of black ants had become more menacing. Lacking any individual character, they are interchangeable "Africans" with stereotypical bulging eyes, neck rings, and spears. Camping in the jungle-like wilderness, Donald attempts to eat outdoors, only to have his picnic food stolen by ants playing "war drums" (giant mushrooms) and speaking an unintelligible "language" of Hoola Boola gibberish. The racist trope was recycled again in *Uncle Donald's Ants* (1952), an indoor assault on Chef Donald involving a large jar of maple syrup, the proverbial stand-in for civilizing the wilderness. In the films, the predictable plot portrayed the black ants as completely unwelcome guests at Disney picnics, whether indoors or outdoors. The media's selective depiction of UP picnics on the edge of the wilderness was similarly effective.

PICNICKING IN THE CLOVERLAND

Regeneration was part of the exuberance of the timber industry. The region's former logging areas gave rise to cleared fields of clover and larger crops of berries and berry-pickers. The preferred nickname for the Upper Peninsula, explained the *Cloverland Tourist's Guide, 1932*, was "Cloverland," the name applied "by pioneer settlers due to the wild growth of clover in areas cleared of timber" beginning in the 1920s.[26] The guide, whose cover featured tourists in an automobile traveling through a landscape of lakeshore and woods, recommended taking the one-thousand-mile driving circuit around the UP, while claiming that "any road in Cloverland leads to an ever-changing panorama of scenic beauty and rugged splendor."[27] The scourge of deforestation and industrialization was cleverly rebranded. Old logging roads and abandoned mines had become quaint tourist attractions. Berry-picking itself inspired millions of picnics for visitors and locals alike across the generations.

Native to the Upper Peninsula were many kinds of summer berries, including huckleberries, which grew wild near marshes, ripened in late July and early August, and figured heavily in the early menus of logging camps. This association is not surprising, since many of the berries commonly appear as part of the natural ecological succession in clear-cut regions and areas ravaged by forest fires. Devastating forest fires were recorded in 1871 and 1881, burning more than two million acres, with smaller, but also deadly fires in 1896, 1908, and 1911. The *Cloverland Tourist's Guide, 1932* contained numerous warnings about the dangers of forest fires, cautioning readers toward safe practices. Native peoples and early settlers would burn and clear land intentionally only to stimulate the next year's berry crops. Now, in the aftermath of massive logging, there were expansive fields of fruit. Local favorites included wild lowbush blueberry, wild strawberry, wild raspberry, wild black currant, black chokeberry, and the very tiny and rare thimbleberry, which was among the most favored of elite berry crops.

The association of berry-picking with picnics was thus long-standing in the Upper Peninsula. Advertisements in local newspapers alerted would-be harvesters to the time of ripening. On July 23, 1897, an advertisement for "Fresh Strawberries" appeared in an issue of the *Calumet News*. The advertisement announced that "the strawberries on the Brunneau farm are just ripe for gathering and can be had in large or small quantities by applying to Mrs. Ed Brunneau, Phoenix, Keweenaw County."[28] The anticipation of bountiful berry harvests propelled the picnickers and would-be jam makers into action.

The heart of the original picnic season was berry-picking near farm fields often reached on foot. Although Iola May Bly (1888–1981) recorded life in the Upper Midwest as an endless cycle of cooking, washing, and ironing chores, school, church, camp meetings, and visiting friends and family, her journal entries also reveal the special ordinariness of berries ripening in local July fields. She wrote: "We picked strawberries in the forenoon," on July 7, 1906. The next day, berry-picking again was followed by ice cream and a walk to the lake, where George "cut our initials on the birch tree."[29] On July 9 and 11, Iola went berry-picking for strawberries and then for currants. The berry season gave way to bags of apples by the end of the month.

Not every picknicker traveled by automobile in a leisurely fashion. Other opportunities for berry-picking were seasonal occasions for a rare outing. The special excursion trains on the weekend reached into public lands near the lakeshore.

In the novel *Inga of Porcupine Mine* (1942), set in the iron mining Upper Peninsula, author Caroline Stone recalls an earlier generation of berry-picking through her main character, the daughter of a Cornish father and Finnish mother, and her friends:

> The train [to Pine Plains] was crowded as the girls climbed aboard. . . . As soon as the passengers reached the ground, they began to scatter like ants in all directions. On all sides stretched the sandy plains on which blackberries and raspberries grew in abundance—the tall bush and the low bush blueberry, and the ruby-colored raspberry.[30]

The Pine Plains trains eventually were replaced by the caravans of automobiles swarming into the berry fields.

IMAGINING THE PICNIC WORLD

The first automobile in Copper Country had arrived in 1905. Whereas steam and electricity propelled a few earlier horseless carriages in France and Scotland, the German and American models built at the end of the nineteenth century revolutionized the world of the picnic. Their combustion engines resulted in greater drivability, durability, and mobility. In 1911, two Ford dealerships owned by Edward G. Kingsford (married to Henry Ford's cousin) were operating in Marquette and Iron City. By 1914, multiple-auto collisions were being reported in the local news as the number of vehicles expanded.[31] Automobiles and the roads they necessitated made the berry fields accessible and further shaped the local transportation scene around a seasonal tourism.

None described the berry better than the artist William Donahey (1883–1970) and his wife, writer Mary Dickerson, who, although they braved winters in Chicago, were longtime summer residents of Grand Marais in the Upper Peninsula. Donahey was best known for the tiny two-inch cast of characters who occupied a miniaturized world he created just for them.[32] In this world of exaggeration, the single berry could satisfy a family. Transportation might be via tiny automobiles, boats, and trains or aboard magical birds, a

The Teenie Weenies carve a giant strawberry in a kitchen scene from William Donahey, *The Teenie Weenies Under the Rosebush* (Chicago: Reilly & Lee, 1922).

grasshopper, or a snail. Donahey's invented characters interacted with food and with the natural world. They had picnics. His universe included entire families and a variety of occupations, such as sailor, policeman, and cook, who appeared with a black assistant called Gogol. Working together, the Donaheys also helped to compile and edit a cookbook collection of Grand Marais recipes in the 1930s and gained notoriety when they lived in their "picklehouse" cottage, actually a custom-built set of two giant pickle barrels (both built by Donahey in 1926, and one of them a kitchen) that made the couple appear to lead the miniature lives Donahey had created in his books and comic strip, *The Teenie Weenies*.[33] The Northwoods were also an inspiration for the insects, birds, fish, and other animals that populated the Teenie Weenie universe. Donahey's manuscript for *The Teenie Weenies Camping* was never published. His pickle-barrel cottage became a sensational tourist attraction for fans of the Teenie Weenies, but ultimately a nuisance for the Donaheys' reclusive lifestyle. It was eventually ceded to the local chamber of commerce in Grand Marais.

Original artwork assisted another key project that embraced cartoonish advertising designed to promote the Upper Peninsula's tourism efforts between about 1928 and the 1930s. A series of humorous and detailed travel brochures were intended to demonstrate the variety of experiences available to visitors. Illustrated and whimsical county-by-county tourism maps were produced for the Upper Peninsula Development Bureau. The Bureau had been in existence since at least 1919, when it produced, in cooperation with the Northern Michigan Road Builders' Association, the first regional road map in recognition of twelve thousand visitors arriving annually in the UP by automobile.[34] A collection of the promotional tourist brochures was gathered in *The Lure of the Land of Hiawatha* (1928), reprinted in 1996. This early UP tourism marketing campaign emphasized the fishing, hunting, boating, wildlife, and picnicking delights of the region. Images of picnic tables and campfires were scattered across the map, and natural features recalled the names of lakes, forests, and fishing streams. All the tourists depicted on the map were white. Some pointed cameras. Others drove cars or sailed in boats. Some went on picnics. Others fished. In other words, the map was much more than a navigational tool. The map was an instructional guide meant to demonstrate the sociable relationship between the wilderness and the white tourist. An advertisement produced by the Les Cheneaux Chamber of Commerce likened the region's romance and its water adventures to an island fairyland, calling the area the "Venice of Michigan." Notably, these portrayals of the distinctive regions of the UP as unique and individual tourist destinations brought families, women, and children to the center stage of the northern wilderness. At their heart was an uncomfortable contradiction.

REJECTION OR RETREAT

Not every community bought into the automobile culture of the 1920s. Mackinac Island residents had found the horseless carriages of the 1890s annoying. They informally began to ban cars during this era, preferring to maintain a nostalgic and picturesque environment for residents and tourists alike. At the end of the nineteenth century, the federal government had set aside portions of the island as protected lands, also regulating and restricting development. The carriage drivers had found that automobiles frightened their horses on the narrow streets, hotel owners wondered where visitors would park their vehicles, and so residents managed to initiate a temporary ban in 1898 and permanent local laws banning them beginning in 1923. The island was just under four square miles in area, making the prohibition on modern transport possible. In place of cars, bicycles were embraced on Mackinac Island. Since the 1920s, both tourists and horses have retreated to warmer pastures in the winters.

In contrast to this aberrant rejection of automobilism, Ford and the other Vagabonds celebrated the links between the picnic and touring by car. Between 1929 and 1946, the Ford Motor Company heavily marketed picnic "kits" for grilling on portable grills with charcoal briquettes alongside automobiles. The kits were given away and later sold through an advertising campaign that exalted the virtues and menus of the roadside picnic. John Sellman recalled the weekly occasions of traveling picnics in the Upper Peninsula. Not only tourists but also locals embarked on picnics. According to Sellman, "Early in the morning, several automobiles were loaded with necessary food and sometimes a tent or two. Off went the caravan to a township park. Almost any park within a fifty-to-one-hundred-mile range would do."[35] The picnic images in advertising were gendered by expectations that men would drive the women and families, and women would prepare the modern picnic foods. Any earned time away from the household would reward women with relaxation, suggesting that women were still the homemakers, even at picnics. An advertisement for prepared food (a can of Campbell's Pork and Beans with Tomato Sauce) in the *Saturday Evening Post* on June 12, 1920, promised that "[even] housekeepers can rest" if they rely on prepared foods.[36] Finally, a new wave of cookbooks explained how to travel with picnic foods that could be easily cooked or reheated over campfires and even over the heat of the car engine itself.

Classical Picnic Diplomacy

As their economies moved increasingly toward the significant reliance on tourism, the UP picnic remained an imaginative and appealingly affordable affair that could easily be promoted. In the interim, the picnic also had become quintessentially American. Although it was debated for months in her newspaper column, "My Day," First Lady Eleanor Roosevelt eventually displayed the audacity to serve the visiting English royalty a *picnic* of hotdogs at her Hyde Park, New York, residence, where she famously hosted King George VI and Queen Elizabeth at a Sunday gathering in the summer of 1939. Other iconic American foods were also served, including ham and smoked and plain roast turkey, but the validated hotdog grabbed the headlines: "King Tries Hotdog and Asks for More."[37] The *New York Times* reporter Felix Belair Jr. claimed a symbolic "American" meaning for the lowly picnic fare:

> The picnic was a big event for all concerned and the King and Queen rounded out a most democratic interlude shaking hands with the retainers of the Roosevelt homestead from the family cook, Miss Mary Campbell, to the keeper of the roads, Frank Drive, who was on hand with nine of his ten children. It would be difficult to imagine a more representative cross section of American democracy than was to be found among the relatives, friends and neighbors of the Roosevelts who received invitations to the picnic.

Eleanor's choice of picnic foods was also representative of the range of popular American cuisines, including both the South's Virginia ham and the ubiquitous strawberry shortcake. Hotly debated and decidedly political, the "hotdog-sandwiches" were the big hit. After watching the royalty eat hotdogs, guests were also regaled by two Indian entertainers, "artists dressed in full tribal regalia," who were filmed by the king.

The nonroyal hotdog was, of course, a version of the "wiener" or "frankfurter," a sausage in casing, which German and other European immigrants to the UP had continued to make locally from hunted and trapped game. Far from purely nationalist, their variations represented regional identities. The Coney (sans Island) Dog (with bean-less chili, raw onion, and yellow mustard) was a Michigan favorite from Down Below, where the Hamtramck Polish dog also held sway. The "Michigan" with chili meat sauce was popular in upstate New York.[38] So-called Chicago-style hotdogs on poppy seed buns were ketchup free, but called for pickles, peppers, relish, onions, celery salt, and mustard. The Cincinnati Cheese Coney, a chili dog topped with grated cheddar, was invented in about 1922 by a Greek immigrant, who added a beef stew seasoned with onions, peppers, cinnamon, and cloves to the hotdogs he sold. A Detroit version used beef heart and omitted tomatoes. Like the Old California picnic recipe for tamale croquettes made of local foods (corn, oysters, graham crumbs, and eggs), new inventions appeared alongside picnic potato salad. In this way, regional favorites emerged in distant picnics, taking their inspiration from the local population's variety of ethnic origins.

In the UP, northern Italian immigrants made pork and venison sausage, an Ishpeming-Negaunee original, known locally as the "Gudighi" (or *cudighi*), flavored with red wine and cinnamon, nutmeg, cloves, garlic, and allspice from the Caribbean. They served them as flattened patties in homemade rolls from a food truck beginning in 1936. Many earlier UP cookbooks similarly included recipes for croquettes, hash, chopped meats, and meatloaf, and they also used scraps and leftovers economically and nonstop from the turn of the century onward.[39] Hotdogs became so commonplace that they rarely appeared in recipes (see below). *The Cooking Pots of Grand Marais* (c. 1930s) offered "How to Vary the Roasted Wiener" by roasting it with onion, wrapping it with bacon, or adding cheese and a dash of mustard.[40]

There was both enthusiasm and concern expressed by the locals, who observed the increase in the number of tourists arriving in the Upper Peninsula. As early as 1846, the sentiment of a lost UP wilderness had already sprung forward, leaving some with "a kind of regret on the time which, I suppose is near at hand, when its wild and lonely woods will be intersected with highways, and filled with cottages and boarding-houses."[41] For others, who both celebrated the wilderness and gained pleasure and wealth from sharing its remarkable character, the region's tourism industry offered alternative livelihoods at the very moment when timber, mining, and fishing declined. Without a doubt the world of the wilderness had shrunk, while dining on its edge had gained ground in the popular imagination.

When permanent changes in transportation and an inevitably altered landscape eventually did arrive, they only served to underscore the exaggerated and enduring appeal of the wilderness in the American imagination. The twentieth century would bring greater leisure time, family vacations, and the means and ability to make pockets of wilderness accessible to the average American. Political promises allegedly advertised the proverbial "chicken for every pot" and "two cars in every garage."[42] They may well have promised a vacation with forest and lake view, for this had become an extension of the American worker's dream, which included the paid vacation. In response, the audience for picnics exploded. Within decades, the ownership of automobiles had altered the expectations of travel to the wilderness now reached by travel in groups, who crowded the roads. In 1941, the Upper Peninsula Development Bureau could proclaim that "all roads lead to Michigan's Upper Peninsula."[43] And these roads had picnic parks. According to the Development Bureau, "An innovation in Michigan and a popular one is the practice of placing roadside picnic tables at convenient points along the state trunkline highways. Last year [1940], some 3,200 tables—enough to accommodate 19,000 persons at one time—were placed along Michigan roads."[44] The distribution of even more picnic tables was reportedly underway.

By the 1940s, state organizations like the American Automobile Association exhorted the public to travel and cook outdoors:

And today, literally thousands of Michigan cars carry portable grills as part of the summer equipment, for the Michigander has learned the thrill that goes with roadside and park cookery. The state parks have their grills. . . . Thousands of Michiganders have grills and fireplaces in their gardens. . . . And you won't need elaborate dishes, for there's always an appetite in the open air—and all food will taste good.[45]

The notion of simplicity had been around for a long time. "Mrs. M.S.," writing in the *Los Angeles Times Cook Book* (1905), suggested that "going on a picnic one does not care to work all the day before to prepare an elaborate lunch and go feeling so tired they cannot enjoy the outing. . . . Take plenty of sandwiches and less cake."[46] Women were instructed to take along thin wooden dishes (precursors of disposable paper plates) that could be thrown away after eating. Although the picnic fare was touted as plain and simple, the art of preparing to eat outdoors eventually required attention and training directed to the next generation.

KETTLES AND CAMPFIRES

Cooking over the camp stove was something that would be taught to millions of young scouts in the twentieth century. In *Kettles and Campfires: The Girl Scout Camp and Trail Cook Book* (1928), the experiences of "preparing, cooking and eating meals out-of-doors" were no longer ordinary activities. In the increasingly urban environment, they had become "novel."[47] To camp cooking belonged its own aesthetics of "food combinations and table arrangements," demonstrating to another generation that "an attractive meal served in an attractive place is eaten with increased relish."[48] In contrast, the original *Boy Scouts Guidebook* (1911) had recognized the need for also teaching young boys about supplies and recipes (receipts) for three meals each day while camping or hiking: breakfast, dinner, and supper. Instructions included how to cook over a campfire's limited surface: "mouth-watering" griddle cakes, coffee, cocoa, bacon, frog legs, and potatoes, as well as recipes that employed canned and fresh fish. The image of the Boy Scout who hiked and therefore would need to be fed "When a Fella's Good and Hungry" was soon employed by advertisers in the 1920s, when they reminded women shoppers: "No man likes a feminine sandwich, he wants something substantial."[49] The cooking and camping merit badges eventually were dropped from the Eagle Scout requirements, while conservation practices were included in 1972.[50] Yet something even conservationists could not solve was the supply problem of dwindling fuel in a shrinking wilderness. For the Girl Scout in regions of scarce woods, handbooks told girls that they must either be satisfied with the "quick growing rapid burning woods" or else:

> [they] must console themselves with corn cobs, buffalo or cow chips, low growing greasewood, sagebrush, even tightly rolled grass clumps or weathered cactus stalks or fibers. Where abundance fails, imagination mounts high, for Girl Scouts can always use a little ingenuity in their camping.[51]

The general decline in outdoor skills paralleled the increasing reliance on family automobiles before and after World War II. For the adult drivers of automobiles, picnic kits were marketed for one dollar (available at Ford dealerships), and a five-pound bag of Ford's charcoal briquettes was only twenty-five cents. A portable, steel picnic grill came free with the purchase of an automobile beginning in the 1930s. The reference to a picnic sold more than automobiles. In 1954, a new, plaid Scotch picnic cooler was awarded to the purchaser of a Frigidaire refrigerator in Chicago, and it was large enough to hold the food for ten picnickers.[52] The Ford Motor Company even published a magazine for would-be outdoor diners and drivers, by viewing them as a single, inseparable market. The *Ford Times* cajoled the consumer by presenting repetitive, bucolic scenes of red Fords, usually convertibles parked near the lake's edge. There was only one way to access the wilderness and it was reached by driving in a shiny red car.

Picnic tables laden with seasonal bounty and enamel cookware with Chinese blue-and-white porcelain patterns completed the picnic portrait. *The Ford Times Traveler's Cookbook* purported to provide "quick ways to prepare good food on the road, [including] Impromptu meals the whole family will enjoy:

Ford Times Traveler's Cookbook (1965, cover). Copyright Ford Motor Company.

delicious sandwiches, one-dish meals, salads, and local delicacies you can prepare on-the-spot."[53] By 1966, picnic recipes routinely employed time-saving
elements: aluminum foil and selected prepared ingredients, such as canned
vegetables, boxed potato flakes, canned Hollandaise sauce, frozen lemonade,
and instant tea. Recipes stopped short of suggesting a driving speed, instead
warning "when you have nice weather and a good spot, take your time."[54]

"FOR THE PEOPLE AND POSTERITY"

The year following the 1923 Vagabond picnics, a major Ford company marketing scheme recognized the ecological reality embedded in the company's
relationship with the wilderness. The early automobiles, including the Model
T, had used substantial amounts of wood rather than steel for the body frame
and other parts, not just for the vehicle's decorative elements. On the one hand,
the acquisition of automobiles was promoted as giving individuals unprece-
dented access to the countryside and to the northern Michigan forests that
beckoned. However, the lumber requirements of the Ford manufacturing operations amounted to over a million board feet per day and relied on the logging
of 450,000 acres of Upper Peninsula forests. Sawmills were proliferating, and
wood was dried in kilns and distilled for use. Ford bragged that the company
had "revolutionized the handling of wood for automobile bodies" by joining
the operations together: "Logging, sawmill operation, drying wood in kilns,
body parts fabrication and wood distillation have been joined in a program
of efficiency and economy that is without precedent."[55] Ford pledged not to
cut small trees with trunks under one foot in diameter. The forest underbrush
was being burned to prevent further risk of forest fires. Recovery of scrap for
the manufacture of thirty-four different by-products (like the charcoal briquettes) was touted as another solution to the problem of industrial waste.

Being responsible for largely deforested hardwood regions of the wilderness
was portrayed as the cost of doing business economically and efficiently. Kingsford
alone had acquired more than three hundred thousand acres of UP timberland,
sawmills, and a chemical plant. He also owned the automobile dealerships in the
region. Under the signature logo of the Ford Motor Company was the prideful

Early Ford dealership with Edward Kingsford on the left, Marquette, c. 1911. Courtesy Jack Deo/Superior View.

tagline that might seem alarming today: "Owning and operating coal and iron mines, timber lands, sawmills, coke ovens, foundries, power plants, blast furnaces, manufacturing industries, lake transportation, garnet mines, glass plants, wood distillation plants and silica beds." The sum of these activities both paralleled and accelerated the disappearing wilderness of the tourist and picnicker.

BRIDGING THE PAST

Since their introduction in the early twentieth century, automobiles had steadily increased their impact on life in the Upper Peninsula. While ferries once had carried railway cars across in the 1880s, by 1921, automobiles regularly had boarded ferries and steamships, crossing the waters of the Straits, where Lake Michigan and Lake Huron met. Vehicle traffic crossing the Straits of Mackinac by ferry transport had gone from 59,484 cars in 1925 to 133,697, double the number of vehicles in 1929, and again doubling to 274,748 in 1937.[56] During peak seasons, drivers would line up and wait four or five hours for their turn to cross by ferry, consoled only by the car-to-car vendors hawking warm pasties and smoked whitefish to their captive customers. Since the 1880s, bridges and tunnels had been proposed as a solution to the isolation of the UP, especially during the winter. Inspired by the Brooklyn Bridge (1883) and Scotland's Firth of Forth Bridge (1889), local leaders seemed convinced of the inevitability of spanning the Lower and Upper Peninsulas.

Then, in 1934, the headline of Hamel's *Les Cheneaux Breezes* triumphantly declared, "Huge Bridge across Mackinac Straits Will Be Built."[57] In actuality, the construction of the Mackinac Bridge was still an aspirational dream in the 1930s. It would take two decades to raise the funds and secure government approval to build a bridge. Finally, groundbreaking ceremonies on Friday, May 7, 1954, included a parade in St. Ignace, with bands and floats and ten inches of new snow. The bridge opened to traffic on schedule, on November 1, 1957. When the five-mile suspension bridge finally opened, it was the world's longest, as measured between cable anchorages.[58] It was suspended by forty-two thousand miles of cable wires, enough to encircle the earth nearly twice. By 1984, thirty years after the groundbreaking ceremonies, fifty million vehicles had crossed the "Mighty Mac."

The Mackinac Bridge quickly became a tourist destination of its own. The Bridge View Park in St. Ignace was built by the Mackinac Bridge Authority to provide scenic views of the bridge and ensure a prime area for picnickers. The two activities were coupled in the region, known as one of the most popular of nearly *all* American tourist destinations. Completion of the bridge had an enormous impact on tourism, increasing wilderness access and encouraging the commodification of local cultural icons. Catering to the driving traveler, Lehto's Pasties first opened in 1947. Ten years later, the St. Ignace pasty shop had become a famous stopover on the way to and from Down Below. Other popular tourist destinations remained water- and woodland-based "nature" sites throughout the twentieth century.[59]

PORCUPINES AS ROADKILL

Picnics became more intentional experiences of the wilderness and its "woods culture" as the increased individual ownership of automobiles provided

Dedication of the Mackinac Bridge with a giant cake (1957). Courtesy of the Mackinac Bridge Authority, Michigan Department of Transportation.

Lehto's Pasties, with picnic tables situated near the Mackinac Bridge, opened in 1947. Photograph by the author.

opportunities for organized camping and quickly produced new traditions that linked the urban and rural more easily. The experience of the wilderness became as manufactured as the automobiles that carried picnickers to its edge. Thanks to the automobile, the social landscape of tourism was also changing. The exclusive men's hunting clubs gave way to a promotion of family experiences, of which the picnic was a peak. Motoring hotels appeared along the routes and became popularly known as "mo-tels." The first, called the "Milestone Mo-Tel," was built in California in 1925, but the concept soon caught on around the world. Gas stations were needed for refueling along the way, and their convenience stores provided outlets for selling postcards and souvenirs to the tin-can tourists.

Among the driving enthusiasts was the travel writer and naturalist Edwin Way Teale. Teale's four-volume series reached a wider audience than ever before as he traveled across the United States, season by season. With his wife, Nellie, Teale drove thousands of miles across America, seeking the wilderness and beauty of the natural world, without it needing to be "untouched." They reached the Upper Peninsula, the American North Coast, in 1957, the year of the bridge opening. Describing the UP in his *Journey into Summer: A Naturalist's Record of a 19,000-Mile Journey through the North American Summer* (1960), Teale wrote about the amazement of tourists observing through their windshields the bears that were ravaging the garbage dump at Copper Harbor for meals.[60]

In Teale's view, nature and culture were one comingled life experience. His tales of the road had tails—dead ones—and he noted the sightings of the porcupines and other critters killed by speeding cars in his spiral-bound notebook: "With morning mist entangled in the treetops and crows flapping up from feasts where porcupines had been killed on the road, we traversed the Hiawatha National Forest."[61] His sightseeing in nature was not simply apprehending the beauty of a pristine wilderness engineered and then manufactured by the National Park Service. Teale also drove ten miles down a gravel road to reach Tahquamenon, the Dark River, and then motored to Seney, listening from a position prone on the ground for the adventure of sandhill cranes, loons, herons, marsh hawks, mallards, and this "hidden singer," the whippoorwill. He and Nellie ate pasties every day and everywhere they could, including on their picnic during a twilight walk east of Manistique.[62] But mostly Teale preached that Nature could teach us how to live and "that to stop, just to enjoy nature, has its own significance."[63] His books struck a chord for a postwar generation, who

Roadside picnic using a tree stump as a table, 1930. From the Collections of the Henry Ford. Gift of Ford Motor Company, THF 120736.

vacationed by packing the family troops into automobiles and taking it all in.[64] The newest generation of picnickers also drove their children to the drive-in and the drive-through establishments born in the automobile era.

The creation of public parks and state and federally funded rest stops further encouraged families to travel prepared for camping at any number of impromptu roadside locations. Intended to protect the dwindling wilderness, the actions had unintended consequences. The increasing number of motorists speeding along on paved roads meant death for the porcupines and countless other slower-moving critters on the scenic byways. Maps began to identify tourist attractions and enabled drivers to locate marked picnic sites as their preferred destinations. Vacations and picnics were becoming commodified. Cars themselves were useful commodities in the pursuit of leisure. Commercial advertisements provided cultural instructions for enjoyment of the "new" outdoor cookery, which shifted again toward the masculine identity of grill master. By the 1950s, a Sears advertisement suggested that in the hands of a man, picnics could be turned into banquets.[65] The family itself would become the star of automobilism as the picnic played a critical role in the expression of touring to discover the scenery of the reconstructed wilderness. The landscape of picnics and porcupines would be forever changed by what John Burroughs had called the "large, generous way of looking at things [that] kindles the imaginations and touches the sentiments more."[66]

A QUARTET OF VAGABOND SANDWICHES (C. 1923)

We were favored with a mighty good cook in Sato. He is a treasure. He was always very willing and did his best to please us all and succeeded admirably.
—Letter from John Burroughs to Mrs. Ford, August 20, 1919[67]

After these trips, Mr. Ford would be a changed man—noticeably refreshed and rested. He was just living another life over just like we'd be—turn us loose in the wilderness and live and have food and everything out there.
—Reminiscences of F. W. Loskowske, Ford Company employee in the 1920s

Henry Ford and Edward Kingsford stand in front of the kitchen truck in Western wear at the Vagabonds camping trip in the UP, 1923. From the Collections of the Henry Ford. Gift of Ford Motor Company, THF 122603.

Sandwiches were a regular part of the Vagabonds' travels. They contrasted with the more elaborate camp-style meals prepared by Chef Sato. As early as the turn of the century, sandwiches were viewed as the quintessential picnic food because they were easily prepared and offered endless variations. According to the *Los Angeles Times* (1905), women should not spend endless hours preparing foods so complicated that they would not enjoy the outdoor picnic repast themselves. Individually wrapped sandwiches, whether chicken, ham and pickle, egg salad, or plain butter, made a jolly picnic lunch that was universally liked.[68]

Enduring Baked Bean Sandwich

A bottle of Heinz ketchup can be viewed in photographs of the condiments on the Vagabond camp table's lazy Susan. First made in 1876, ketchup was a popular condiment and recipe ingredient, savored across classes and cultures. Other Heinz products soon followed in the wake of its popularity. Van Camp's Baked Beans (from the 1880s) and Heinz Baked Beans (since 1901) were popular picnic items paired with frankfurters and eaten in sandwiches. And, of course, beans, toast, and "bangers" became the consummate British breakfast. The following recipe appears in an 1899 Michigan church cookbook.[69]

Recipe: Mash cold baked beans to a paste, season with onion juice, a little mustard, add some finely chopped celery and parsley and spread between buttered bread, either brown or white.

Hyla Hamel's Radish and Butter Sandwich

Gertie's last child was Hyla Hamel Goucher, who loved to make this sandwich. The pairing would bring back memories from her Cedarville childhood of the 1930s.

Recipe: Butter 2 slices of freshly baked white bread. Cut 3 or 4 radishes into thin slices and spread the discs in circular, ringed rows on one of the bread slices, starting in the center and continuing so that the radishes overlap slightly. Sprinkle with salt and pepper. Close it up with the second bread slice. Buttering both slices of the bread will help keep the radishes in place.

Ramped Up Sandwich

Wild leeks ("ramps" or *Allium tricoccum*) were a form of wild onion abundant at the beginning of the picnic season, when they appeared in alluvial floodplains and moist woods. The tiny white bulbs and the tender, early leaves were the first signs of spring on the forest floor and were favored by many.

Recipe: The harvested ramps should be clean and dry. They can be added raw to a sandwich of leftovers, whether beef or fish or sliced ham. They also can be used with a boiled egg to spice up the fresh, buttered bread brought along as the simplest and most easily transportable picnic fare.

Mrs. Margaret Spoor's Sweet Chocolate Sandwich

Places called "Chocolay" are found near Harvey and Marquette along the Lake Superior tributary in the Upper Peninsula. These place-names for muddy rivers, estuaries, and their townships likely reflect the early French influence from the seventeenth century (the French pronunciation of the word for "chocolate"—*chocolat*—sounds like "sho-co-la"). Sandwiches made with chocolate were rare treats even for the wealthy, and the addition of nuts helped to stretch the chocolate. This 1921 recipe is a precursor to the more famous recipe for the "Some More" of 1927 and later years (see below).[70]

Recipe: Two squares chocolate, 2 tablespoons butter, 1 cup powdered sugar, 3 tablespoons cream, ⅔ cup finely chopped nuts, slices of buttered, white bread. Melt chocolate over gentle heat, add butter, sugar, and cream, then cook 5 minutes over hot water, add nuts and mix. Cool slightly before spreading between the slices of buttered bread.

THE PICNIC HOTDOG

By the 1930s, the quintessential picnic fare was the hotdog, fit for kings and made famous globally by Eleanor Roosevelt. Its origins have been claimed by the German city of Frankfurt (whose residents celebrated the five-hundredth anniversary in 1987) and German immigrants alike.[71] The hotdog was so commonplace in the American picnic that the only recipes required were ways to provide variety. Mrs. William N. Boller offered her advice to the members of the Grand Marais Woman's Club in their cookbook produced by the Donaheys.

How to Vary the Roasted Wiener[72]

1. Make a small slit lengthwise of wiener. Insert a thin slice of onion and roast.

2. Insert a thin slice of cheese, add a dash of mustard, and wrap wiener with thin slice of bacon. Fasten with little bits of green twig and roast as usual.

THE PICNIC POTATO SALAD

Picnic lunches invariably included the ubiquitous potato salad, which could feed a large crowd of hungry picnickers. Although chefs like James Beard decried their generally bland taste and ordinariness, potato salad recipes were sacred and did not appear in cookbooks without a characteristic twist. Cook the potatoes in beef consommé, suggested Mrs. Dengle, add some vinegar or pickles for brightness, or season with cayenne pepper were among the secrets shared. Hot potato salad was associated with German immigrants. Some salads used mayonnaise (initially an elite luxury); others invented dressings that better held up to the conditions of the summer outing before refrigeration or vacuum technology. Popular since the nineteenth century, here is a crunchy version of potato salad from the *Superior Cook Book* (1905), reflecting the colorful summer bounty of the local kitchen garden.

Mrs. Walters's Potato Salad[73]

Recipe: [Take] 12 good-sized potatoes and boil in jackets. When cool slice and add 2 cucumbers cut in small pieces, 1 large onion chopped fine, 2 bunches of red radishes cut fine, and 1 cup of green peas. Mix thoroughly with the following French dressing: One tablespoonful of vinegar, 3 tablespoonfuls of oil, 1 saltspoonful [¼ teaspoon] of salt, and 1 saltspoonful of pepper.

He went to sea in a thimble of poetry without sails or oars or anchor.
—Jim Harrison, *Songs of Unreason*[74]

[There was] such an abundance of wild strawberries,
raspberries and blackberries that they fairly perfumed the
air of the whole coast with fragrant scent of ripe fruit.
—Andrew Blackbird, Ottawa (early 1800s)[75]

Picking berries in the newly deforested landscapes often entailed an entire summer day's outing. There was never a better reason for a picnic with family and friends. Hungry berry pickers returned to join the group picnic after swooping in for buckets of strawberries, blueberries, raspberries, and other sweet berries. They enjoyed the fruits of their labors as part of the picnic spread and brought the rest home for making jams and preserves.

The thimble is a frequent prop in the stories of the Teenie Weenies. From William Donahey, *The Teenie Weenies Under the Rosebush* (Chicago: Reilly & Lee, 1922).

Teenie Weenie Thimbleberry Jam

The Teenie Weenies do a mighty fine job of taking care of themselves. . . . There are many two-, three-, and four-drop jars, which the Tennie Weenies have made out of clay, and these are filled with jam, jelly, and some vegetables.
—William Donahey, "No Rationing Here," *The Teenie Weenies*, n.d.

At first it was fun to feed the little chicken. The Teenie Weenie Cook didn't mind cooking a thimbleful of corn but when the chicken began eating several thimblefuls a day he began to grumble.
—William Donahey, "A Problem Child," *The Teenie Weenies*, April 8, 1945[76]

In William Donahey's original book *The Teenie Weenies* (1917), the miniaturized characters go for a picnic in the shade afforded by a geranium pot, and they undertake to fish the local pond. In later books, they enjoy outdoor cooking and purchase single slices of enormous cherries sold like watermelon at fruit concession stands. With considerable difficulty, two characters harvest a single strawberry in *The Teenie Weenies Under the Rosebush* (1940). Their tiny recipe for thimbleberry jam is imagined below from the vantage point of Copper Country advice found much later in *Favorite Recipes: Upper Peninsula of Michigan* (1978).[77]

Thomas Nuttall had identified the thimbleberry of the Great Lakes (*Rubus parviflorus*) as early as 1810.[78] Most thimbleberry jam recipes called for nearly equal parts of berries and sugar to counter the sour taste of the fruit. The Keweenaw Peninsula was and is particularly recognized for its thimbleberry crop and award-winning jams. The thimbleberries reportedly will "ripen in the latter part of July and the beginning of August—go away from the road, where they will not be as dusty and dirty." Harvest the berries and bring them home. Many thimbleberries have a floral quality and need nothing other than sugar. They are also a favorite food of black bears across the UP.[79]

Recipe: To 1 cup Thimbleberries, add ¾ cup sugar with a dash of lemon juice. Boil 2 to 3 minutes. No pectin will be needed. Pour in a sterilized jar and seal.

SOME MORE PICNICS (1927-1930S)

*For the open fires of summertime . . . [i]f campfires play a part
in your vacation activities, take along some Ford Charcoal
Briquets. . . . Their hardwood aroma imparts a delicious
flavor, and they burn without soot or spark.*
—Advertisement, Ford Charcoal Briquets, 1929

Marshmallows on sticks had been toasted over campfires by earlier generations, and chocolate sandwiches were an old-time favored picnic and teatime treat (see above); combined they became a modern tradition promoted on a national level. In the late 1920s, an increased desire and ability of young people to travel into the wilderness emerged through day and overnight camping and picnicking experiences. The recipe below from the Girl Scout handbook *Tramping and Trailing with the Girl Scouts* (1927) made the beloved S'mores a shared, national phenomenon that eventually transcended region and generation.

"Some More"

The original Girl Scout recipe allots two marshmallows, one chocolate bar, and two graham crackers per person.

Ingredients

8 sticks (for roasting)   8 bars plain chocolate
16 graham crackers   16 marshmallows

Instructions

Toast two marshmallows over the coals to a crisp gooey state and then put them inside a graham cracker and chocolate bar sandwich. The heat of the marshmallow between the halves of chocolate bar will melt the chocolate a bit. Though it tastes like "some more" one is quite enough to satisfy the picnicker.

Girl Scout *Kettles and Campfires* cover (1928). Collection of the author.

Marguerites (c. 1930)

Despite the original appearance of the classic S'mores recipe the year before, the recipe did not make the cut for the definitive scouting cookbook for campfire experience in 1928. Instead, dessert recipes included "Surprise," which directs the boiling of a can of condensed milk in a kettle of water, roasting bananas, and stewing raisins. The old-fashioned toasted marshmallow recipe for fire-baked "Marguerites" appears below.[80]

Recipe: Fill a reflector pan full of saltines. Put a marshmallow and a few chopped nuts or raisins on each. Let them brown in front of the coals. For a richer dessert, place a piece of chocolate bar under each marshmallow before heating.

Quilly

The authenticity of picnic fare embraced the key elements of modernity and mobility in the age of automobiles. Tinned food and packaged ingredients became commonplace. Manufactured marshmallows and powdered gelatin were widely available. Even fruit was canned. These time-saving ingredients suited the busy housewife, but they also called on the remembrance of childhood favorites. Savory gelatin-based aspics or "Jell-O" salads were popular in the 1930s, when they were often categorized by their color. Pink salad had hot tomato juice added as the liquid (with celery, carrot, and red pepper), and the memorable green salad used lime Jell-O mix and often relied on some combination of evaporated milk, cottage cheese, and mayonnaise with sweet, canned fruit added in the 1950s.[81]

The gelatin recipe below is a modern riff on a favorite Southern dessert that had traveled from the English to the French and then to the American plantation kitchens run by enslaved Africans. A recipe for the Southern Charlotte appears in *The Virginia Housewife*, published in 1824 by Mrs. Mary Randolph.[82] That Randolph writes "Stew any kind of fruit, and season it in any way you like best" may account for the popularity of this variety of dessert, whose other ingredients were butter-soaked bread and sugar, grilled with an iron salamander.[83] The version below was Martin Luther King Jr.'s favorite childhood dessert among his mother's recipes from the 1930s. A twist on the earlier bread pudding, it used stale cookies and was called "Quilly" by her children. The name was possibly derived from the distortion of "Chantilly," a lightly whipped cream (often added to bread puddings), and perhaps inspired by the image of porcupine "quills" made by arranging spiky shards of thin cookies or wafers as garnish.[84]

Ingredients

1 tablespoon gelatin	¼ pound chopped almonds
¼ cup cold water	6 macaroons, stale and crumbled
¼ cup boiling water	1 dozen marshmallows
1 cup sugar	1 can fruit salad, well drained
1 pint heavy cream, whipped	1 teaspoon vanilla or rum extract

Instructions

Soak 1 tablespoon gelatin in ¼ cup cold water for 5 minutes. Then dissolve in ¼ cup boiling water. Add 1 cup sugar. When mixture is cool, add 1 pint of heavy cream whipped, chopped almonds, stale macaroon crumbles, 1 dozen marshmallows, and 1 can of fruit salad. Flavor with vanilla or rum extract. Pour into a quart mold which has been rinsed in cold water. At serving time decorate with sugar wafers. The recipe serves about 8.

6

THE POLITICS OF PICNICS AND PORCUPINES

Where the porcupine is I don't know but I hope
it's high up on some pine bough . . .
—Mary Oliver, "Porcupine"[1]

What we see here is not so much a natural world, but
one made by human decisions and ingenuity.
—Robert Archibald[2]

INTRODUCTION

In the small town of Menominee on Lake Michigan, a memorable nighttime picnic took place on the chilly evening of March 29, 1935. Not only porcupines were out in search of food under the starry sky. After a long winter, the spring's stream temperatures finally had reached the forties, causing the smelt to run. Crowds of people swarmed the town bridges, where, standing side by side, they lowered nets into the water, scooping up hundreds of the small, silvery fish. The year before, the record catch was more than two tons of fish caught by just two intrepid fishermen in five hours. Along the UP shorelines, the scene was repeated. At the Escanaba Annual Smelt Run Jamboree, His Royal Highness, "Kingfish Long of Smeltiana" ruled the festivities. Along inland streambeds, children scooped up the shimmering, wriggling fish with their hands.[3] There was the faint scent of cucumber in the air, before that gave way to the smell of hot cooking oil, smoke, and crispy critters. The night was filled with bonfires and deep-fried fish. What was so remarkable was that the species of the little fish was an imposter, an invasive species, having hitched a ride from its Atlantic Ocean home to the Great Lakes sometime after Gertie's Bois Blanc picnic, between 1912 and the 1920s.

The coming of springtime marked the beginning of the picnic season. Modern picnics, including the nighttime festivals of imposter smelt, were meals that continued to connect their diners to a place in the landscape throughout the long twentieth century. In the Upper Peninsula, the picnic's place was among the features of a vastly diminished and ever-changing wilderness of water and woods. Once upon a time, the wilderness had been an edible landscape. Its shorelines and trees had supplied the products and inspiration for meals consumed on the edge of the forest. The arrival of new cuisines and changing technologies altered the picnicscapes of earlier days. As they gained undeniably global characteristics and even greater mobility, these moveable feasts became less predictable, as if mistakenly anchored in the uncertainty of economic hardships, technological changes, and the environmental challenges of the twentieth century.

GERTIE'S LATER PICNICS

Gertrude Meyer and Robert Hamel were married on November 28, 1916. While they were courting, there surely had been shared boat rides and picnics. Family picnics followed their marriage. There were picnics in the 1920s and early 1930s before Gertie died, picnics with her children, Arlo (1919–2014), Ivan (1922–88), Elda (1924–2013), and my mother, Hyla Rae (1931–2015). Photographs from these later family picnics are missing from the album in my possession, but other grandchildren hold some picnic photos thought to be from the early 1920s. These photos show the exuberant embrace of family life by the young Gertie. Her husband and son hold a lake fish. She sits on a box crate and cooks food in an iron skillet on the campfire. The family meal of grilled fish and biscuits takes place at a low, makeshift "picnic" table on a newspaper "tablecloth" amidst wooden crates and barrels, with the forest and lake and maybe a porcupine in sight. Gertie turns and grins for the obligatory camera pose that briefly interrupts her picnic.

The charm of picnics across generations meant that individuals were assured their places within a longer tradition and a deeper landscape of belonging. Remembering also could conjure up an awareness of the changes in foodways and the transformed picnic landscapes. As the region absorbed the economic uncertainty of hard times, many picnickers looked to the local environment to mitigate these global forces. Renewed interest in accelerating the extraction of ores and timber hastened the changing landscapes of the picnic.

One of Gertie's many family picnics with fresh walleye served at the lake after her marriage, c. 1920s. Collection of Alana Kemper.

Changing technologies both provided access for thousands more picnickers and further diminished the wilderness.[4]

GLOBAL AND LOCAL FOOD CHALLENGES

The people who had experienced the hard times of the First World War era and the Great Depression found solace and social sharing in the continued availability of picnic gatherings.

Accommodations had been made in picnic recipes when ingredient shortages were encountered, resulting in recipes for foods such as Tomato Soup Cake, but the magical expectations of picnics had endured.[5] The lean years of the Great War and the Great Depression were followed by more years of food rationing during the Second World War. Marquette resident William Donahey's newspaper column once suggested that the rural folks of the UP were considered better able than most Americans to weather shortages by being both capable of self-sufficiency and skilled in preserving food for the long winters. Most homes and even summer cottages had deep root cellars for storing foodstuffs beyond their season. Moreover, even the local smelt runs ended up in canning jars.

President Theodore Roosevelt had been inspired by the early wildlife photographs of George Shiras III to initiate public policy and secure conservation legislation to curb hunting to seasons that would favor the nesting patterns of migratory birds and other species that were facing extinction. By the 1930s, the changing landscape required a similar investment in forestry. President Franklin Roosevelt's Civilian Conservation Corps (the CCC, sometimes referred to as "Roosevelt's Tree Army") was one attempt to bring relief to American families by employing men in labor schemes designed to improve the wilderness resources across the nation. Targeting the fields of stumps left behind by logging, the CCC reached into the Upper Peninsula, with the first two hundred men arriving in the Hiawatha National Forest, west of Sault Ste. Marie, in the spring of 1933. Soon there were CCC camps across the forestlands of the UP, including at Newberry, at Big Bay, in Chippewa County (Camp Marquette, which employed First Peoples, north of Eckerman), and at Seney, where

Hemingway had picnicked. Now the men of Company 3626 established a National Wildlife Reserve in 1935 and seeded wild rice to feed the waterfowl. The CCC was responsible for planting acres of trees and stocking fish, as well as fighting forest fires, building infrastructure and campgrounds, and revitalizing the national and state park systems.[6] The Women's Land Army (1943–47) and victory gardening were similarly among northern Michigan's contributions to war efforts. The sense of purposeful community building often neglected some regions while enhancing others. Electricity and refrigeration came late to the region, leaving hotels and homes to continue to rely on traditional remedies: the annual harvesting of ice blocks and the canning, smoking, and drying of local meats and fish. Food rationing might alter even the most familiar of recipes equally anchored in the global and national networks of ingredients—butter, sugar, bacon, tea, and coffee among them.

The World War II era also changed the demographics of vacationers and picnickers. The 1941 *Lure Book* produced by the Upper Peninsula Development Bureau targeted women traveling alone during the war years. Proclaiming that "women will find plenty of companionship," the publication showed women could catch their own fish and row their own boats.[7] Women tourists arrived on buses, trains, ferries, and airplanes to engage in winter sports and explore geologic wonders. These changes in transportation mediated the picnic, giving it a timetable. Women were invited to pick berries in the hills of Dickinson County, but they were singularly warned: "A suggestion to women . . . do not make this climb wearing silk stockings."[8] Nonetheless, they often brought their families to the UP for summer vacations during the otherwise bleak years of war and sacrifice.

Seasonality had always been essential to the UP picnic. And seasonality drove the local economy, not only the spectrum of seasonal tourism businesses. Many residents, including those who worked in the tourist industry in some capacity, drew unemployment benefits every winter beginning in 1935, when the federal Social Security Act was signed into law by President Roosevelt.[9] Poverty and unemployment had grown dramatically during the Great Depression, causing public perceptions about social welfare to shift. That shift also allowed the summer visitor–dependent tourism to flourish.

Diets were called upon to adjust to the era's fluctuations in the availability and safety of local foods. Widespread concerns over the safe consumption of fish out of the Great Lakes changed the local diets even as easily transported and prepared foods became more readily available. As early as 1912–14, the International Joint Commission with Canada studied the pollution in the trans-boundary river basins. At that time, the bacterial pollution in the Great Lakes was recognized as a serious public health concern. A century later, the concerns remain in the public arena, and the longitudinal studies have been continued.[10]

In the mid-twentieth century, government-recommended limits began to be placed on monthly and annual consumption of certain species of local fish, causing many to eat smaller fish and to avoid the fish skins, where higher levels of toxins were stored. Consequently, favorite UP recipes turned away from fish and relied more and more on chicken and beef. The next generation of picnics adjusted to more than the changing availability and cost of fish. Hotdogs, pasties, and other sandwiches flourished on picnic menus. Fluctuating periods of economic prosperity and waning industries resulted in many resilient men and women changing their jobs with greater frequency. The reliance on seasonal work left them unemployed for part of the year, adding to uncertainties of the natural world.

In the town of Big Bay, near Marquette, the 1875 sawmill had once dominated local economies. Workers made everything from hardwood flooring to bowling pins until the sawmill finally went out of business in the 1930s, giving way to newer operations in the better-situated town of Marquette. Henry Ford had traveled frequently to the UP. He bought the abandoned mill in 1942 and reopened operations in support of the popular wooden side-paneled autos known as the Ford "Woody" station wagons, whose engines and bodies were primarily manufactured Down Below. Ford also created a *socially* engineered community in the UP by keeping open the lumber industry traditions in the small UP community at Alberta. As in the early communities under the social control of the mining companies, in this community single men received room and board and men with families were given housing. Women were provided allocations of land upon which to grow fruits and vegetables, while their husbands worked in Ford's factory.

Despite hard and uncertain economic times for the greatly diminished forests, "Johnny Carroll's Camp," a lumbering song from 1938, suggested some continuities in the daily routine of the lumberjack's outdoor meals long after the boon of timbering was finished:

Our cooks they are good natured. we get the best of board;
We get the best variety our country can afford:
Potatoes. apples. turnips. beans. and syrup. so pure and sweet.
Although we have no appetite, we cannot help but eat.
There's bread and biscuits. pie and cookies. all seasoned to our taste.
And our cooks be very careful there is nothing goes to waste.[11]

Perhaps the lyrics were wrong to suggest there was no appetite. Whether or not "seasoned to our taste" accurately portrayed that a unity of regional foodways was underway, the foods consumed outdoors reflected the century of global changes that reached the Upper Peninsula. The real and mythic abundance of picnic fare relied on the staples, comprised of both introduced and native foods. The revolutions in transportation—from canoes to steamships to trains to automobiles—had made possible the culinary continuities and the changes experienced by the earlier generations of picnickers. Those technological innovations also had wrought transformations in the picnic's demographics, comprised of locals and tourists.

Ironically, many of the same influencers who brought naturalists and appreciative tourists to the far reaches of the Upper Peninsula also delivered harm and potential death to portions of the wilderness they came to enjoy. Water levels, temperatures, and lake ice have fluctuated greatly between 1860 and the twenty-first century.[12] The commercial exploitation of forests, the industrial pollution from nearby cities, and the automobile's harmful carbon emissions all influenced the health of the Great Lakes region. While the Upper Peninsula advertised itself in opposition to the toxicity of urban life, it would not prove to be remote enough to avoid the impact of industrial cities. Some of these effects were noticeable by the early twentieth century. In the 1920s, industrial chemicals called PCBs (polychlorinated biphenyls) entered the once pure waters of the Great Lakes for the first time. After 1940, other toxic chemicals, including DDT, phosphorus, and mercury, were added to the list of dangerous pollutants that threatened the lake water with excessive algae buildup and contaminated its fish life. By the midcentury, Lake Erie was on its way to its death as an aquatic ecosystem. Although the UP has stepped back from the brink, Lake Erie and the other Great Lakes still rank high on the environmental stress index.[13]

RIGHT: Two loggers, part of the cutting team, Munising, on the southern shore of Lake Superior. Courtesy of Jack Deo/Superior View. **BELOW:** Logging truck, c. 1940s.

ANATOMY AND LEXICON OF A PICNIC

The same transformative processes that had created a nineteenth-century language of lumber camp consumables were at work in the mid-twentieth century. They continued to push picnickers toward food borrowings, brilliant and resourceful culinary moments of adaptation, and a singular, regional cultural identity expressed through food. Some Finns regularly baked Cornish pasties into the 1940s. Others preserved the Scandinavian traditions of lutefisk (salted fish prepared with lye), rye bread baked in rounds, pea soup, and *purro* (porridge prepared with berries).[14] The Italians made sausages, and they fed large picnic crowds with pasta. Fishing communities held their own fish fries.

Many picnic traditions persisted well into the twentieth and twenty-first centuries. Their social welfare purpose reflected in the early church and women's associations cookbooks survived in several local, rural community picnics. The Raber Township-Knights of Columbus annual picnic is also a fundraiser for the volunteer fire department, where an offspring of a favorite Finnish game of *kyykko* (bag toss) persists as the cherished picnic game of "cornhole." Founded by the French, Sault Ste. Marie was irreverently called the "Soo," superimposing its English (phonetic) spelling. The same was true for the Les Cheneaux (probably a distortion of the French word for channels), contorted by English-speakers into the nonsensical and common, if incorrect, translation, "The Snows." Similarly, the French Bois Blanc (meaning "white wood") had been hijacked by the name of Bob-Lo by 1911 and, while it appears on no official maps, this remains the insider's local name for the place in Lake Michigan.

How did the picnic assist in the complex process of transforming ethnic identities into a singular regional culinary and cultural spread? While some community church picnics or political picnics might feed a cross-section of picnickers from a variety of origins, other picnics also brought people together in cherished social gatherings connected to immigrant homelands and their imported cuisines. In their unique picnic meals, Italian, Finnish, German, and other immigrant families held events showcasing their foods and food memories. Larger picnics would be based on broader church, work, community, or fraternal groupings that syncretized the ethnic and cultural differences and promoted unity for a common cause, such as building a church or organizing for labor rights.

The syncretic picnic gained traction as regional solidarity grew in response to the influx of outsiders with picnic baskets of their own. The term "Yoopers," meaning people from Michigan's Upper Peninsula, first appeared in print around 1977, but Da Yoopers, a musical band, was founded in Ishpeming a few years earlier (in about 1975). Their song lyrics were popular and humorous, making fun of the shared but quintessential experiences of the UP's year-round residents, from the culture of deer camps to rusty cars that survived long winters. In sharp contrast, Yoopers used the term "Fudgies" to refer derisively to tourists as cultural outsiders, particularly those visitors to Mackinac Island's seemingly endless row of shops selling fudge in the summer months.[15] Locals were "Yoopers," well, just because "Upper Peninsula" had long ago turned into the acronym "UP," a regional identity to which "UP-ers" belonged. The *Da Yoopers Glossary: A Tourist's Guide to a Better Understanding of the Yoopanese Language* (n.a., revised edition 1998) became a necessary reference tool.[16] This was not the first nor would it be the final notice of a unique regional shaping of cultural identity. From the many came one singular sense of belonging on the island-that-was-not-an-island.

Mid-twentieth-century novels also suggested the complex ways that the dual identities inside of multiethnic families were created from intermarriages and believed to play out among rising social tensions and their resolution. In Caroline R. Stone's young adult novel, *Inga of Porcupine Mine* (1942), the protagonist is the daughter of a Finnish mother who is the best pasty-maker on the Porcupine Mountain range and a Cornish father who works in the iron mines. The dual ethnic identities are fed by dueling cuisines. Recipes are not written down—they are exchanged verbally and through endless hours of home kitchen observation. In the story, the secrets of expert pasty-making are revealed in the book's first chapter:

Instead of using any drippings or lard, you must use suet for the shortening. . . . Then when you get the dough made, you fold it into sort of little bags, and fill 'em with slices of raw potatoes, onions, carrots and small chunks of beef—and, for the grand flavor, Cousin Jennie says "use turnits" [turnips].[17]

Stone's 1942 novel is set in the twentieth-century north country, where only some women and young girls still baked (and ate) pasties in the community but everyone still picked berries with seasonal regularity, accompanied by a picnic comprised of pasties, sandwiches, and hard-boiled eggs. *Not* eating pasties defined Finnish heritage for some immigrants as much as consuming saffron bread and sour-cream gravy. Ultimately, making their own food for sharing with others yielded income for a struggling family and provoked life-changing cultural choices. Picnic season increased the demands for pasties for the tourists and locals to eat at beach picnics or while berry-picking. Each summer, visitors would become predictable consumers of the jams made from crops of raspberries, thimbleberries, and blueberries that grew in "Pine Plains," the fields left behind from timbered forestlands and that were reachable by train. Repetition played a role in the preservation of memory and identity across the generations, but change was also a constant companion reflected in the landscape.

The lawyer-turned-novelist Robert Tarver (aka John Voelker) wrote *Anatomy of a Murder* (1958) and peopled his midcentury story with plenty of local characters indicative of the Upper Peninsula world around Marquette, where the bestseller was inspired by a sensational murder trial in which John Voelker himself was the real-life defense attorney. *Anatomy of a Murder* was made into a 1959 film by the same name. Directed by Otto Preminger, it starred James Stewart and Lee Remick. Its opening scene shows defense attorney Stewart returning home from a fishing trip. Against a backdrop soundtrack score by Duke Ellington, Stewart hurriedly empties his knapsack, filled with fish, into the kitchen sink. He's been out fishing "in a rowboat on some godforsaken backwater." We don't see whether the fish are eaten for dinner or if the catch gets added to the refrigerator already so overflowing with fish that "if this refrigerator gets any more fish in it, it will swim upstream and spawn all by itself." After meeting his client for the first time, Stewart himself has a meal outdoors—he peels a hard-boiled egg—with a busy construction crane operating behind him. This is not the only signal of the transformed midcentury landscapes. While most of the film takes place in the confines of the courtroom, the jail, or Stewart's law office/home, after the small-town jury declares the defendant "not guilty," the successful lawyer drives to the nearby wooded camping grounds to learn that he's been cheated out of his legal fees. Despite the small-town feel, the film's setting subtly evoked the wilderness from a perspective situated inside of the midcentury modern time and place. It was sophisticated and worldly in town, but there were hints that a rural wilderness existed just outside the camera's view. It was a wilderness both tamed and corrupted by human nature, a wilderness that faced death.

DEATH AND THE PICNIC

Ernest Hemingway had begun picnicking in northern Michigan as a young boy. When he wrote his story "Big Two-Hearted River" set in the desolate UP town of Seney, Hemingway was a twenty-year-old war veteran. The area's landscape reflected the memory of death and war. Today, trails and platforms in the still-remote area immortalized by Hemingway are viewing stations for beaver dams, sandhill cranes, and porcupines. The Anishinaabemowin word for a beaver dam or lodge (*okinum*) literally means the bones of trees.[18] The porcupines still nibble on the salty residue of things touched by humans in this ghost forest preserve. Today the preserves at Two Hearted River Forest, its watershed, and Laughing Whitefish Lake (where George Shiras III took his legendary nighttime photographs of the porcupine) are among the many once-threatened UP areas now protected by the Nature Conservancy.

For Hemingway, a "moveable feast" was more than a picnic; it was a celebration that lingered beyond the moment, inviting reminiscence. The author wrote equally about memory as hunger: "There are so many sorts of hunger. In the spring there are more. But that's gone now. Memory is hunger."[19] Picnicking that took place within a ruined landscape would become a twentieth-century theme in literature and film, according to picnic historian Walter Levy.[20] During and after the world wars, picnics in films, poems, and novels were often held in cemeteries, among the ruins of ancient buildings, or even in the trees overlooking battlefields. The picnic meme figured prominently in the political cartoons of Herbert Block (known as "Herblock"), for whom the picnic basket was negatively associated with agricultural policy, the economy out of control, and the disruptions of World War II.

Politicians and artists mimicked the historical associations of picnics with memory and death when they staged their commemorative events. A

After Waiting So Long for Nice Weather

Cartoon depicting Hitler and Goering during air operations of World War II in springtime, "After waiting so long for nice weather." A 1942 Herblock Cartoon, © The Herb Block Foundation.

controversial meme for the link between the picnic and death had occurred quite by accident, when onlookers had brought picnic baskets to the famed "Picnic Battle," the Battle of Bull Run (1861), and picnickers (including "ladies as spectators") reportedly had anticipated an easy victory.[21] The claim that during the Jim Crow era and the terror lynching of African Americans the word "picnic" had another origin (the "n" word) is unfounded, although brutal racial killings were said to have been observed in the American South in a "picnic-like [celebratory] atmosphere."[22] Such haunting images compelled Abel Meeropol to compose a poem, which became the famous lyrics sung by Billie Holiday in "Strange Fruit." When Winston Churchill picnicked on the Dutch side of the Rhine in 1944 after the Allied invasion of Germany, the sandwiches were viewed as political weapons.[23] Arthur Conan Doyle's description of the remembered battle at Vaalkrantz during the earlier Boer War (1899–1902) similarly leaned on the reference to the picnic as a consummate symbol of gaiety and spectacle, yet somehow also on the "fringe of death."[24] How did both the edge of the forest and the shoreline become UP spaces on the fringe of death?

FISH TALES

Writer Robert Tarver, like Hemingway, was also a well-known fishing geek. The author of *Trout Madness: Being a Dissertation on the Symptoms and Pathology of This Incurable Disease by One of Its Victims* (1960) and *Trout Magic* (1974), Tarver wrote about, lived, and breathed local fly-fishing in the UP. He was not the only one capable of fish tales. Cedarville entrepreneur Guy Hamel, Gertie's brother-in-law, began publishing *Les Cheneaux Breezes* in 1933 as a tool to promote the area and his personal real estate business. A regular feature was the column called "A Fish Story" and later "Fish Tales," an ideal place for sharing local fishing experiences. In 1939, Hamel published the tale of Mrs. O. P. Westervelt of Peoria, Illinois. She recounted how her first catch, the 18-pound, 11.5-ounce, 41-inch northern pike, was promptly shipped home and served to friends, no doubt with a fish-tale sauce.[25] In August of the same year, Horace Johnson of Akron, Ohio, a regular summer visitor since 1908, received a certificate for having caught the month's largest small-mouth bass (5 pounds, 14.6 ounces, 21 inches in length, with a girth of 15.25 inches) and arranged for Cedar Inn to cook it.[26] Bass were commonly caught with a bait of live frogs, in turn captured by local boys and sold to the hotel guests.[27] Advertisements in the *Les Cheneaux Breezes* offered not only the delights and varieties of local fishing (rainbow trout, speckled trout, northern pike, walleyes, muskellunge, and black bass) and the services of guides, they also guaranteed hay fever relief to the tourists. Hamel and others touted the area as the "Venice of Michigan," devoid of ragweed and blessed with "waterwashed air [which] is free from pollen."[28]

The ups and downs of the natural (and unnatural) history of UP lake fish drove the real-life fortunes of both local commercial fishing and the tourist industry. As with the lumbering of earlier days, the rewards of fishing went from absolute abundance to endangered occupation, and sometimes the pendulum swung back again. Fishing was first observed in the 1690s by Antoine de la Mothe de Cadillac, who claimed in his own time that "there is no family which does not catch sufficient fish in the course of the year for its subsistence."[29] Early exploration over the next century assumed a continuation of this seemingly limitless supply. Yet already by the mid-1800s, there were signs of overfishing and other imbalances. Observations of the behavior of species like

Les Cheneaux realtor Guy Hamel showed lakefront properties from his boat, a family tradition carried on by John Griffin, the husband of his great-niece Jeri, in Cedarville. Courtesy Jack Deo/Superior View.

the fatty trout called siscowet (from Ojibwe, meaning literally "to cook itself") were made by part-time naturalist and theologian James Strang on Beaver Island, who noted in the 1840s that there existed an interrelatedness of various fish populations, which coexisted in a complex choreography of depth, speed, and season. In the big-fish-eats-the-little-fish world of the Great Lakes, the sis-cowet consumed other smaller lake trout, which were still quite large at the time (more than fifty pounds). In the winters, Strang reported that the siscowet even were competing favorably with fishermen, who were ill-equipped to snag the large trout through the ice: "The moment the bite is felt the fisherman throws the line over his shoulder, and runs with all his might, in a direct line, till the fish is on the ice."[30] And it turned out that the siscowet also liked the smelt.

Non-native smelt were not the only invasive species. With the building of canals beginning in the 1830s, the sea lamprey also had arrived from the Atlantic Ocean. Conservation writer Edwin Way Teale described the destruction brought about by the lamprey, "this nightmare creature," when he wrote how "a whole industry collapsed as the spreading blight of the sea lamprey upset the balance of nature."[31] The construction of the St. Lawrence Seaway, a system of locks, canals, and channels, enabled larger ships filled with ocean ballasts to enter from the Atlantic to the Great Lakes in the 1950s. Known as "salties," the ships brought undesirable consequences with their overseas cargoes. The inherent changes intensified a longer and larger process of globalization, affecting human populations and wildlife.

The commercial fishing of the 1930s had hauls consisting of millions of pounds of fish, with Michigan producing more than 30 percent of the Great Lakes catches and more than 18 percent of freshwater yield nationally.[32] More than half of that state yield came from Lake Huron, where the Hamel family fished.[33] Now, in the 1950s, this had dwindled to less than one hundred pounds. A century after its invasion began, the sea lamprey was making a significant dent in the populations of whitefish and trout.[34] In the 1870s, another invader had been the common carp, which ravaged other native fish, including herring, whitefish, perch, and trout.[35] When the alewife (herring) populations increased, the perch decreased. Commercial harvesting of the lake trout once exceeded 6.5 million pounds of fish.[36] By 1950, the industry had come to a sad end, leaving room for little more than sportfishing and scientists debating the causes of the industry's collapse. Was it due to overfishing or the invasions of the sea lamprey in the 1930s and 1940s?[37] The ecological consequences of some changes also revealed the linked chain of the natural world. Later introductions of quagga and zebra mussels were discovered in the 1990s to have ingested biological pollutants and so were placed on the list of lake fish that humans should avoid consuming. But the mussels were being eaten by larger fish, which were in turn consumed by wild birds, to the detriment of all living creatures on land and water. Bird populations had suffered because of diminishing forest habitats and now they suffered along the lakeshores. Another introduced species was the chinook, an invasive species of salmon from Pacific Northwest hatchlings that peaked in the 1980s. In the ecosystem of Lake Huron, where migrating alewives from the Atlantic (since the 1920s) were eating baby trout, but being chased by salmon, the payoff was positive for the native species.[38]

Environmental scholars have demonstrated the entanglement of ecological and human-centered concerns around public policy decisions.[39] Some

The Grayling, by Samuel A. Kilbourne (1836–81). The 1880 original was published as a chromolithograph in *Game Fishes of the United States* (Boston: Armstrong and Co., 1878–81). Once abundant in the Great Lakes region, the Arctic grayling declined precipitously before its reintroduction.

Robert Hamel repairing his fishing nets, c. 1957. Although women have been recorded pulling gill nets in Lake Michigan in the nineteenth century (for example, seventeen-year-old Magdalene Burfeind set her nets near North Manitou Island in 1869), most commercial fishing was done by all-male crews. Collection of the author.

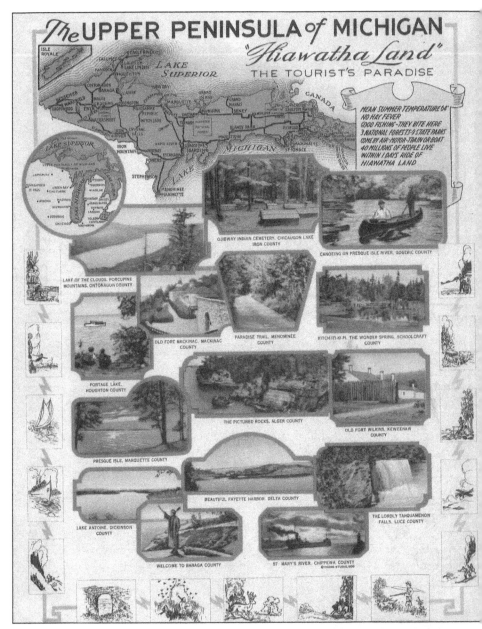

Pre-1957 tourist map of "Hiawatha Land" showing the three national forest areas and tourist sites from the westernmost Menominee on Lake Michigan to Mackinac Island and Cedarville in the eastern regions of Lake Huron, with the Keweenaw Peninsula jutting into Lake Superior in the north. Employing the name "Hiawatha" continued to romanticize the wilderness by emphasizing its connections to "wild" Indigenous people. Lake Superior Press (Guelff Printing), Marquette.

have argued that the problems are "erroneously labeled invaders and invasive species—terms that temper human complicity and instead blame the problem species."[40] The commercial interests of an international fishing industry straddled the Great Lakes boundaries between Canada and the United States. Global warfare pushed the economies toward increased food production in support of the war effort. The two nation-states jointly established the Great Lakes Fishery Commission in 1955. But fluctuations in fishing spilled over into the rest of the economy and culture of the Great Lakes region. If festivals could be invented for invasive species, what else was possible? In 1934, Guy Hamel had predicted a curious future for the region, one that was dependent upon the automobile *and* the boat. What would the visitor to the Les Cheneaux vacationland find in one, two, or three decades into the future? Hamel took a stab at a prophecy, when he wrote: "I can see a growing colony of summer homes along the scenic highway and shorelines east of Les Cheneaux. . . . Electricity and telephone service will quickly follow into these districts served by this artery of life—highways." According to Hamel, fishing would need to be maintained and improved "by regular plantings of fish and a closed season on hook and line."[41] Interventions would be required to offset the impact of tourism and its colonizing growth. Hamel's arteries of life were getting clogged.

THE BUTTERFLY'S PICNIC

Not only fish and bird populations registered the impact of changing climate and increased levels of pollution. By the mid-1950s, the habitats of butterflies were threatened by disturbances such as road building and the mobility of larger and larger human populations. Of the sixty species of butterflies found in Michigan, three of them are endangered or threatened: the Karner blue butterfly (*Plebejus melissa samuelis*) that feeds on the rare wild blue lupine, the Mitchell's satyr (*Neonympha mitchellii mitchellii*) in grassy wetlands, and the more familiar monarch (*Danaus plexippus*), which feeds on milkweed. The final generation of each year's monarchs overwinters in Mexico two thousand miles away. Monarch butterflies in the UP have established a major staging area for their current migrations. It is located on Peninsula Point (near Escanaba) on

Lake Michigan. There, in sight of about ten picnic tables, the butterflies leave the Upper Peninsula and fly south. The Karner blue is one of about thirty Michigan species that belong to the Lycaenidae family of butterflies. These species are known for their sociability with ants.

Scientists describe the relationship between butterflies and ants as one of mutuality (myrmecophily) or symbiosis, meaning that each species gains something from the species's interactions. As with other adult butterflies, the eggs of the Karner blue butterflies hatch into larvae or caterpillars, which feed on leaves and eventually hang upside down on one of them to form a pupa (chrysalis). This final stage undergoes a further metamorphosis to become a butterfly. The larvae of the Lycaenidae family have special organs on their backs that secrete a sugary substance with a unique chemical profile that attracts ants. In exchange for the "picnic" of nectar, the ants protect the caterpillars and pupa from predators like birds, who don't appreciate the bitter taste of ants. This may be the one picnic at which ants are welcome guests.

LOSING AND FINDING THE PORCUPINE'S HABITAT

The Hamel family played their role in the region's dwindling forests by their homesteading, timbering, and boat- and dock-building enterprises, through commercial fishing, and through the promotion of tourism. Trees were cut to construct civilization's homes, docks, and boats, even while other family members were marketing the access to the forests that visitors required and expected. The woods that had once defined the wilderness gave way to train tracks and automobile roads. Improved transportation and more effective sawmills and mining operations were powered by steam and electricity and thus enabled the lucrative exploitation of forests.

Delivering lumber to his future father-in-law had likely led to Robert Hamel's early romantic encounters with and marriage to Gertie Meyer. Her father, Ernst Meyer, was the chief engineer at the Hoeft and Sons Stave and Heading Mill Company, whose docks in Rogers City shipped lumber out to England and France, as well as to Detroit, Chicago, Buffalo, and Montreal. That lumber included maple for furniture; elm for staving salt barrels; cedar for paving sidewalks, for fencing farms, for making shingles, and for use in railroad beds; plus Norway and white pine, driven from lumber trains. Meyer, originally recruited as a steam boiler expert, used the train's steam haulers to move goods to the docks.[42] The passenger railroad arrived there in 1911, also the year of Gertie's memorable picnic. The picnic grounds of P. H. Hoeft State Park on the heavily wooded shores of Lake Huron provided scenic views of these shipping lanes after the land was donated to the state by Paul Hoeft in 1922. It is likely that Meyer played a guiding role in sharing the rudiments of steam technology with his son-in-law Robert. In this way, the early residents and their descendant families "built a nation out of a wilderness."[43] But perhaps the wilderness always was destined to be consumed.

Today global warming threatens the future of the planet and all the air, lands, forests, and waters of the Upper Peninsula. The UP's five inland seas provide the world with more than 20 percent of the planet's fresh surface water. Ten species of fish found in the UP are now endangered, as are the moose, trillium, Kirtland's warbler, and spotted turtle. The wild UP is no longer the wilderness it once was. In part, it is a managed landscape, and its sustainability is threatened. Yet the hunger for its forest paths continues. The region's history also contains many more stories beyond the ones in this book. They include the stories of individual lives and global forces beyond their reach, the stories of picnics and porcupines shared within the landscapes these individuals have inhabited, visited, and infused with meaning and purpose.

The picnic's history has demonstrated the ways in which a single meal can be a microcosm of global processes. Participants and ingredients were driven by the global economy, by migration, famines, bounties, technology, popular culture, and wars. The picnic's past on the edge of the wilderness revealed an intensive, yet highly localized set of influences that brought about transformations in foodways and other cultural and environmental understandings. Whether real or imagined, experienced and curated, the elements of picnicking in the Upper Peninsula suggested the same tensions and intimate tenderness of any dinner table indoors. But the adage "never discuss politics at the dinner table" was left behind in the mid-twentieth century, when the picnic became political. Picnics had been held by churches, women's associations, union groups, and companies, so why not by political candidates? Political campaigns in the twentieth century used picnics to meet and greet communities, engineering a social occasion that could make the otherwise elite seem to be "one of them."

By the 1960s, the interplay of natural wilderness and human-made attractions was even more obvious. Guy Hamel spoke to this around 1963, when he remarked that "Mother Nature has been kind to Michigan . . . [and] Nature, indeed, produced the unusual here in Les Cheneaux."[44] The human-made attractions were equally important. Hamel suggested a combination of the two experiences by developing the traditional early summer lifting of the commercial pond nets as a tourist attraction. Pond nets differed from the gill nets that were being illegally installed in local waters to the detriment of sportfishing. Although "the crop of whitefish, like [lake] water levels, seems to have its own cycles of ups and downs," Hamel saw the potential appeal of pond nets to residents and tourists alike:

> Over the years interested parties, from time to time, have taken advantage of seeing these nets raised and, in some cases, have purchased one or more of these freshly-caught whitefish and headed for a beach "fish fry" and what tastes better than a really fresh whitefish cooked to the Queen's taste over an open fire?[45]

Hamel goes on to suggest the place for these picnics on Government Island, once the site of his family's turn-of-the-century steam-powered sawmill. In the 1960s, Government Island had become a federally owned island, where cookout places were being built. This was the perfect storm for a tourist industry that could receive public support and private investment while walking the tightrope of sportfishing and commercial harvesting.

Generations of resistance and acceptance also helped consolidate native claims to the Upper Peninsula's lands and fishing waters protected by the early treaties. A cultural resiliency preserved foodways across generations. Transmitted to tribal members and shared with the many cultures that eventually inhabited the UP, the First Nations foodways were grounded in the local landscape and its rich resources. They could not remain unchanged. Besh-a-min-ik-we, known locally as "Mrs. Shabaway," the widow of the son of the 1836 treaty-signer Chief Chabowaywa, was interviewed by Frank Grover in 1901. According to Besh-a-min-ik-we, the family "raised corn and potatoes, and had apple and plum trees and gooseberry bushes."[46] Besh-a-min-ik-we was also a grandmother. The early twentieth-century photograph of Besh-a-min-ik-we suggests the full arc of history. Nearly a century after Agassiz and Cabot hoisted their iron

Besh-a-min-ik-we
(Mrs. Shabaway), Hessel,
c. 1930. Courtesy Les Cheneaux
Historical Museum, Cedarville.

cooking pot onto the prow of their canoe, Besh-a-min-ik-we sits on her Hessel home's porch while a metal pot hangs behind her like a trophy on the wall.

Conclusion

There is no singular history of the past, any more than there was one defining menu for every small island of humanity. My grandmother's picnic and other picnics were both intimate, social occasions and the products of global forces. The diverse histories of the picnic reveal unique national, regional, and cultural characteristics. The changing foods and landscapes also suggest some patterns that can reveal the emergence of shared identities. The meals consumed outdoors in Michigan's Upper Peninsula were critical points of intersection, where the many mouths spoke different languages and ate different foods. In the wilderness that was always partly imagined, recreated, and then consumed, these differences came together, seeking the constancy of environment. Constancy was a myth, although the landscape of the picnic was a place where the intimate, local experience of regularity, seasonality, and custom met the global forces of change. The changes resonated in the shorter lives of locals like my grandmother, who nonetheless transferred the emotion-driven meanings of the picnic and landscape to her children and to theirs. Somehow both the landscape's porcupines and its picnics survived through the long twentieth century.

The picnic was a unique type of meal that not only connected people to a place within the wilderness landscape of Michigan's Upper Peninsula. The picnic comprised the art of edible memory, in which its foods linked picnickers to meaningful moments in their own histories, both imagined and remembered. "To collect photographs is to collect the world," wrote Susan Sontag.[47] Gertie's album of photographs opened her world to me. Photographs of picnics, friends, and family spoke to me; their sequential points of consumption included moments that possessed meaning for my grandmother and now for me, in different ways. Picnics embraced the endless abundance of fruit in the summer season, when the field, lake, and forest were in full bloom. As a form of memory, the picnic's food was also transcendent, connecting self and surroundings that were both natural and social. Outdoor meals became vehicles for accessing the trails that led from past to present, from vague mystery to empowering meaning. The language of the picnic was among the languages "in which all is said without a word being uttered."[48] When environmentalist Aldo Leopold wrote about the shrinking wilderness in his *Sand County Almanac* (1949), Lake Superior was already "losing the last large remnant of wild shoreline on the Great Lakes," and, as Leopold observed, "no single kind of wilderness is more intimately interwoven with history, and none nearer the point of complete disappearance."[49] For more than a century, the UP picnic had marked and celebrated the relationships between the wilderness, its animals, forests, waters, and people. However fundamental, these were not unchanging relationships immune to local politics or to the global forces of migrations, industrial capitalism, family, imperialism, slavery, racism, competing foodways, technological transformation, war, or environmental change. In 1911, they were, as they remain, fragile but dynamic ecologies of mind and heart.

GOVERNOR'S PICNIC (1953)

Governor G. Mennen "Soapy" Williams was the featured guest at a UP Governor's Picnic at Birch Lodge, Trout Lake, on Sunday, July 19, 1953. The day's picnic featured a buffet luncheon, boat races, and a ball game. Governor Williams was a popular six-term governor and a presidential prospect in the 1950s, with a decidedly global perspective. This wasn't Williams's first picnic in the UP. Three years earlier he had attended a picnic in the copper-mining community of the Champion Company (Painesdale, Marquette County), just one day after having been attacked by prisoners wielding a kitchen knife and a four-foot-long metal onion masher during a Marquette Branch Prison visit. The governor was investigating the impact of budget cuts on the prison, and he had wanted to taste the lima beans being served in the prison mess hall at the time of the attack. In the 1960s, John F. Kennedy appointed Williams to the African post (assistant secretary of state for African affairs) at the State Department, and later President Johnson named him US ambassador to the Philippines. He also served on the Michigan Supreme Court. Williams's remains were interred on Mackinac Island.

Bow Tie Summer Salad

G. Mennen "Soapy" Williams wore a characteristic, old-fashioned bow tie into the 1950s and 1960s, but the ingredients of this salad are metaphorical, since fancy bow tie pasta (*farfalle* or "butterfly") was not likely to have been used at the time of the Birch Lodge picnic (macaroni was more commonly eaten). Community events hosting political figures would have been occasions to show off Michigan regional and family recipes to the governor and other guests. Picnic salads during the 1950s might have included caraway coleslaw, jellied saladettes, or the nearly unimaginable Spam-aroni picnic salad.[50] Curries and chutneys, popular globally from colonial India to England, appear in UP cookbooks from the 1880s onward, but the recipe below is also a riff on Queen Elizabeth II's coronation luncheon (that recipe credits Rosemary Hume's famous coronation chicken as its inspiration). On the other side of the Atlantic, it was served to the Queen of England a little more than a month before the governor's picnic, on June 2, 1953.

Ingredients

2 cups cooked chicken, diced
2 cups farfalle pasta, cooked
1 cup frozen peas, thawed
½ cup golden raisins
½ cup mayonnaise

1 teaspoon tomato ketchup
1 teaspoon curry powder
½ teaspoon ginger, finely minced
1 tablespoon lime zest
1 tablespoon lime juice

Instructions

Place the first four ingredients above in a large bowl, before making the dressing. In a smaller bowl, blend together the remaining ingredients with a whisk and add the mixture to the large bowl. Combine dressing with pasta and chicken, gently stirring until all the ingredients are coated with dressing. Let sit at least an hour before serving.

Governor Sauce (c. 1930s)

A persistent holdover from the influence of maritime cuisines is the prevalence of smoked fish and the pepper sauce that livens up the dreary and repetitive menus of an isolated region. The global reach of interests never disappeared for the immigrants from overseas territories. Their descendants have continued to reproduce the regional treasures. This pepper sauce was always on the picnic table, for spicing up the grilled fish and wild meat that were so prevalent. The recipe comes from "Mrs. McIver" in *The Cooking Pots of Grand Marais*, published in the 1930s and reprinted in 1976.[51]

Ingredients

1 peck of green tomatoes
1 cup salt
2 cups cider vinegar
1 cup water
1 cup brown sugar

4 large onions
6 green peppers
1 teaspoon whole cloves
1 teaspoon ground allspice
1 teaspoon ground cinnamon

Instructions

Slice 1 peck of green tomatoes, sprinkle with 1 cup of salt, let stand overnight, drain off liquor and rinse with clear, cold water. Cover with 2 cups vinegar and 1 cup water, 1 cup brown sugar,

The author at a beach picnic at Lake Huron, c. 1955. From left to right: grandmother Lena, mother Hyla, father Russ, and Candice Goucher. Collection of the author.

4 large onions and 6 green peppers chopped fine, 1 teaspoon cloves, Allspice, and cinnamon. Simmer until cooked. Keep airtight.

MIDCENTURY MODERN BEACHED PICNIC (1960s)

And all the pines wept stardust for a while.
—Great Lakes Myth Society, *Marquette County, 1959*[52]

Grandma's (Lake) Superior Fried Chicken with Strawberry Jam[53]

By the 1960s, many locals had some serious qualms about eating too many fish from polluted waters. Fifty years earlier chicken would have been unimaginable as a feast for a crowd. The Mackinac Bridge (completed in 1957) had made possible the menu substitutions by other foods that were now inexpensive and more widely and regularly available. The combination of savory and sweet was a family favorite.

Ingredients

1 whole chicken, cut up for frying, or 3 pounds of assorted breasts, cut in half, and bone-in thighs and legs

Salt and pepper

1½ cups buttermilk, seasoned with 1 teaspoon salt

1 cup and ½ cup flour, separated

1 tablespoon Old Bay seasoning or other Creole spice mixture

2 tablespoons parsley, finely chopped

1 cup cornmeal

2 eggs, beaten

¼ cup cooking oil (peanut or canola)

Instructions

Clean and wash the chicken pieces. Soak chicken in salted buttermilk for at least two hours in the refrigerator. Remove chicken and season lightly with black pepper. Set aside to approach room temperature. Prepare three "dipping baths" of (1) ½ cup flour; (2) beaten eggs; and (3) cornmeal mixed with remaining flour, seasoned with Old Bay and parsley. In that order, cover each piece with a light bath of flour, then dip each in egg, and finally in the seasoned cornmeal and flour mixture.

Heat the oil in a deep skillet until it reaches 350 degrees. Add chicken a few pieces at a time, turning halfway through, and cook until the skin is crisp and golden brown and the meat is done (about 160 degrees for 15 minutes). Alternatively, the breaded chicken can be baked on racks in the oven, allowing the fats to collect below in a baking dish. Don't overcrowd the pan or the temperature will drop too suddenly. Rest on paper towels to cool and serve with homemade biscuits and strawberry jam.

Elda's Canned Smelt[54]

Although the smelt season was brief, it was also intense. What did fisherfolk and cooks do with overabundance? During the smelt festival in Escanaba, members of the local Rotary Club packed up excess fish (nearly 2,500 pounds worth) and shipped them to fellow Rotarians in distant places. My Aunt Elda canned hers.

Ingredients

Smelt, freshly caught, enough to pack into a pint jar	3 tablespoons ketchup or barbecue sauce
1 teaspoon salt	2 teaspoons vinegar
1 teaspoon oil	

Instructions

Clean smelt and pack tightly in sterilized jars. Add ingredients above to each pint jar. Seal with lids and place in pressure cooker/canner. Process for 50 minutes at 10 pounds pressure. After timing, let the pressure go down without disturbing.

CHURCH PICNIC (1960s)

Prayer of the Woods: I am the bread of kindness and the flower of beauty. Ye who pass by, listen to my prayer: Harm me not.
—Author unknown, public roadside sign near
Lower Tahquamenon Falls State Park[55]

[This is a nature] that is accessible, that stimulates wonder without overwhelming the senses.
—Jon Saari, "Upper Peninsula Summer Camps"[56]

Although churches were less important venues for social gatherings in the 1960s than they had been in the past, UP congregations continued to welcome visitors into their flocks in the summer months. They became important meeting places for locals and visitors. Church camps occupied former logging sites and offered expertly managed, outdoor experiences to families and youth. Among the popular youth activities that the camps managed was collecting maple syrup. The widespread UP substitution of maple syrup for provisions of sugar persists from the earliest days of the voyageurs in the seventeenth and eighteenth centuries until today.

Maple Ice Cream

Ingredients

⅔ cup Grade B maple syrup, reduced
  by a quarter by boiling
1¾ cups heavy cream

¾ cup whole milk
4 large egg yolks, beaten until light
¼ teaspoon fine salt

Instructions

Mix cream and milk together and heat. Slowly add ¼ cup of this mixture to the egg yolks to temper them before adding the eggs to the custard base. Slowly cook, while constantly stirring. The mixture should just begin to boil slightly. When it thickens so that the custard will coat the back of a wooden spoon, add the syrup and salt. Place the mixture briefly in a bowl of ice or in the freezer to cool rapidly for about an hour. Transfer custard bowl to the refrigerator, where your ice cream freeze's metal container also should be chilling. Turn the fully chilled mixture into the cold ice cream maker container surrounded by ice and salt, according to maker directions. Crank to churn the ice cream until thick. Freeze and serve.

Camp-Meeting Cake

Fiery preachers on the Michigan frontier also inspired early social gatherings with simple cakes like the one below (from the ladies of the Order of the Eastern Star, a Masonic-affiliated group) that dated from the 1890s. In the 1950s and 1960s, Reverend Paul Beymer of the First Union Church in Cedarville continued this long tradition when he purchased a secondhand school bus to transport boys and girls for Sunday fellowship picnics.[57]

Recipe: One cupful of sugar, ½ cupful of butter, ½ cupful of milk, 2 eggs, 2 teaspoonsful baking powder, 2 cups flour. Sprinkle the batter with sugar before putting in the oven. Bake at 350 degrees until done.

YOOPERS VS. FUDGIES PICNIC (C. 1977)

When you have nice weather and a good spot, take your time.
—Dearborn Ford Motor Company, 1965

It isn't very far as highways lie
I might be back by nightfall, having seen
The rough pines, and the stones, and the clear water.
—Mary Oliver, "Going to Walden"[58]

Greater ease in reaching the UP by automobile after 1957 meant a predictable swarm of tourists each summer, sparking the inevitable battle of the Fudgies (outsiders) vs. Yoopers (insiders). In my family it was a more complicated "us vs. them" affair because, although my mother and I had been born in the UP, we had moved away. When we came home to visit, we yearned to take the ferry and be "Fudgies" on Mackinac Island, if only for the day. Once we even stayed overnight in the Truscott family house on the island, home to my great-grandmother Ida (Gertie's mother-in-law) and her family. After 1990, it had become a bed-and-breakfast establishment called the Market Street Inn. Tourism had begun there during the nineteenth century, when the early island shops sold Indian curios and confections. Indeed, at the bottom of the Fort Hill on Mackinac Island, hawkers around the turn of the century offered Indian-made picnic baskets for sale. At about the same time, a fudge "craze" hit North America. Any Yoopers and Fudgies picnic likely would have agreed on this recipe, which lacks the classic ingredient of milk. It comes from the *Superior Cook Book* (1905).[59]

Winifred Colby's Chocolate Fudge

Recipe: Two cups sugar, 2 cups water, 1 teaspoonful cornstarch, 2 tablespoons butter, 3 squares bitter chocolate. Boil until, when tested by putting a little in a saucer and creaming with a teaspoon, it forms a soft but not a sticky ball. Set to cool. When cold, stir until it may be taken in the hands and creamed. Flatten out on a plate and cut into squares.

Remembering Gertie's Candy Penoche (c. 1925)

This is Gertie's own recipe for penoche (penoche or penuche is a fudge-like confection made with milk). The recipe was passed down by Gertie to her brother Ronald's wife and their daughter Joyce Meyer Pines, who preserved it in the family book of heirloom recipes.[60] Joyce liked to add a small amount (1 tablespoon) of light corn syrup to the mixture to prevent overcrystallization. Without a candy thermometer, Gertie would have tested and watched the candy form a soft ball in cold water. Its maple flavors made it a popular treat.

Ingredients

3 cups brown sugar (or use maple sugar)   1 teaspoon vanilla
1 cup whole milk   ½ cup nuts (pecans, peanuts,
1 teaspoon butter   or walnuts), optional
¼ teaspoon salt

Instructions

Boil together all ingredients, except vanilla and optional nuts, until a soft ball forms while continually stirring. This stage is usually reached at about 234 degrees Fahrenheit on a candy thermometer. Remove the pan from the fire. Cool the candy briefly, before adding vanilla (and nuts). Beat the mixture until it begins to grain and loses its gloss. Pour on a buttered plate or spread into a pan lined with parchment paper.

Bob Hamel with his
second wife, Phyllis
Dunn, and two sons,
eating watermelon
at a picnic, c. 1960.
Collection of the author.

NOTES

Acknowledgments

1 Robert Macfarlane, *The Old Ways: A Journey on Foot* (New York: Viking, 2012), quoted in Rob Nixon, "Paths of Enlightenment," *New York Times*, December 7, 2012.

Introduction

1 See the concept of opacity in Édouard Glissant, *Poetics of Relation*, trans. Betsy Wing (Ann Arbor: University of Michigan Press, 1997), especially 185–88.

2 Charles and Ray Eames directed *Powers of Ten: A Film Dealing with the Relative Size of Things in the Universe and the Effect of Adding Another Zero* (7 min. color film, 1968 prototype, re-released in 1977, and made for IBM). It was based on *Cosmic View: The Universe in Forty Jumps* (1957), a book with text and graphics intended for schoolchildren by the Dutch educator Kees Boeke. The scientific knowledge was updated in a similar film made by the BBC in 2022. The updated version carries the viewer of a picnic in Sicily toward a scale of one hundred billion light years away.

3 Charles and Ray Eames revealed the coded message of their environmental agenda in a showing of the early (1968) version of the film at Harvard University in 1970. See Eric Schuldenfrei, "Powers of Ten," Library of Congress essay, www.loc.gov/static/programs/national-film-preservation-board/documents/powers_of_ten.pdf, citing Charles Eames, "Norton Lecture One," *Harvard Norton Lecture Series*, Cambridge, MA: Eames Office Archives, October 26, 1970.

4 While fully aware of the anachronisms created, I have broadened the original definition of the term "picnic" that evolved from the French (1649) eating indoors to the English and American meaning of eating outdoors for pleasure, to be able to make comparisons and examine the culinary history of the UP wilderness across

225

categories of time, gender, class, race, and culture. For a discussion of the more culturally specific term, see Walter Levy, *The Picnic: A History* (Lanham, MD: AltaMira Press, 2014). The volume is part of *The Meals* series, Rowman & Littlefield Studies in Food and Gastronomy.

5 See especially, William Cronon, "The Trouble with Wilderness: Or, Getting Back to the Wrong Nature," *Environmental History* 1, no. 1 (1996): 7–28; Robert Michael Morrissey, *People of the Ecotone: Environment and Indigenous Power at the Center of Early America* (Seattle: University of Washington Press, 2022).

6 Cronon, "The Trouble with Wilderness," 7, 8.

7 See the discussion in Morrissey, *People of the Ecotone*, 11–12.

8 Morrissey, *People of the Ecotone*, 27–29.

9 Morrissey, *People of the Ecotone*, 21–22, 57–59.

10 This anonymous and perhaps apocryphal quote appears frequently among quotes describing the wilderness as something alternately fearful, in opposition to "civilization," and transcendent. For more quotes, see "Learn About Wilderness" (Wilderness Connect, Wilderness Institute, University of Montana), accessed January 30, 2024, https://wilderness.net/learn-about-wilderness/quotes.php.

11 See below, chapter 2.

12 Histories of the picnic have mostly focused on the western experience. In addition to Levy, *The Picnic*, see Levy's website "Picnicwit: The History, the Food, the Stories," www.picnicwit.com; Walter Levy, "Picnics," in *The Oxford Companion to American Food and Drink*, ed. Andrew F. Smith (Oxford: Oxford University Press, 2007), 453–54; Karen Eyre and Mireille Galinou, *Picnics* (London: London Museum, 1988); John Burns and Elisabeth Eaton, *The Urban Picnic* (Vancouver: Arsenal Pulp Press, 2004), 9–39.

13 John Knott, *Imagining the Forest: Narratives of Michigan and the Upper Midwest* (Ann Arbor: University of Michigan Press, 2012).

14 The Central Algonquian language family comprises several Indigenous peoples, including Anishinaabe cultural groups. Among these are the Great Lakes people called Ojibwe, the official government name used in historical treaties. See R. Horton, "Anishinaabemowin: Ojibwe Language," in *The Canadian Encyclopedia* (Toronto: Historica Canada, 2023), www.thecanadianencyclopedia.ca/en/article/anishinaabemowin-ojibwe-language.

15 See, for example, the oral history interview (October 11, 1976, by Helen Armstrong), "Eva Koopikka," Finnish Folklore and Social Change in the Great Lakes Mining Region Oral History Collection, Finlandia University, Finnish American Historical Archive and Museum; although Eva's mother made pasties, they were considered to be foreign (i.e., not Finnish) and thus were referred to as "American."

16 Ronald Takaki, *A Different Mirror: A History of Multicultural America* (Boston: Little, Brown, and Company, 1993), 128.

17 See below, chapter 6, for a discussion of the Civilian Conservation Corps efforts.

18 Mark Kurlansky, ed., *The Food of a Younger Land: A Portrait of American Food from the Lost WPA Files* (New York: Penguin, 2009).

19 Grand Marais Woman's Club, *The Cooking Pots of Grand Marais* (1930s; repr., Grand Marais, MI: Voyager Press, 1976).
20 Larry B. Massie and Priscilla Massie, *Walnut Pickles and Watermelon Cake: A Century of Michigan Cooking* (Detroit: Wayne State University Press, 1989).
21 Katherine S. Kirlin and Thomas M. Kirlin, *Folklife Cookbook* (Washington, DC: Smithsonian Institution Press, 1991).
22 Russell M. Magnaghi, *Prohibition in the Upper Peninsula: Booze & Bootleggers on the Border* (Charleston, SC: American Palate, 2017) and *Upper Peninsula of Michigan: A History* (Morrisville, NC: Lulu, 2017).
23 Isabella Beaton, *Beeton's Book of Household Management* (London: S. O. Beeton, 1861), 960.
24 Linda Hull Larned, *One Hundred Picnic Suggestions* (New York: Charles Scribner's Sons, 1915).
25 May E. Southworth, *The Motorist's Luncheon Book* (New York: Harper & Brothers, 1923); C. F. Leyel, *Picnics for Motorists* (London: G. Routledge & Sons, 1936).
26 According to Beard, "Ever since I was a child in the Pacific Northwest, I've had a passion for picnics"; see "Portable Feasts," in James Beard, *Beard on Food* (Philadelphia: Running Press, 1974), 262. See also Fisher's essay (first published in 1957) in M. F. K. Fisher, "The Pleasures of Picnics," in *A Stew or a Story: An Assortment of Short Works by M. F. K. Fisher*, ed. Joan Reardon (Emeryville, CA: Shoemaker & Hoard, 2006), 199–207.
27 Jeremy Jackson, *Good Day for a Picnic: Simple Food That Travels Well* (New York: HarperCollins, 2005); Marnie Hanel et al., *The Picnic: Recipes and Inspiration from Basket to Blanket* (New York: Artisan, 2015).
28 Levy, *The Picnic*, 1.
29 Martha Reardon Bewick, *Tranquility Grove: The Great Abolitionist Picnic of 1844* (Mt. Pleasant, SC: Arcadia Publishing, 2018).

Chapter 1

1 Steven C. Brisson, *Wish You Were Here: An Album of Vintage Mackinac Postcards* (Mackinac Island, MI: Mackinac Island State Historic Press, 2002), v.
2 Gertrude Meyer was born June 4, 1892, in Fair Haven, near Detroit. Her parents, Ella Jane Sprangle (Sprankle) and Ernst Meyer (also "Myers"), appear on the 1900 census in Fair Haven, Ira, Michigan (Sheet 11/197/196) with their first child, "Gerthy," and they also appear on the 1910 census, with six of the couple's eight children residing at their home on Second Street in Rogers City, where her father worked for the sawmill as an engineer. Gertrude's brother Alva was born in Rogers City in 1902.
3 *Oxford English Dictionary*, s.v. "Picnic."
4 Levy sets his sights on Europe, England, and the United States in Walter Levy, *The Picnic: A History* (Lanham, MD: AltaMira Press, 2014), 1.

5   Isabella Beeton, *Beeton's Book of Household Management* (London: S. O. Beeton, 1861), 1000. See also Susan Zlotnick, "On the Publication of Isabella Beeton's *Book of Household Management*, 1861," in *BRANCH: Britain, Representation, and Nineteenth-Century History*, ed. Dino Franco Felluga, extension of Romanticism and Victorianism on the Net (website), accessed February 3, 2019, https://branchcollective.org/?ps_articles=susan-zlotnick-on-the-publication-of-isabella-beetons-book-of-household-management-1861.

6   Martha Reardon Bewick, *Tranquility Grove: The Great Abolitionist Picnic of 1844* (Stroud: America Through Time/Fonthill Media, 2018), 18. The "neats' tongues" served at Tranquility Grove were cuts of beef (from the tongues of both cow and ox), often dried and smoked or pickled.

7   Bewick, *Tranquility Grove*, 35.

8   Maki refers to the distinctive fault or crevice in the island's limestone; the *Ojibwe People's Dictionary* contains "mikinaak" for snapping turtle. See the online dictionary, Department of American Indian Studies and University Libraries, University of Minnesota, *Ojibwe People's Dictionary*, ed. Nora Livesay, accessed January 31, 2024, http://ojibwe.lib.umn.edu.

9   Letter from Charlotte to John O'Brien, quoted in Edward Nicholas, *The Chaplain's Lady: Life and Love at Fort Mackinac* (Mackinac Island, MI: Mackinac Island State Park Commission, 1987), 7, 36, 37.

10   Quoted in Walter Levy, *The Picnic: A History* (Lanham, MD: AltaMira Press, 2014), 23.

11   James Beard, *Beard on Food* (Philadelphia: Running Press, 1974), 262.

12   See Yvonne Lockwood, "Pasties in Michigan: Foodways, Interethnic Relations and Cultural Dynamics," in *Creative Ethnicity*, ed. S. Stern and J. A. Cicala (Logan: Utah State University Press, 1991), 3–20. Cornish miners also brought the pasty to the Anaconda copper mines in Butte, Montana, sometime after 1881, and miners moved easily between the two mining regions, Montana and Michigan. Similarly, Cornish pasties appear in the cuisines of Hidalgo, Mexico, in Pachuca and Mineral del Monte in 1825, as "el paste," filled with potatoes, "swedes," meat, peppers, and sometimes pineapple. Pasties differ from empanadas because their ingredients typically are sealed in the dough when raw and baked inside.

13   On this point, I am grateful for the insights of the Australian executive chef Barney Hannagan, Proud Mary Cafe, in Portland, Oregon, who has baked on three continents. Personal communication, November 16, 2018.

14   Quoted in Arthur W. Thurner, *Strangers and Sojourners: A History of Michigan's Keweenaw Peninsula* (Detroit: Wayne State University Press, 1994), 137.

15   Lorraine Uitto Richards, *The Pasty of the Copper Country of Keweenaw: Everything You Always Needed to Know about Pasties* (self-pub., c. 1990), 5.

16   See the nineteenth-century "Cornish fish pie" and modern pasty with carrots and rutabaga in *Did They Really Eat That?: A 19th Century Cookbook That Acquainted Immigrants with Northwoods Pioneer Fare* (Calumet, MI: Copper Sun Publications, 1992), 10, 40.

17 See "Anna" Clemenc's profile as a Michigan Women's Historical Center & Hall of Fame Honoree in 1996, web.archive.org/web/20120309000704/http://hall .michiganwomen.org/honoree.php?c=0&A=126~127~125~122~128~121~123 ~124.

18 Ana Clemenc, "A Woman's Story," *Miners Bulletin*, October 2, 1913.

19 See Lyndon Comstock, *Annie Clemenc and the Great Keweenaw Copper Strike* (self-pub., 2013), 32.

20 Jean Ellis and JoAnn Shaffer, eds., *The Calumet Women's Club: Beginning Its 115th Year of Service to the Community, 1901–2016* (Calumet, MI: Calumet Women's Club, 2016).

21 Cousin Joyce Pine's assembly of family recipes has historical notes and modern favorites: *Heirlooms: Then and Now* (Waverly, IA: G&R Publishing, 1996).

22 For example, one early advertisement read, "Wanted: a good lady clerk who can speak Scandinavian languages" (*Copper Country Evening News* [Calumet], July 3, 1896, 2).

23 Ladies' Aid Society, Laurium Methodist Episcopal Church, *Copper Country Cookery* (Laurium, MI: Methodist Episcopal Church, 1902), [4].

24 Maria Parloa, *Camp Cookery: How to Live in Camp* (Boston: Estes and Lauriat, 1878), 11–12.

25 Recipe for "Fried Oysters," Ladies' Aid Society, *Copper Country Cookery*, 27; compare "Little Pigs in Blanket," Ladies' Aid Society, *Copper Country Cookery*, 28–29 and "Little Pigs in Blankets" in Maria Parloa, *Miss Parloa's New Cook Book and Marketing Guide* (Boston: Estes and Lauriat, 1880), 120.

26 See Susan Koolman, "The Great Oyster Craze: Why 19th Century Americans Loved Oysters," MSU Campus Archaeology Program, February 23, 2017, campusarch.msu.edu/?p=4962.

27 Ladies' Aid Society, *Copper Country Cookery*, 83.

28 Adelaide Keen, *With a Saucepan Over the Sea; Quaint and Delicious Recipes from the Kitchens of Foreign Countries* (Boston: Little, Brown, and Company, 1902).

29 Lyman Beecher Stowe has argued for this attribution, claiming Twain made the remark at the New York City restaurant Delmonico's in 1905; see quoteinvestigator .com/2018/10/15/eat/, accessed February 1, 2024.

30 Women's Auxiliary of Grace Church, *Superior Cook Book* (Ishpeming, MI: Peninsular Record, 1905).

31 Women's Auxiliary of Grace Church, *Superior Cook Book*, 146.

32 Advertised in the *Copper Country Evening News* (Calumet), January 6, 1896, 2.

33 Edward Robert Bulwer-Lytton, "The Dinner Hour," poem quoted in Ladies' Aid Society, *Copper Country Cookery*, [5].

34 See Thurner, *Strangers and Sojourners*, 149.

35 Malinda Russell, *A Domestic Cook Book* (Paw Paw, MI: T. O. Ward, 1866); see also Toni Tipton-Martin, *The Jemima Code: Two Centuries of African American Cookbooks* (Austin: University of Texas Press, 2015), 18–20. The *Superior Cook Book* has recipes for "Chicken Southern Style" and "Southern Sweet Potatoes,"

"Southern Corn Cakes," and "South Carolina Biscuits," Women's Auxiliary of Grace Church, *Superior Cook Book*, 29, 57, 70, 64.

36 Walter Levy, "Picnics," in *The Oxford Companion to American Food and Drink*, ed. Andrew F. Smith (Oxford: Oxford University Press, 2007), 454.

37 Phil Porter, ed., *A Boy at Fort Mackinac: The Diary of Harold Dunbar Corbusier, 1883–1884, 1892* (Mackinac Island, MI: Mackinac State Historic Parks and The Corbusier Archives, 1994), 10, 42, 54–55, 92–94.

38 Porter, *A Boy at Fort Mackinac*, 55.

39 Quoted in David Maynard and Donald N. Maynard, "II.C.6 Cucumbers, Melons, and Watermelons," in Kenneth F. Kiple and Kriemhild Connee Ornelas, eds., *The Cambridge World History of Food* (Cambridge: Cambridge University Press, 2000), 1:306. Twain's novel examines racism and racial identities through the biting satire of two boys switched at birth, one growing up as mistakenly "white" and the other as mistakenly "black." The story was made into a silent film in 1916.

40 See Kat Eschner, "There Never Were 57 Varieties of Heinz Ketchup," *Smithsonian Magazine*, October 11, 2017.

41 Heinz global reach advertisement from the *Ladies' Home Journal*, 1924, H. J. Heinz Company Records, MSS 057, Detre Library & Archives, Senator John Heinz History Center, Pittsburgh, PA.

42 Paul W. Handel, *The Outdoor Chef* (New York: Harper Brothers, 1950), 57.

43 Betty K. K. Zane, *Planning Consumer Education Material for the Agricultural Extension Service in Hawaii: "The Well-Selected Picnic Basket . . ."* (East Lansing: Michigan State College, Home Management and Economics of the Family, 1953), 5, 8.

44 Levy, "Picnics," 454.

45 Young Woman's Auxiliary of the First Presbyterian Church, *Cloverland Cookbook* (Escanaba, MI: The Mirror, 1913), 120.

46 Young Woman's Auxiliary, *Cloverland Cookbook*, 12, 35, 119.

47 Young Woman's Auxiliary, *Cloverland Cookbook*, 31.

48 Ladies' Aid Society, *Copper Country Cookery*, 46.

49 *Food & Wine* editors, "Our Best Sandwiches to Pack for a Spring Picnic," *Food & Wine*, April 2021, www.foodandwine.com/cooking-techniques/7-best-sandwiches -pack-spring-picnic#:~:text=Sandwiches%20are%20the%20centerpiece %20of,make%20for%20a%20spring%20picnic.

50 See Helen C. Shoberg, *Early Hotels in the Les Cheneaux Islands* (Cedarville, MI: Helen C. Shoberg, 2003).

51 It is possible to place this transition around 1949, early in the postwar era.

52 William Cullen Bryant, August 20, 1846, quoted in Eugene T. Peterson, *Mackinac Island: Its History in Pictures* (Mackinac Island, MI: Mackinac State Historic Parks, 1973), endpaper.

53 Charles Lanman, *Summer in the Wilderness: Embracing a Canoe Voyage up the Mississippi and round Lake Superior* (New York: Appleton, 1847), 142.

54 Lanman, *Summer in the Wilderness*, 162, 165.

55 Lanman, *Summer in the Wilderness*, 166.
56 Henry R. Schoolcraft, *Narrative Journal of Travels . . . in the Year 1820* (Albany: E. and E. Hosford, 1821), 122; Schoolcraft traveled as a mineralogist on this early expedition and later became an Indian agent.
57 Gustav Unonius, quoted in Brian Leigh Dunnigan, *A Picturesque Situation: Mackinac before Photography, 1615–1860* (Detroit: Wayne State University Press, 2008), 246.
58 Lanman, *Summer in the Wilderness*, 149.
59 Advertisement for Edward J. McAdam's gift stores and an undated photograph's shop sign in Peterson, *Mackinac Island*, 68, fig. 2 and 69, fig. 7.
60 See Steven Brisson, *Picturesque Mackinac: The Photographs of William H. Gardiner, 1896–1915* (Mackinaw, MI: Mackinac State Historic Parks, 2007); David Tinder tentatively dates Gardiner's earliest photograph on Mackinac Island to the summer of 1894 in David V. Tinder, "William H. Gardiner," *Directory of Early Michigan Photographers*, ed. Clayton A. Lewis (Ann Arbor: William L. Clemens Library, University of Michigan, 2013).
61 Detroit and Cleveland Steam Navigation Company, with Cummings D. Whitcomb, *A Lake Tour to Picturesque Mackinac; Historical and Descriptive* (Detroit: O. S. Gulley, Bornman & Co., 1884), 10.
62 Detroit and Cleveland Steam Navigation Company, *Lake Tour*, 88, 92.
63 Detroit and Cleveland Steam Navigation Company, *Lake Tour*, 5–6.
64 Detroit and Cleveland Steam Navigation Company, *Lake Tour*, 88.
65 See below, chapter 2.
66 William H. Gardiner, *Mackinac Island: The Ancient Michilimackinac* (Buffalo, NY: W. G. MacFarlane, 1908).
67 Porter, *A Boy at Fort Mackinac*, 94.
68 Shoberg, *Early Hotels*, 10; Doris Beach, "Vancel Hodeck," in Philip M. Pittman, ed., *The Les Cheneaux Chronicles: Anatomy of a Community* (Charlevoix, MI: Peach Mountain Press for the Les Cheneaux Centennial Committee, 1984), 341.
69 Robert Heuck, *Early Recollections of the Snows* (printed privately by Heuck family, 1982), 41.
70 Ernest Hemingway, in *A Moveable Feast* (New York: Charles Scribner's Sons, 1964), wrote about memory as hunger; see page 204 in chapter 6.
71 A twenty-first-century photoshopped image of the White House lawn as a watermelon field accompanied Barack Obama's election as the nation's first African American president in US history.
72 In the same family album, another photograph of my grandmother shows her standing in front of the Hoeft family store in Rogers City.
73 Kyla Wazana Tompkins, *Racial Indigestion: Eating Bodies in the 19th Century* (New York: New York University Press, 2012), 106.
74 Erica L. Taylor, "Little Known Black History Fact: Colored American Day," Black America Web, accessed January 28, 2019, blackamericaweb.com/2013/08/26/little-known-black-history-fact-colored-american-day/.

75 E. A. Modlin Jr., "A Market or 'a Relic of Barbarism'? Toward a More Inclusive Analysis of Social Memory on Postcards," in *Social Memory and Heritage Tourism Methodologies*, ed. Stephen P. Hanna, Amy E. Potter, E. Arnold Modlin, Perry Carter, and David L. Butler (Abingdon: Taylor & Francis, 2015), 173.

76 Adapted from a 1906 Kalamazoo recipe from the Charlotte *Michigan State Federation Cook Book* (1909), 65, and a recipe by Mary Barber and Sara Corpening called "Watermelon Rind Pickles" published in *Bon Appétit* (August 1998), 44; by comparison see also Women's Auxiliary of Grace Church, *Superior Cook Book*, 157.

77 "Minniehaha [*sic*] Cake" appears in: Joyce Pines, comp., *Heirlooms: Then and Now* (Waverly, IA: G&R Publishing, 1996), 37.

78 Schoolcraft's twenty-five-year residency in the Upper Peninsula not only facilitated the 1836 acquisition of about thirteen million additional acres of native lands by the government and homesteaders but also provided the basis for romanticizing the Ojibwe nation's history and luring many generations of future residents to the UP.

79 *The World's Fair Recipe Book* (Philadelphia: Jacob Landis, 1893), 18, https://babel .hathitrust.org/cgi/pt?id=loc.ark:/13960/t12n5mr0f&view=1up&seq=20&skin= 2021.

80 Women's Auxiliary of Grace Church, *Superior Cook Book*, 132.

Chapter 2

1 Naila Moreira, "Porcupine," *Cider Press Review* 22, no. 3 (October 14, 2020). Moreira's poem evokes the porcupine as a stenographic statement of the wilderness and recalls the use of the word "bristling" by George Shiras III (below, this chapter). The wild is viewed as potentially dangerous and most certainly uncomfortable.

2 Among the first night photographs, black-and-white images of an albino porcupine on a floating log were taken repeatedly by Shiras between 1897 and 1904 at Whitefish Lake near Lake Superior; see George Shiras III, *Hunting Wildlife with Camera and Flashlight* (Washington, DC: National Geographic Society, 1935), 1:342. See also Finis Dunaway, "Hunting with the Camera: Nature Photography, Manliness, and Modern Memory, 1890–1930," *Journal of American Studies* 34, no. 2 (2000): 207–30, www.jstor.org/stable/27556807.

3 See another trope for cultural appropriation, coined as the "Jemima code" by Toni Tipton-Martin, *The Jemima Code: Two Centuries of African American Cookbooks* (Austin: University of Texas Press, 2015).

4 Shiras, *Hunting Wildlife*, 1:400–401.

5 Alan B. Shabel, Anthony D. Barnosky, Tonya Van Leuvan, Faysal Bibi, and Matthew H. Kaplan, "Irvingtonian Mammals from the Badger Room in Porcupine Cave: Age, Taphonomy, Climate, and Ecology," in *Biodiversity Response to Climate*

Change in the Middle Pleistocene: The Porcupine Cave Fauna from Colorado, ed. Anthony D. Barnosky (Berkeley: University of California Press, 2004), 312–13.

6 Roger A. Powell and Robert B. Brander, "Adaptations of Fishers and Porcupines to Their Predator Prey System," in *Proceedings of the 1975 Predator Symposium*, ed. Robert L. Phillips and Charles Jonkel, 45–53, American Society of Mammalogists 55th Annual Meeting, June 16–19, Montana Forest and Conservation Experiment Station, University of Montana, Missoula (printed in 1977).

7 Shiras, *Hunting Wildlife*, 1:327.

8 R. B. Brander, "Longevity of Wild Porcupines," *Journal of Mammalogy* 52, no. 4 (November 1971): 835.

9 See *Ojibwe People's Dictionary*, s.v. "jigaakwaa." Department of American Indian Studies and University Libraries, University of Minnesota, *Ojibwe People's Dictionary*, ed. Nora Livesay, accessed January 31, 2024, http://ojibwe.lib.umn.edu.

10 Roger Williams, *A Key into the Language of America* (London: Gregory Dexter, 1643), 13.

11 Williams, *Language of America*, 11.

12 Antonio Rossano Mendes Pontes, José Ramon Gadelha, Éverton R. A. Melo, Fabrício Bezerra de Sá, Ana Carolina Loss, Vilacio Caldara Junior, Leonora Pires Costa, and Yuri L. R. Leite, "A New Species of Porcupine, Genus *Coendou* (Rodentia: Erethizontidae) from the Atlantic Forest of Northeastern Brazil," *Zootaxa* 3636, no. 3 (2013): 421–38.

13 Gregory Forth, *Why the Porcupine Is Not a Bird: Explorations in the Folk Zoology of an Eastern Indonesian People* (Toronto: University of Toronto Press, 2016), 110–15.

14 R. A. F. De Reaumur, "Observations sur le porc-epic; Extraites de memoires et de lettres de M. Sarrazin, Medicin du Roy a Quebec et Correspondant de l'Académie," *Mémoires de l'Académie Royale des Sciences* (Paris) (1727): 383–96.

15 Kathryn A. Young, "Crown Agent–Canadian Correspondent: Michel Sarrazin and the Académie Royal des Sciences, 1697–1734," *French Historical Studies* 8, no. 2 (Autumn 1993): 416–33, 432n73.

16 Uldis Roze, *The North American Porcupine*, 2nd ed. (Ithaca: Cornell University Press, 2009), 10.

17 Henry R. Schoolcraft, *Narrative Journal of Travels . . . in the Year 1820* (Albany: E. and E. Hosford, 1821), 125–26.

18 See Christopher D. E. Willoughby, *Masters of Health: Racial Science and Slavery in U.S. Medical Schools* (Chapel Hill: University of North Carolina Press, 2022), 44, 76, 143.

19 See Stephen Jay Gould, *The Mismeasure of Man* (New York: W. W. Norton, 1981), 42–50.

20 Louis Agassiz, "The Diversity of Origin of the Human Races," *Christian Examiner* 49 (1850): 110–45; see the extensive discussion of Agassiz and tropicality in Nancy Leys Stepan, *Picturing Tropical Nature* (London: Reaktion Books, 2001), 98–112.

21 Louis Agassiz and James Elliot Cabot, *Lake Superior: Its Physical Character, Vegetation, and Animals, Compared with Those of Other and Similar Regions* (Boston: Gould, Kendall and Lincoln, 1850), facing page 78.

22 Agassiz and Cabot, *Lake Superior*, 89.

23 Agassiz and Cabot, *Lake Superior*, 89.

24 As Jesuit missionary Father Claude Dablon (1618–97) reported in his *Relation de . . . la Nouvelle France* (Paris, 1672), quoted in Brian Leigh Dunnigan, *A Picturesque Situation: Mackinac before Photography, 1615–1860* (Detroit: Wayne State University Press, 2008), 12.

25 National Ocean Service, NOAA, "Do the Great Lakes Have Tides?" See ocean service.noaa.gov/facts/gltides.html.

26 Plate 36, a hand-colored lithograph, in J. J. Audubon, *The Viviparous Quadrupeds of North America* (New York, 1845–54).

27 E. L. Palmer, *Field Book of Nature-Study* (Ithaca, NY: Slingerland-Comstock Co., 1928), part 2:2; see also the collection of the Cornell University Library, Division of Rare and Manuscript Collections, #4128, 2662-900-1140, 2662-900-1150.

28 Jean Lipman, *Calder's Universe* (New York: Viking Press, 1976), 82.

29 John Burroughs, "An Astonished Porcupine," accessed February 2, 2024, fullreads .com/literature/an-astonished-porcupine/.

30 Charles G. D. Roberts, "In Panoply of Spears," in *The Kindred of the Wild: A Book of Animal Life* (Boston: L. C. Page & Company, 1902), 357.

31 Roze, *The North American Porcupine*, 16–17.

32 James H. McCommons, *Camera Hunter: George Shiras III and the Birth of Wildlife Photography* (Albuquerque: University of New Mexico Press, 2019).

33 Sonia Voss, quoted in Jessie Wender, "Meet Grandfather Flash, the Pioneer of Wildlife Photography," *National Geographic*, November 20, 2015, www .nationalgeographic.com/photography/proof/2015/11/20/meet-grandfather -flash-the-pioneer-of-wildlife-photography/#close.

34 Alexander Agassiz and George R. Agassiz, *Letters and Recollections of Alexander Agassiz: With a Sketch of His Life and Work* (Boston: Houghton Mifflin, 1913), 73.

35 Lewis H. Morgan, *The American Beaver and His Works* (Philadelphia: J. B. Lippincott, 1868), viii, x.

36 Morgan, *The American Beaver*, 22–23. Roze, *The North American Porcupine*, 42, reports an average weight of 4.59–5.53 kg, or less than half the maximum weight.

37 Roze, *The North American Porcupine*, 93, 104.

38 Shiras, *Hunting Wildlife*, 1:342; currently part of Laughing Whitefish Lake Preserve.

39 Shiras, *Hunting Wildlife*, 1:320.

40 Shiras, *Hunting Wildlife*, 1:333.

41 Roze, *The North American Porcupine*, 81.

42 Terry Reynolds and Virginia Dawson, *Iron Will: Cleveland-Cliffs and the Mining of Iron Ore, 1847–2006* (Detroit: Wayne State University Press, 2012).

43 Robert Macfarlane, *The Wild Places* (New York: Penguin Books, 2008), 169; see also Christopher Tilley and Kate Cameron-Daum, *An Anthropology of Landscape:*

The Extraordinary in the Ordinary (London: University College London Press, 2017).

44 Charles Bert Reed, *Masters of the Wilderness* (Chicago: University of Chicago Press, 1914), 71.

45 Reed, *Masters*, 67.

46 Schoolcraft, *Narrative*, 125.

47 Reed, *Masters*.

48 For a full history of the distinct periods of logging and forest industry, see Theodore J. Karamanski, *Deep Woods Frontier: A History of Logging in Northern Michigan* (Detroit: Wayne State University Press, 1989).

49 See Calumet Woman's Club, *Sharing Our Best of Copper Country Recipes* (Calumet, MI: Calumet Woman's Club, 1952); see Agassiz and Cabot, *Lake Superior*, 27, 34, 40, 44, and 115.

50 Arthur W. Turner, *Strangers and Sojourners: A History of Michigan's Keweenaw Peninsula* (Detroit: Wayne State University Press, 1994), 160.

51 Stewart Edward White, *The Blazed Trail* (New York: Grosset & Dunlap, 1902), chap. 5.

52 Stewart Edward White, *The Forest* (New York: Grosset & Dunlap, 1903), 31.

53 White, *The Blazed Trail*, 4.

54 Near Cedarville, "Hungry Hill" was near the site of an early steam-powered sawmill. See Robert Heuck, *Early Recollections of the Snows* (printed privately by Heuck family, 1982).

55 Roze, *The North American Porcupine*, 46–47.

56 Powell and Brander, "Adaptations," 46.

57 Powell and Brander, "Adaptations," 47–48.

58 Powell and Brander, "Adaptations," 51.

59 Julie Anderson, "Nebraska Wildlife Rehab's Ark Is Bursting at the Seams," *Omaha World-Herald*, June 24, 2015; Sid Perkins, "Porcupine Quills Reveal Their Prickly Secrets," *Science*, December 10, 2012: Harvard research has shown thirty thousand quills, each with as many as seven hundred to eight hundred barbs.

60 See Donald A. Spencer, "Porcupine Population Fluctuations in Past Centuries Revealed by Dendrochronology," *Journal of Applied Ecology* 1, no. 1 (1964): 127–49, doi.org/10.2307/2401593.

61 Keith R. Widder, *Mackinac National Park, 1875–1895* (Williamston, MI: Mackinac Island State Park Commission, 1975), 9.

62 The text of the Wilderness Act of 1964 (Public Law 88-577, 16 U.S.C. 1131–1136) may be accessed at wilderness.net/learn-about-wilderness/key-laws/wilderness-act/default.php.

63 Aldo Leopold, foreword to *A Sand County Almanac, and Sketches Here and There* (1949; repr., New York: Oxford University Press, 1989), viii.

64 Leopold, *Sand County Almanac*, 225. John Knott might disagree; his *Imagining the Forest: Narratives of Michigan and the Upper Midwest* (Ann Arbor: University of Michigan Press, 2012) explores a select literary history of the region's forests.

65 Leopold, *Sand County Almanac*, 221.
66 Quoted by William Eaton, ed., "The Solitudes of This America," *Zeteo*, July 23, 2015, accessed August 21, 2017, zeteojournal.com/2015/07/23/de-tocqueville -quinze-jours-dans-le-desert/. See Alexis de Tocqueville, *Democracy in America: Historical-Critical Edition of De la démocratie en Amérique*, ed. Eduardo Nolla, trans. James T. Schleifer (Indianapolis: Liberty Fund, 2010), vol. 4, accessed August 21, 2017, oll.libertyfund.org/titles/2288#lf1532-04_footnote _nt825, and Alexis de Tocqueville and Gustave de Beaumont, *Journey to America*, trans. George Lawrence, ed. J. P. Mayer (New Haven: Yale University Press, 1959).
67 Shiras, *Hunting Wildlife*, 1:333.
68 Shiras, *Hunting Wildlife*, 1:338.
69 See a discussion of this phrase in Stephen Jay Gould, *The Mismeasure of Man* (Boston: W. W. Norton, 1981).
70 See J. W. Attig, L. Clayton, and D. M. Mickelson, "Correlation of Late Wisconsin Glacial Phases in the Western Great Lakes Area," *Geological Society of America Bulletin* 96 (1985): 1585–93.
71 See Robert Macfarlane, *The Wild Places* (New York: Penguin Books, 2008), 93–94.
72 Agassiz and Cabot, *Lake Superior*, 49.
73 Agassiz and Cabot, *Lake Superior*, 124–25.
74 *The Standard Guide to Mackinac Island and Northern Lake Resorts* (New York: Foster & Reynolds, 1899), 11.
75 Robert Louis Stevenson, "An Autumn Effect," in *Essays of Travel* (London: Chatto & Windus, 1905), 130.
76 Stevenson, "An Autumn Effect," 106.
77 Henry David Thoreau, "Journals," in *The Writings of Henry David Thoreau*, ed. John C. Broderick and Robert Sattelmeyer (Princeton, NJ: Princeton University Press, 1984), 165.
78 John Gatta, "Sacramental Communion with Nature: From Emerson on the Lord's Supper to Thoreau's Transcendental Picnic," *Religions* 9, no. 2 (2018): 48, doi.org/ 10.3390/rel9020048.
79 Henry David Thoreau, *Wild Fruits: Thoreau's Rediscovered Last Manuscript*, ed. Bradley P. Dean (New York: W. W. Norton, 2000), 52.
80 Thoreau, *Wild Fruits*, 52.
81 Tocqueville and Beaumont, *Journey to America*, 334–37.
82 Charles Lanman (before 1846), quoted in Brian Leigh Dunnigan, *A Picturesque Situation: Mackinac before Photography, 1615–1860* (Detroit: Wayne State University Press, 2008), 231.
83 Adapted from a recipe by Constance Sullivan (Waaseya Anang Ikwe, "Bright Star Woman"), a member of the Keweenaw Bay Indian Community Ojibwe tribe. See Constance Sullivan, "Fry Bread Recipe—Native American Heritage Month," Potawatomi Casino/Hotel Blog post, November 27, 2018, https://www.paysbig .com/blog/fry-bread-recipe-native-american-heritage-month.

84 Sean Sherman with Beth Dooley, *The Sioux Chef's Indigenous Kitchen* (Minneapolis: University of Minnesota Press, 2017), 9.

85 From the Ladies' Aid Society, Laurium Methodist Episcopal Church, *Copper Country Cookery* (Laurium, MI: Methodist Episcopal Church, 1902), 9.

86 In Mark Kurlansky, ed., *The Food of a Younger Land* (New York: Penguin, 2009), 219.

87 Adapted from The Committee, "Recipe for Porcupine Stew," in *Favorite Recipes: Upper Peninsula of Michigan*, comp. and ed. Cy Meier (Calumet, MI: District 1 Michigan Federation Business & Professional Women, 1978).

88 Grand Marais Woman's Club, *The Cooking Pots of Grand Marais* (1930s; repr., Grand Marais, MI: Voyager Press, 1976), 8.

89 Porcupine Meat Balls (made with ground beef, rice, onion, salt, and pepper cooked in tomato soup, water, and chili powder) appeared in the 1952 edition of Calumet Woman's Club, *Copper Country Recipes*.

90 Leopold, *Sand County Almanac*, 210.

91 Leopold, *Sand County Almanac*, 84.

92 Iliana Regan is the owner and chef at Milkweed Inn, a bed and breakfast located near the Hiawatha National Forest in the UP. She describes her relationships with the region's seasons and foods in her memoir *Fieldwork, a Forager's Memoir* (Chicago: Agate, 2023), 39–40. Note that hedgehogs (found in Eurasia and Africa) have quills, but they are unrelated to porcupines.

93 Thomas Vennum Jr., *Wild Rice and the Ojibway People* (St. Paul: Minnesota Historical Society Press, 1988). See www.nativewildricecoalition.com/cultural-importance.html, accessed August 12, 2017.

94 Nancy Kennedy and Mary Augusta Rodgers, *The Ford Times Traveler's Cookbook: Quick Ways to Prepare Good Food on the Road* (Dearborn: Ford Motor Company, 1965), 35.

95 Aldo Leopold, Archives, University of Wisconsin–Madison, Aldo Leopold Papers: 9/25/10-7: Diaries and Journals, Field Notes and misc. cards, 824. [48], accessed February 3, 2024, https://search.library.wisc.edu/digital/A4H7W7SOLVJ6YI8I/pages/A43RM4DXHTJYR48V.

96 This recipe is from the Blue Cornmeal package, Bob's Red Mill Natural Foods, adapted from www.bobsredmill.com/recipes/how-to-make/blue-cornmeal-pancakes/; see also https://www.allrecipes.com/recipe/45145/blue-cornmeal-pancakes/, accessed February 3, 2024.

Chapter 3

1 World historian Anand Yang, speaking about South Asian history in a social media post on Facebook, October 19, 2021.

2 Quoted by William Eaton, ed., "The Solitudes of This America," *Zeteo*, July 23, 2015, zeteojournal.com/2015/07/23/de-tocqueville-quinze-jours-dans-le-desert/.

3 Louis Agassiz and James Elliot Cabot, *Lake Superior: Its Physical Character, Vegetation, and Animals, Compared with Those of Other and Similar Regions* (Boston: Gould, Kendall and Lincoln, 1850), 38.

4 Agassiz and Cabot, *Lake Superior*, facing page 78.

5 Michael Castells, *The Informational City* (Oxford: Blackwell, 1989).

6 Agassiz and Cabot, *Lake Superior*, 124–25.

7 David Waller, *Iron Men: How One London Factory Powered the Industrial Revolution and Shaped the Modern World* (London: Anthem Press, 2016), 37.

8 Quoted in Alvah Bradish, *Memoir of Douglass Houghton, First State Geologist of Michigan* (Detroit: Raynor & Taylor, 1889), title page.

9 Thomas G. Anderson, "Narrative of Capt. Thomas G. Anderson, 1800–1828," in *Report and Collections of the State Historical Society of Wisconsin*, ed. Lyman Copeland Draper (1882; repr., Madison: State Historical Society of Wisconsin, 1909), 9:139.

10 John A. Lomax and Alan Lomax, *American Ballads and Folk Songs* (New York: Macmillan, 1934), 477.

11 Agassiz and Cabot, *Lake Superior*, 99.

12 Agassiz and Cabot, *Lake Superior*, 67.

13 National Park Service, "Isle Royale: SS *America*," February 17, 2021, www.nps.gov/isro/learn/historyculture/ss-america.htm.

14 Russ Green, "Thunder Bay 2010: Cutting Edge Tech & the Hunt for Lake Huron's Lost Ships," *NOAA Ocean Exploration*, accessed February 4, 2024, oceanexplorer.noaa.gov/explorations/10thunderbay/background/plan/plan.html.

15 A beautiful reconstruction of Grandpa's rowboat was built at the Great Lakes Boat Building School in 2012–13. See smallcraftadvisor.com/our-blog/?p=3529 for photographs of local boatbuilding, from cedar, oak, and mahogany, during first- and second-year projects at the school during fall 2012.

16 Ida Hamel gave piano lessons. Among her pupils were her son Edwin, who played piano and violin in a band called Hamel's Night Hawks, and her granddaughters Elda, who was the organist for her church, and Hyla, who fell in love with her husband-to-be, Russell Goucher (also the Cedarville High School music director), while sitting side by side on a piano bench.

17 Handwritten letter from Gertie Hamel to her mother-in-law, Ida Truscott, and family, November 29, 1920.

18 Quoted by Lisa Zyble, comp., "Looking Back: 90 Years Ago, September 24, 1914," *St. Ignace News*, September 23, 2004.

19 Alex Lange, "The Mighty Soo: Construction of the Locks at Sault Ste. Marie, Michigan," *The Unwritten Record* (blog), January 5, 2017, National Archives, unwritten-record.blogs.archives.gov/?s=The+Mighty+Soo.

20 Detroit and Cleveland Steam Navigation Company, with Cummings D. Whitcomb, *A Lake Tour to Picturesque Mackinac; Historical and Descriptive* (Detroit: O. S. Gulley, Bornman & Co., 1884), 8.

21 Advertisement for Lakeside Hotel, Coryell Islands, n.d. (after 1927), in Helen C. Shoberg, *Early Hotels in the Les Cheneaux Islands* (Cedarville, MI: For Helen Shoberg, 2002), 13.

22 Advertisement for Detroit & Cleveland Navigation Company with steamship lines between Detroit, Mackinac Island, St. Ignace, and Chicago, 1925. Detroit Historical Society, 2011.062.011. See also Neil Gale, "Chicago's 'I Will' Motto and 'Y' Municipal Device History," *DRLOIHjournal* (blog), May 10, 2017, drloihjournal .blogspot.com/2017/05/chicagos-i-will-motto-and-y-municipal.html.

23 "75,000 at New Pier," *Chicago Examiner*, July 16, 1916.

24 "Chicago's Municipal Pier," *Chicagology* (blog), accessed October 19, 2021, chicagology.com/?s=municipal+pier.

25 "Coming Pageant of Progress—A Second World's Fair," *Dearborn Magazine*, March 1921, quoted in *Chicagology* (blog), accessed October 19, 2021, chicagology.com/ pageantofprogress1921/.

26 Quoted in Shoberg, *Early Hotels*, 3.

27 Guy H. Hamel, "Boot Island in 1885 Is Scene of Camping Party," *Les Cheneaux Breezes* 10, no. 1 (1942): 27–28.

28 Guy H. Hamel, "Les Cheneaux Winter Was Not a Severe One," *Les Cheneaux Breezes* 10, no. 1 (1942): 10.

29 Guy H. Hamel, "Guides at the Islington Hotel in 1897," *Les Cheneaux Breezes* 11, no. 1 (1944): 17.

30 Florence McKee Heuck, "The Heuck Family," in *The Les Cheneaux Chronicles: Anatomy of a Community* by Philip M. Pittman (Charlevoix, MI: Peach Mountain Press for the Les Cheneaux Centennial Committee, 1984), 440–42.

31 L. Frank Baum, *Father Goose, His Book* (Chicago: George M. Hill Co., 1899), quoted in Timothy Garrett Young, *Drawn to Enchant: Original Children's Book Art in the Betsy Beinecke Shirley Collection* (New Haven: Yale University Press, 2007), 31. Captain Bing was likely Admiral Byng of the Royal Navy.

32 *Buttercup and the Pirates* (1926), with commentary by Dori Heuck Abnee, Alice Heuck Goldfarb, Butzie Wagner Hawley, and Mary Ainslee Heuck Morrison, DVD. Copy courtesy of John Griffin, Cedarville.

33 First Baptist Church (Howell, Michigan), *Howell Cook Book* (Howell, MI: Republican Printing House, Book and Job Dept., 1896), 26.

34 Stewart Edward White, *The Blazed Trail* (New York: Grosset & Dunlap, 1902), chap. 16.

35 Rich Cohen, "Inside Quebec's Great, Multi-Million-Dollar Maple-Syrup Heist," *Vanity Fair*, December 5, 2016.

36 See the research of the Michigan botanist William James Beal in F. W. Telewski and J. A. Zeevaart, "The 120-yr Period for Dr. Beal's Seed Viability Experiment," *American Journal of Botany* 89 (2002): 1285–88, doi.org/10.3732/ajb.89.8.1285.

37 Amelia Simmons, *American Cookery . . . Adapted to This Country, and All Grades of Life* (Hartford, CT: Hudson & Goodwin, 1796), accessed February 4, 2024, d.lib.msu.edu/fa/1.

38 Susannah Carter, *The Frugal Housewife, or Complete Woman Cook* (London: Printed for F. Newberry, 1772).

39 Letter from John Porteous to his father, dated 1767, quoted in Lynn L. Morand, *Craft Industries at Fort Michilimackinac, 1715–1781*, Archaeological

Completion Report Series, no. 15 (Mackinac Island, MI: Mackinac State Historic Parks, 1994), 73.

40 Thus, the North American fruits were called "ice apples" in the Caribbean to indicate they were imported and not local fruit.

41 Peter White, handwritten recipe for Peter White's Punch (July 12, 1905), in Women's Auxiliary of Grace Church, *Superior Cook Book* (Ishpeming, MI: Peninsular Record, 1905), 165, archive.org/details/superiorcookbook00grac/page/165.

42 See the descriptions of ice harvesting in his diary: Phil Porter, ed., *A Boy at Fort Mackinac: The Diary of Harold Dunbar Corbusier, 1883–1884, 1892* (Mackinac Island, MI: Mackinac State Historic Parks and the Corbusier Archives, 1994), 22, 37, 65.

43 See the 1919 brochure containing a steamer schedule, 2011.062.015, collection of the Detroit Historical Society.

44 Patrick Livingston, *Summer Dreams: The Story of Bob-Lo Island* (Detroit: Wayne State University Press, 2008), 39.

45 Livingston, *Summer Dreams*, 80–85.

46 See advertisement, c. 1967, "There's Something Special about a Picnic at Bob-Lo," 2013.062.001, collection of the Detroit Historical Society.

47 Brochure, c. 1958, "Bob-Lo, Where Most Picnics Go," 2013.004.070, collection of the Detroit Historical Society.

48 Thomas W. Pfeiffelmann, *Mackinac Adventures and Island Memories: Growing up on Mackinac* (Boyne City, MI: Harbor, 2004), 59.

49 Rose S. Melchers, *Of Fifty Summers* (Cedarville, MI: Les Cheneaux Historical Association, 1999).

50 The *Eat Safe Fish Guide*, produced by the Michigan Department of Health and Human Services, is updated online and lists the fish that have been tested for PCBs and dioxins, as well as mercury, and how much is safe to consume: www.michigan.gov/documents/mdch/MDCH_EAT_SAFE_FISH_GUIDE_-_UPPER_PENINSULA_WEB_455361_7.pdf.

51 Red Jacket Brewing Company, personal communication, July 27, 2017.

52 Anne Chotzinoff Grossman and Lisa Grossman Thomas, *Lobscouse & Spotted Dog* (New York: W. W. Norton, 1997), 105–7; adapted from the recipe for "duff" in landlocked Charlotte, 1909, *Michigan State Federation Cook Book* (Charlotte, MI: Perry, Nies, & Co., 1909), 281; note that this recipe contains raw eggs and thus is not recommended for children or pregnant women.

53 Based on the published recipe for the "Anaconda" from the Beach Inn in Munising Bay in Russell M. Magnaghi, *Prohibition in the Upper Peninsula: Booze & Bootleggers on the Border* (Charleston, SC: American Palate, 2017), 124, and the Grand Hotel's "Round Island Iced Tea," served on Mackinac Island: "A Tropical Fruit-Flavored Version of a Long Island with Raspberry Vodka, Mango Rum, London Gin, Silver Tequila & Grand Marnier with Pineapple Juice then Topped with Oberon." See www.grandhotel.com/pdfs/Cawthornes_Wine_2013.pdf, accessed August 31, 2017. Round Island is in the Straits of Mackinac and protects

the harbor of Mackinac Island. Usually associated with New York (c. 1972), the original Long Island Tea was invented in the 1920s in Tennessee. The Anaconda likely originates from the migration of miners from the Anaconda mines (in Butte, Montana) to Copper Country in the first few decades of the century. See the article by Arthur W. Thurner, "Western Federation of Miners: The Impact of the Michigan Copper," *Montana: The Magazine of Western History* (Spring 1983): 33.

54 I have fond childhood memories of smelling yeast and cinnamon and finally devouring my mother's baked sticky buns. This recipe comes from a family cookbook from the German side (including her mother, Gertie Meyer Hamel, and Aunt Eileen Radtke, with whom she lived after my Grandma Gertie died). They mostly resided in Rogers City and the Les Cheneaux Islands. See Joyce M. Pines, comp., *Heirlooms: Then and Now* (Waverly, IA: G&R Publishing, 1996), 27.

55 Michael Connell, "Port Huron Once Dominated Chicory Trade," *Times Herald*, October 19, 2014.

56 John J. Sellman, *Martin Reef, Lightship to Lighthouse: Another Chapter in Les Cheneaux History* (Cedarville, MI: Les Cheneaux Historical Association, 1995).

57 Lafcadio Hearn, *La Cuisine Creole: A Collection of Culinary Recipes* (1885; repr., Carlisle, MA: Applewood Books, 2011), 185.

CHAPTER 4

1 Nika Hazelton, *The Picnic Book* (New York: Atheneum, 1969), 123.

2 Jamaica Kincaid, *A Small Place* (New York: Farrar, Straus and Giroux, 1988), 18; Kincaid describes the quintessential tourist on Antigua, an island in the Caribbean.

3 Quoted in Philip M. Pittman, *The Les Cheneaux Chronicles: Anatomy of a Community* (Charlevoix, MI: Peach Mountain Press, 1984), 239.

4 Christian Wolmar, *Blood, Iron, and Gold: How the Railroads Transformed the World* (New York: PublicAffairs/Perseus, 2010), 69.

5 Wolmar, *Blood, Iron, and Gold*, 146.

6 St. Paul Railroad, advertisement, *Calumet News*, July 23, 1897, 3.

7 MDOT, *Michigan's Railroad History, 1825–2014* (Lansing: State of Michigan, 2014), www.michigan.gov/documents/mdot/Michigan_Railroad_History _506899_7.pdf.

8 Dan Egan, *The Life and Death of the Great Lakes* (New York: W. W. Norton, 2017), chap. 2.

9 A lamprey sea pie made a return voyage from the Great Lakes to Gloucester in 2012; see Mark Brush, "Queen to Enjoy 'Great Lakes Sea Lamprey Pie' at Diamond Jubilee," *Here and Now* (Michigan Radio), April 27, 2012. See also the relationship between nineteenth-century "Cornish fish pie" and modern pasty with carrots and rutabaga in *Did They Really Eat That?: A 19th Century Cookbook That*

Acquainted Immigrants with Northwoods Pioneer Fare (Calumet, MI: Copper Sun Publications, 1992), 10, 40.

10   William W. Brown, comp., *The Anti-Slavery Harp: A Collection of Songs for Anti-Slavery Meetings* (Charlottesville, VA: Stephen Railton, Institute for Advanced Technology in the Humanities, 2000), utc.iath.virginia.edu/abolitn/absowwba24t.html.

11   Wolmar, *Blood, Iron, and Gold*, 149.

12   Women's Auxiliary of Grace Church, *Superior Cook Book* (Ishpeming, MI: Peninsular Record, 1905), 29, 57, 70, 64.

13   For example, see Ardashes H. Keoleian, *The Oriental Cook Book: Wholesome, Dainty and Economical Dishes of the Orient, Especially Adapted to American Tastes and Methods of Preparation* (New York: Sully & Kleiinteich, 1913), which includes Turkish coffee, Italian macaroni, and African okra.

14   Walter Levy, *The Picnic: A History* (Lanham, MD: AltaMira Press, 2014), 42–43.

15   Richard A. Fields, *Range of Opportunity: A Historic Study of the Copper Range Company* (Hancock, MI: Quincy Mine Hoist Association and Michigan Technological University, 1997), 5.

16   Fields, *Range of Opportunity*, 6–7.

17   Fields, *Range of Opportunity*, 9–19.

18   "Appalling Disaster on the Northern Pennsylvania Railroad," *Frank Leslie's Illustrated Newspaper* 2, no. 34 (August 2, 1856), 121, microfilm, Knight Library, University of Oregon, accessed February 7, 2024.

19   St. Louis Park Historical Society, "Amusement Parks: Antlers Park," city of St. Louis Park (website), accessed February 5, 2024, slphistory.org/amusementparks/.

20   Caroline R. Stone, *Inga of Porcupine Mine* ([New York?]: Holiday House, 1942); see also chapter 5.

21   Matthew L. Basso, *Meet Joe Copper: Masculinity and Race on Montana's World War II Home Front* (Chicago: University of Chicago Press, 2013), 74.

22   Patrick F. Morris, *Anaconda, Montana: Copper Smelting Boom Town on the Western Frontier* (Bethesda, MD: Swann Publishing, 1997), 102.

23   Morris, *Anaconda, Montana*, 236.

24   See New Zealand History, "Rail Tourism," Ministry for Culture and Heritage, December 20, 2012, nzhistory.govt.nz/culture/rail-tourism/day-excursions.

25   "Portage Lake News," *Calumet News*, July 23, 1897, 3.

26   A third relic was brought to the basilica in the summer of 1960, a gift from Pope John XXIII.

27   See "Copper Range Railroad," May 8, 2023, www.american-rails.com/copr.html.

28   Kevin E. Musser, expert on the Copper Range Railroad, shared the recollections of William Brinkman, "Copper Range Freda Park," Copper Range Railroad (website), accessed February 5, 2024, www.copperrange.org/freda.htm.

29   Fields, *Range of Opportunity*, 34, 43.

30   William Wordsworth, "On the Projected Kendal and Windermere Railway," *Morning Post*, October 12, 1844, https://en.wikisource.org/wiki/Kendal

_and_Windermere_Railway:_two_letters_re-printed_from_the_Morning_Post/
Sonnet:_On_the_Projected_Kendal_and_Windermere_Railway.

31 Wolfgang Schivelbusch, *The Railway Journey: The Industrialization of Time and Space in the Nineteenth Century.* (Berkeley: University of California Press, 2014).

32 Schivelbusch, *The Railway Journey*, chap. 3; see also Nancy Rose Marshall, "On William Powell Frith's *Railway Station*, April 1862," *BRANCH: Britain, Representation, and Nineteenth-Century History*, ed. Dino Franco Felluga, extension of Romanticism and Victorianism on the Net (website), accessed October 30, 2021, www.branchcollective.org/?ps_articles=nancy-rose-marshall-on-william-powell -friths-railway-station-april-1862.

33 Schivelbusch, *The Railway Journey*, chap. 13.

34 Alexander Agassiz and George R. Agassiz, *Letters and Recollections of Alexander Agassiz: With a Sketch of His Life and Work* (Boston: Houghton Mifflin, 1913), 62.

35 Stewart Edward White, *The Blazed Trail* (New York: Grosset & Dunlap, 1902), chap. 1.

36 Ken Kesey, *Sometimes a Great Notion* (New York: Viking Press, 1964).

37 White, *The Blazed Trail*, 4.

38 White, *The Blazed Trail*, chap. 1.

39 Russell M. Magnaghi, *Upper Peninsula of Michigan: A History* (Morrisville, MI: Lulu Press, 2017), 94.

40 White, *The Blazed Trail*, chap. 5.

41 White, *The Blazed Trail*, chap. 37.

42 "Hungry Hill," near Cedarville, marked the site near an encampment of the old sawmill owned by my grandfather. See Robert Heuck, *Early Recollections of the Snows* (printed privately by Heuck family, 1982).

43 Ernest Hemingway, *A Moveable Feast* (New York: Charles Scribner's Sons, 1964), 76.

44 Ernest Hemingway, "Big Two-Hearted River," in *In Our Time* (New York: Boni & Liveright, 1925).

45 This recipe was collected on October 11, 1976, during an oral history interview with Eva Koopikka by Helen Armstrong for the Finnish Folklore and Social Change in the Great Lakes Mining Region Oral History Collection, Finlandia University, Finnish American Historical Archive and Museum.

46 Adapted from a recipe by Chef David Sapp, Park Kitchen, Portland, Oregon, July 1, 2017.

47 Charles A. Anderson, "Diaries of Peter Dougherty: Introduction," *Journal of the Presbyterian Historical Society* 30, no. 3 (1952): 175–92.

48 "Marshmallow Roasts. There Is Much Amusement but Little Excitement in a New Fad," Morning Call (San Francisco), August 18, 1892, 6, https://chronicling america.loc.gov/lccn/sn94052989/1892-08-18/ed-1/seq-6/.

49 Adapted from a recipe from Gemma Stafford, *Gemma's Bigger Bolder Baking* (website), accessed February 5, 2024, www.biggerbolderbaking.com/homemade -marshmallows-recipe/.

50 Wolmar, *Blood, Iron, and Gold*, 14.

CHAPTER 5

1 John Burroughs, quoted in Francis Champ Zumbrun, "Famous Travelers: Edison, Ford, Firestone; The Vagabonds Continue Two Week Camping Trip in Western Maryland," Maryland Department of Natural Resources, accessed February 5, 2024, dnr.maryland.gov/pages/md-conservation-history/travelerspart4.aspx. Another version is published as part of the essay by John Burroughs, "Straight Seeing and Thinking," in *John Burroughs' America: Selections from the Writings of the Hudson River Naturalist* (1951; repr., Mineola, NY: Dover, 1997), 54.

2 Steven C. Brisson, *Wish You Were Here: An Album of Vintage Mackinac Postcards* (Mackinac Island, MI: Mackinac Island State Historic Press, 2002), 64.

3 See the reprint of Rose S. Melchers, *Of Fifty Summers* (Cedarville, MI: Les Chene- aux Historical Association, 1999), 70–72. Melchers's account was first published in 1955; it is a memoir of the Islington Hotel, built in 1895.

4 See Gijs Mom, *Mobilizing Automobilism: Exuberance and the Emergence of Layered Mobility, 1900–1980* (New York: Berghahn, 2020); Katherine J. Parkin, *Women at the Wheel: A Century of Buying, Driving, and Fixing Cars* (Philadel- phia: University of Pennsylvania Press, 2017); and Gijs Mom, *Atlantic Automo- bilism: Emergence and Persistence of the Car, 1895–1940* (New York: Berghahn Books, 2015).

5 Uldene Rudd LeRoy, *Six on an Island: Childhood Memories from Lake Huron* (Chicago: Adams Press, 1956), 23; see also the historical remembrance by Uldene Rudd LeRoy (Dodo's) great-grandson Joshua Lycka, "Off of the Island: Reflec- tions through Memory" (2012), Honors Projects, Grand Valley State University, scholarworks.gvsu.edu/honorsprojects/368.

6 Linda Hull Larned, *One Hundred Picnic Suggestions* (New York: Charles Scrib- ner's Sons, 1915), cover. The separate recipe section for the "Motor Hamper" calls for toasted and trimmed sandwiches of the like of "Club Sandwich de Foie Gras" and "Lobster Creole, Hot." See also Walter Levy's essay, "Linda Larned's *One Hundred Picnic Suggestions* (1915)," Picnicwit: The History. The Food. The Stories (website), accessed February 5, 2024, www.picnicwit.com/foodanddrink/ cookbooks/linda-hull-larneds-one-hundred-picnic-suggestions-1915/.

7 C. F. Leyel [Hilda Winifred Waughton], *Picnics for Motorists: Lure of Cookery Series* (London: Routledge, 1936). Leyel was a champion of seasonal and local ingredients, alongside pigeon pies and caramel soufflés.

8 James Beard, *Beard on Food* (Philadelphia: Running Press, 1974), 262.

9 Rhyming "Lucille" with "Oldsmobile," Fleischer Studios' suggestive *In My Merry Oldsmobile* was an animated short film made in 1930; its bouncing-ball sing-along song was originally composed in 1905, with music by Gus Edwards and lyrics by Vincent P. Bryan.

10 Norman Brauer, *There to Breathe the Beauty* (Dalton, PA: Norman Brauer Publications, 1995).

11 Mary B. Mullett, "Four Big Men Become Boys Again," *American Magazine* 87, no. 2 (1919): 34.

12 U.S. Government Patent Office, patent no. 667,050, Machine for Making Artificial Fuel, filed by Ellsworth B. A. Zwoyer, August 1, 1900, and granted January 29, 1901.

13 Ford Motor Company, "Experiments Yield Wood Briquettes for Fuel," *Ford News* 2: IIF:4, vol. 2, no. 11 (January 8, 1923): 4, Benson Ford Research Center, Henry Ford Museum.

14 Frank E. Brimmer, "Forty-Four Million Awheel: National Motor Tourist Business Aggregates $3,590,400,000 in 1928," *American Motorist* 21, no. 1 (1929): 33–36.

15 The Ford picnic advertisements were not the first of their kind. Picnics had advertised everything from canned fish to Guinness and Coca-Cola. See the website by Walter Levy, PicnicWit: The History. The Food. The Stories, www.picnicwit.com.

16 John Burroughs (1921), quoted in Brauer, *There to Breathe the Beauty*, xii. Unpublished "meticulous" notes on the trips by Firestone are held by the Bierce Library, University of Akron.

17 See 1920 United States Federal Census, Thomas Sato, Dearborn, Wayne County, Michigan, ACC 1, Box 34, Folder 10; Japanese Reliable Employment Agency, ACC 285, Box 876, 1928-989; Box 171/159 7/24, Letters from Liebold to Thomas Edison July 21, 1923, and Washuya, Japan, June 4, 1923, Letter from Thomas Sato to Mrs. Henry Ford; ACC 512, Box 6, Vagabonds, Letter from Burroughs to Mrs. Ford August 20, 1919, Woodchuck Lodge, Roxbury, NY (Benson Ford Research Center, Henry Ford Museum, Dearborn, MI).

18 American Automobile Association, *A Story of Service* (Washington, DC: American Automobile Association, 1957).

19 Mom, *Atlantic Automobilism*, 373.

20 Brauer, *There to Breathe the Beauty*, 200–201.

21 See *Ford News* 2, no. 8 (1922): 2 and 5.

22 See Jon L. Saari, "Upper Peninsula Summer Camps: An Historical Look at Their Place in Our Lives and Nature," in *A Sense of Place: Michigan's Upper Peninsula, Essays in Honor of William & Margery Vandament*, ed. Russell M. Magnaghi and Michael T. Marsden (Marquette, MI: Northern Michigan University, 1997), 177–93.

23 See Beverly E. Bastian, "Elmwood: The Archeology of Twentieth Century African-American Pioneers in the Great North Woods," in *I, Too, Am America*, ed. Theresa A. Singleton (Charlottesville: University Press of Virginia, 1999); see also www.blackpast.org/aah/elmwood-michigan-1926-1929, accessed September 22, 2017.

24 Personal communication, February 13, 2019, Vancouver, WA; see her poem "tobermory heaven," written in memorium and dedicated to her father, the late Siegel G. Clore II, in Melba Joyce Boyd, *the province of literary cats* (Ferndale, MI: Past Tents Press, 2002), 51–52.

25 May Bragdon, quoted in Anya Jabour, "A Paradise for Single Ladies," *Atlas Obscura*, March 1, 2022, www.atlasobscura.com/articles/single-women-paradise -georgian-bay.

26 Henry A. Perry, ed., *Cloverland Tourist's Guide, 1932* (Menominee, MI: Herald-Leader Co., 1932), 2.

27 Perry, *Cloverland*, 2; "Land of Hiawatha" and "Roof Garden of the United States" were two other names. See also Aaron Shapiro, "Promoting Cloverland: Regional Associations, State Agencies, and the Creation of Michigan's Upper Peninsula Tourist Industry," *Michigan Historical Review* 29, no. 1 (2003): 1–37; Aaron Shapiro, *The Lure of the North Woods: Cultivating Tourism in the Upper Midwest* (Minneapolis: University of Minnesota Press, 2013); and Olivia Ernst, "From Cut-Over to Clover: Rebranding the Upper Peninsula," *Michigan History* (July/August 2013): 44–48.

28 Advertisement, "Fresh Strawberries," *Calumet News*, July 23, 1897, np.

29 Iola May Bly, *Journal* (Gordon, MN: unpublished, 1904–11), 1:73–75. I'm grateful to Iola's grandson Daniel Gray for sharing her journals.

30 Caroline R. Stone, *Inga of Porcupine Mine* ([New York?]: Holiday House, 1942), 72–73.

31 "Automobiles Collide: Cars Come Together at Corner of School and Rockland Streets," *Calumet News*, October 5, 1914, 8.

32 Joseph M. Cahn, *The Teenie Weenies Book: The Life and Art of Willian Donahey* (La Jolla, CA: A Star & Elephant Book, The Green Tiger Press, 1986).

33 Grand Marais Woman's Club, *The Cooking Pots of Grand Marais* (1930s; repr., Grand Marais, MI: Voyager Press, 1976); William Donahey, *The Teenie Weenies in the Wildwood* (Chicago: Rand McNally, 1923).

34 Upper Peninsula Development Bureau [John A. Doelle, secretary-manager], *Annual Report 1919* (Marquette, MI: Upper Peninsula Development Bureau, 1919).

35 John J. Sellman, *Martin Reef, Lightship to Lighthouse: Another Chapter in Les Cheneaux History* (Cedarville, MI: Les Cheneaux Historical Association, 1995), 67.

36 See Katherine J. Parkin, *Food Is Love: Advertising and Gender Roles in Modern America* (Philadelphia: University of Pennsylvania Press, 1997).

37 *New York Times*, June 12, 1939.

38 Found in Plattsburgh, New York, since the 1920s, the Michigan claim to "Red Hots" has a murky history. A UP Michigan sauce is produced by Vollwerth's in Hancock, Michigan.

39 For example, see Ladies' Aid Society, *Rogers City Cook Book 1922: Book of Recipes* (Rogers City, MI: St. John's Evangelical Lutheran Church, 1922), 7, 9, 11.

40 Grand Marais Woman's Club, *Cooking Pots of Grand Marais*, 29.

41 William Cullen Bryant, August 20, 1846, quoted in Eugene T. Peterson, *Mackinac Island: Its History in Pictures* (Mackinac Island, MI: Mackinac State Historic Parks, 1973), endpaper.

42 Republican Party's "Vote for Hoover" political advertisement, *New York Times*, October 30, 1928. See the advertisement in question, history.iowa.gov/history/ education/educator-resources/primary-source-sets/great-depression-and -herbert-hoover/chicken.

43 Upper Peninsula Development Bureau, *The Lure Book of Michigan's Upper Peninsula* (Ann Arbor, MI: Ann Arbor Press, 1941), 83.

44 Upper Peninsula Development Bureau, *Lure Book*, 77.

45 "The Old AAA Traveler," Grill and Skillet AAA Club of Michigan, 1942.

46 Los Angeles Times, *Los Angeles Times Cook Book, No. 2: 957 Cooking and Other Recipes by California Women* (Los Angeles: Times-Mirror Co., 1905), 98.

47 *Kettles and Campfires: The Girl Scout Camp and Trail Cook Book* (New York: Girl Scouts, 1928), 5.

48 *Kettles and Campfires*, 6.

49 See the advertisement for Underwood Pure Deviled Ham in the *Ladies' Home Journal*, June 1926, 137. The association of mom's deviled ham sandwich with fathers and sons remained potent into the 1950s; see also the *Ladies' Home Journal*, September 1950, 105.

50 Boy Scouts of America, *The Official Handbook for Boys* (Garden City, NY: Doubleday, Page and Company, 2011), 149–53.

51 *Kettles and Campfires*, 99–100.

52 See advertisements in the *Chicago Tribune*, August 12, 1954, pt. 2, 6.

53 Nancy Kennedy and Mary Augusta Rodgers, ed., *The Ford Times Traveler's Cookbook: Quick Ways to Prepare Good Food on the Road* (Dearborn, MI: Ford Motor Company, 1965), cover.

54 Kennedy and Rodgers, *Ford Times Traveler's Cookbook*, 15.

55 Ford Motor Company, "For the People and Posterity" Ford Motor Company Institutional Message Advertising Campaign, 1924 (THF95509), Benson Ford Research Center, Henry Ford Museum, www.thehenryford.org/collections-and -research/digital-collections/artifact/350931/.

56 James H. Cissel, "A United Michigan," *Les Cheneaux Breezes* 1 (1939): 3.

57 Guy H. Hamel, "Huge Bridge across Mackinac Straits Will Be Built," *Les Cheneaux Breezes* 2, no. 1 (1939): 1.

58 The official length of the bridge is 26,372 feet, about 28 feet short of five miles long, one of the longest bridges in the world and still the longest in the Western Hemisphere, according to the Mackinac Bridge Authority website: www .mackinacbridge.org/about-the-bridge/frequently-asked-questions/.

59 See Gail A. Vander Stoep, "Perceptions and Status of Michigan as a Heritage Tourism State: Results of an Eleven-Month Telephone Survey," in *Proceedings of the 1997 Northeast Recreation Research Symposium*, ed. H. Vogelsong (Burlington, VT: USDA Forest Service, Northeastern Forest Experiment Station, 1998).

60 Edwin Way Teale, *Journey into Summer: A Naturalist's Record of a 19,000-Mile Journey through the North American Summer* (New York: Dodd, Mead, 1960), 152–57.

61 Teale, *Journey into Summer*, 121.

62 Teale, *Journey into Summer*, 121.

63 Edwin Way Teale, *Wandering through Winter* (New York: Dodd, Mead, 1966), 85. For a discussion of Teale's significance in the postwar era, see also Thomas R. Dunlap, "National Nature through the Windshield: Edwin Way Teale's American Seasons," *Environmental History* 16, no. 4 (2011): 633–50.

64 See Susan Sessions Rugh, *Are We There Yet? The Golden Age of American Family Vacations* (Lawrence: University Press of Kansas, 2008).

65 Sears Roebuck and Co., *Let's Cook Outdoors: Sears Handy Guide to What to Cook—How to Cook It—And the Equipment Needed for Best Results* (Recipe Booklet), 1954; the front cover has a photograph of a man grilling while two women are seated next to the barbecue, with the tagline: "Turn Picnics into Banquets with Sears Portable Grills and Gay Accessories for Outdoor Eating," University of South Carolina Library, Jered Metz Collection, digital.tcl.sc.edu/digital/collection/jmetz/id/424/rec/1.

66 John Burroughs, "The Art of Seeing Things," in *American Earth: Environmental Writing since Thoreau*, ed. Bill McKibben (New York: Library of America, 2008), 151.

67 Letter from John Burroughs to Mrs. Ford, August 20, 1919, Benson Ford Research Center, Henry Ford Museum.

68 Los Angeles Times, *Los Angeles Times Cook Book*, 96–99.

69 Ladies of the First Presbyterian Church of Kalamazoo, *A Friend in Need . . .* (Kalamazoo, MI: Ihling Bros & Everard, 1899).

70 Ladies of Corinthian Chapter No. 123 Order of the Eastern Star, *Book of Recipes* (Kalamazoo: n.p., 1921). The French word *marais* (as in Grand Marais) also refers to a marsh or swamp.

71 See the definitive history of the hotdog as cultural icon and more: Bruce Kraig, *Hot Dog: A Global History* (London: Reaktion Books, 2009).

72 Grand Marais Woman's Club, *Cooking Pots of Grand Marais*, 29.

73 Women's Auxiliary of Grace Church, *Superior Cook Book* (Ishpeming, MI: Peninsular Record, 1905), 50.

74 Jim Harrison, *Songs of Unreason* (Port Townsend, WA: Copper Canyon Press, 2011). Jim Harrison was a gourmand, poet, and writer of both fiction and essays. He kept a picnic table in his UP backyard.

75 Andrew Blackbird, *History of the Ottawa and Chippewa Indians of Michigan; A Grammar of Their Language, and Personal and Family History of the Author* (Ypsilanti, MI: Ypsilantian Job Printing House, 1887).

76 The Chicago Tribune Syndicate Archive; Donahey's drawings and stories appeared between 1917 and 1970, in newspapers, books, and advertisements. In *Too Much Jelly*, Dunce falls in a jelly jar and eats jelly for supper, sleeps in jelly,

and has jelly for breakfast; says he, "I'm pretty well fed up on jelly" (January 16, 1944).

77 Cy Meier, comp. and ed., *Favorite Recipes: Upper Peninsula of Michigan* (Calumet, MI: District 1 Michigan Federation Business & Professional Women, 1978), 295.

78 Russell M. Magnaghi, *Upper Peninsula of Michigan: A History* (Marquette, MI: 906 Heritage, 2017).

79 Local, wild thimbleberries and chokecherries are among the fruits still gathered, preserved, and sold by the monastery brothers at the Jam Pot, Poorrock Abbey, near Jacob's Falls, Keweenaw Peninsula.

80 *Kettles and Campfires: The Girl Scout Camp and Trail Cook Book* (New York: Girl Scouts, 1928), 126.

81 See Grand Marais Woman's Club, *Cooking Pots of Grand Marais.*

82 See historian Rachel Snell's website The Virginia House-wife Project, virginia housewifeproject.com, for more information about Mrs. Mary Randolph (1762–1828), considered by many to be the true first American cookbook author.

83 Mrs. Mary Randolph, *The Virginia Housewife: Or, Methodical Cook* (Baltimore: Plaskitt, & Cugle, 1824), 128.

84 See the blog by Fred Opie, "Make Him Quilly," January 15, 2022, www.fredopie .com/food/drkingsfavoritedessert; Opie cites the interview with Alberta King by Poppy Cannon, food writer, *Chicago Daily Defender*, December 12, 1967.

CHAPTER 6

1 Quoted in Gyorgyi Voros, "Exquisite Environments," *Parnassus: Poetry in Review* 21, no.1/2 (1996); Mary Oliver's poetry was rooted in place and the practice of close observation. In this excerpt, she reveals the fragility of the porcupine, who hides in the trees, at once singular and common. Oliver is rooting for the porcupine.

2 Robert Archibald, "An Environmental History of the Upper Peninsula of Michigan: An Outline," *Upper Country: A Journal of the Lake Superior Region* 3 (2015), commons.nmu.edu/cgi/viewcontent.cgi?article=1021&context=upper _country.

3 In Cedarville, Sally VanSickle remembers going out for the smelt runs as a small child: "One of my memories was spring smelt fishing with Dad and Rose, we got in the car and drove to the favorite streams after dark, we loaded nets, some buckets, (the smelt were thick!) and then scooped with our hands. We drove back to their house and had fried smelt! Nothing like it! Such an adventure!" Personal communication posted on Facebook, January 2019.

4 Michigan Department of State Highways Commission, Mackinac Bridge Authority, *Origin-Destination Studies Taken at Mackinac Bridge, Mackinac County for 1967, 1969 and 1970* (Lansing: Michigan Department of State Highways,

[1972?]), 37; the Bridge Authority reported 1.24 million cars in 1958, the first full year of operation (since the bridge opened in November 1957).

5 Diana Hubbell, "This Depression Era 'Magic Cake' Has a Secret Ingredient," *Gastro Obscura*, March 4, 2022, www.atlasobscura.com/articles/what-is-tomato-soup-cake.

6 See Roger L. Rosentreter, "Roosevelt's Tree Army: Michigan's Conservation Corps," *Michigan History*, May/June 1986.

7 Upper Peninsula Development Bureau, *The Lure Book of Michigan's Upper Peninsula* (Ann Arbor, MI: Ann Arbor Press, 1941), 34.

8 Upper Peninsula Development Bureau, *Lure Book*, 34.

9 Voluntary schemes were enacted by some states, including Wisconsin and Ohio, but the federal Social Security Act of 1935 initiated comprehensive benefits. Benefit provisions paid individuals in Michigan sixteen dollars per week in 1938. See Daniel N. Price, "Unemployment Insurance, Then and Now, 1935–85," *Social Security Bulletin* 48, no. 10 (October 1985): 22–32.

10 See Nilima Gandhi et al., "Are Fish Consumption Advisories for the Great Lakes Adequately Protective against Chemical Mixtures?" *Environmental Health Perspectives* 125, no. 4 (2017): 586–93.

11 Recorded by Alan Lomax and Harry B. Welliver, in *Songs of the Michigan Lumberjack, from the Archive of Folk Song*, ed. E. C. Beck (Washington, DC: Library of Congress, 1960), 10.

12 See US EPA, "Climate Change Indicators: Great Lakes Water Levels and Temperatures," accessed August 28, 2017, www.epa.gov/climate-indicators/great-lakes.

13 Nick Walker, "Pollution in the Great Lakes: Mapping the Environmental Woes of the Great Lakes," *Canadian Geographic*, July 1, 2013.

14 "Karkanen, Julia," "Hogback, Laina," and "Hill, Jean," interview by Helen Armstrong, Finnish Folklore and Social Change in the Great Lakes Mining Region Oral History Collection, Finlandia University, Finnish American Historical Archive and Museum.

15 Individual shops on the island called America's fudge capital manufacture as much as five hundred pounds daily in the summer tourist season; see one version of the confection's contested history: www.cbsnews.com/news/the-history-of-fudge-did-a-mistake-create-a-sweet-treat/?fbclid=IwAR18mNwpqROHaatlvv CqyTfrd288G-6klU7gIVMoQQt9mHK51vTyqgI67eA.

16 [Richard Bunce?], *Da Yoopers Glossary: A Tourist's Guide to a Better Understanding of the Yoopanese Language* [Ishpeming, MI: Da Yoopers Tourist Trap?, 1998].

17 Caroline R. Stone, *Inga of Porcupine Mine* ([New York?]: Holiday House, 1942), 14.

18 See the play by Canadian writer/actress Emilie Monnet, *Okinum* (Toronto: Scirocco Drama, 2022), which interweaves the themes of memory and death in three languages: English, French, and Anishinaabemowin.

19 Ernest Hemingway, *A Moveable Feast* (New York: Charles Scribner's Sons, 1964), 56–57.

20 Walter Levy, *The Picnic: A History* (Lanham, MD: AltaMira Press, 2014), 116.

21 Kat Eschner, "Was the First Battle of Bull Run Really 'The Picnic Battle'?" *Smithsonian Magazine*, July 21, 2017, www.smithsonianmag.com/smart-news/was-first-battle-bull-run-really-picnic-battle-180964084/.

22 Bryan Stevenson, director, *Lynching in America: Confronting the Legacy of Racial Terror*, 3rd ed. (Montgomery, AL: Equal Justice Initiative, 2017), lynching inamerica.eji.org/report/.

23 Levy, *The Picnic*, 129.

24 Arthur Conan Doyle, *The Great Boer War* (London: Smith, Elder, & Co., 1900), chap. 16.

25 Mrs. O. P. Westervelt, "My Fish Story," *Les Cheneaux Breezes* 1 (1939): 14.

26 Horace B. Johnson, "Letter to Mr. G. H. Hamel," January 20, 1939, *Les Cheneaux Breezes* 1 (1939): 16.

27 See the accounts by C. H. Reiter of Cincinnati, Ohio, in *Les Cheneaux Breezes* 1 (1939): 14; and Robert Heuck, *Early Recollections of the Snows* (printed privately by Heuck family, 1982).

28 See Murray Hill Hotel (Sault Ste. Marie) and Les Cheneaux Chamber of Commerce advertisements in *Les Cheneaux Breezes* 1 (1939): 20, 23.

29 Milo M. Quaife, ed., *The Western Country in the 17th Century: The Memoirs of Lamothe Cadillac and Pierre Liette* (Chicago: Lakeside Press, 1947), 12–13.

30 James Strang, quoted in Dan Egan, *The Death and Life of the Great Lakes* (New York: W. W. Norton, 2017), 44.

31 Edwin Way Teale, *Journey into Summer: A Naturalist's Record of a 19,000-Mile Journey through the North American Summer* (New York: Dodd, Mead, 1960), 146.

32 Kent LaCombe, "Lake Huron's Entangled Eden: Fish, Fisheries, and Lost Opportunities in Freshwater Borderlands, 1900–1940," *Michigan Historical Review* 41, no. 1 (Spring 2015): 25–56. See also Margaret Beattie Bogue, *Fishing the Great Lakes: An Environmental History, 1783–1933* (Madison: University of Wisconsin Press, 2000) and Robert Doherty, *Disputed Waters: Native Americans and the Great Lakes Fishery* (Lexington: University Press of Kentucky, 1990).

33 LaCombe, "Lake Huron's Entangled Eden," 52.

34 Egan, *Death and Life*, 53.

35 Egan, *Death and Life*, 88.

36 Egan, *Death and Life*, 46.

37 Great Lakes Fishery Commission, *Reassessment of the Lake Trout Population Collapse in Lake Michigan in the 1940s*, Technical Report, 65 (2002): 25–27; this report concluded that overfishing predated the collapse by reducing the spawning population, whereas the sea lamprey's appearance (first seen in Lake Huron in about 1937) could not have been responsible.

38 Jeff Gillies, "Alewives: The Trouble They Cause and the Salmon That Love Them," *Great Lakes Echo*, September 3, 2009.

39 LaCombe, "Lake Huron's Entangled Eden," 25–26.

40 LaCombe, "Lake Huron's Entangled Eden," 54.

41 Guy Hamel, "A Prophecy: Les Cheneaux of the Future," quoted in the *Evening News* 88, no. 157 (August 11, 1988).

42 Karl L. Vogelheim, "Reminiscences—Reflections—Rumors, Rogers City," in *Rogers City: Its First 100 Years*, ed. Arthur D. Josephson (Rogers City, MI: Centennial Committee, 1971), 101.

43 Vogelheim, "Reminiscences," 112.
44 G. H. Hamel, Untitled manuscript, 5 pp., c. 1963, Les Cheneaux Historical Museum, Cedarville, MI.
45 Hamel, Untitled manuscript, 4.
46 Frank R. Grover, *A Brief History of Les Cheneaux Islands: Some New Chapters of Mackinac History* (Evanston, IL: Bowman, 1911), 73.
47 Susan Sontag, *On Photography* (New York: Penguin, 1979), 174.
48 Jean-Jacques Rousseau, *Essay on the Origin of Languages*, published 1781 (*Essai sur l'origine des langues*), quoted in Edouard Glissant, *Caribbean Discourse, Selected Essays* (Charlottesville: University of Virginia Press, 1989), epigraph.
49 Aldo Leopold, *A Sand County Almanac, and Sketches Here and There* (1949; repr., New York: Oxford University Press, 1989), 266–67.
50 See the American Dairy Association's *Let's Eat Outdoors: Recipes and Ideas for Picnics, Barbecues, Patio Parties, Camping* (mid-1950s pamphlet), thevodkaparty.com/food/lets-eat-outdoors-mid-50s, 6, 7, 8.
51 Grand Marais Woman's Club, *The Cooking Pots of Grand Marais* (1930s; repr., Grand Marais, MI: Voyager Press, 1976), 84.
52 See greatlakesmythsociety.com/track/marquette-county-1959; these lyrics refer to the filming of *Anatomy of a Murder* (1959). The film, about the 1952 small town murder in Big Bay, was shot in Marquette, Ishpeming, and Michigamme. Its stars included Lee Remick, Eve Arden, Ben Gazzara, as well as James Stewart.
53 Adapted from the recipe for "Breaded Chicken" in Women's Auxiliary of Grace Church, *Superior Cook Book* (Ishpeming, MI: Peninsular Record, 1905), 30.
54 This recipe from my aunt, Elda Hamel Nye, is found in Joyce M. Pines, comp., *Heirlooms: Then and Now* (Waverly, IA: G&R Publishing, 1996), 237.
55 Claimed to be a Portuguese inscription and quoted in *American Forestry* 26 (1920): 692.
56 Jon L. Saari, "Upper Peninsula Summer Camps," in *A Sense of Place: Michigan's Upper Peninsula, Essays in Honor of William & Margery Vandament*, ed. Russell M. Magnaghi and Michael T. Marsden (Marquette, MI: Northern Michigan University, 1997), 191.
57 Judy Cason, "My Grandfather, Reverend Paul Beymer . . . As I Remember Him," in *First Union Church, Cedarville Michigan, 1894–1994*, comp. ed. Helen Shoberg (Cedarville, MI: First Union Church, [1994?]), 31–33.
58 Mary Oliver, "Going to Walden," in *New and Selected Poems, Volume One* (Boston: Beacon Press, 1992). In this poem, Oliver, like many writers before her, referenced the 1845 journey of Henry David Thoreau to Walden Pond, where he sought an appreciation of nature.
59 Women's Auxiliary of Grace Church, *Superior Cook Book*, 172.
60 Pines, *Heirlooms: Then and Now*, 68.

INDEX

charcoal briquets (briquettes).
   See Ford Motor
   Company: briquets and
cherry, 48, 149
Chicago: Columbian
   Exposition, 24, 47, 50,
   104; Elmwood and, 163;
   hotdogs, 172; Hull House,
   28; iron ore trade, 139,
   144–45; lumber trade,
   104, 212; Motor Club,
   161; steamships and, 97,
   103–4; summer visitors
   from, 103, 167; trains
   and, 41, 128
chicken, 23; breaded, 252n53;
   cold, 24; coronation, 217–
   18; "for every pot" slogan,
   173; fried, 24, 34, 219–20;
   roasted, 159; sandwiches,
   183; Southern Style, 133,
   229n35; substitute for
   fish, 198, 219; Teenie
   Weenies and, 187
Chinese immigration, 131–32.
   See also Asians
chocolate, 10, 30, 38, 51, 223;
   fudge, 223; marguerites,
   189; sandwich, 184;
   S'mores, 188
churches: building funds for,
   29–30, 32, 201; camps,
   221–22; cookbooks,
   29–31, 33, 149, 183, 201;
   mining companies and,
   135; mission, 40; picnics
   and, 21, 136, 138, 201,
   213, 221; recipe sharing
   and, 148
Civilian Conservation Corps
   (CCC), 8, 196–97
Clemenc, Ana Klobuchar, 27,
   229n17
Clemens, Samuel. *See* Twain,
   Mark
Cloverland: name for UP, 165;
   picnics, 165; tourism,
   165–66, 245n27
coffee and tea: chicory and,
   122; expected, 26; logging
   camps and, 122, 143;
   picnics and, 21, 23, 30, 35,

44, 106; rationing, 197;
   scouts and, 174; supplies,
   30, 92, 147; Vagabonds
   and, 159
Columbian Exposition,
   Chicago (1893). *See*
   Chicago: Columbian
   Exposition
cookbooks: authors, 30, 132–33,
   229n5, 232n3; barbecues
   and, 10; church, 29–31;
   community, 8, 25, 29, 31,
   201; as historical sources
   and, 2, 9; international
   recipes in, 31, 38, 48, 133,
   185, 217; meat scraps and,
   172; pasties in, 27; picnic,
   10, 12, 24, 185; Southern,
   34, 132–33; travel and,
   170, 244n6; wild game
   meat in, 70, 81, 85;
   women and, 28, 30, 201
Corbusier, Henry Dunbar, 34–
   35, 115
Croatians, 7, 26–27, 29, 45
cudighi ("Gudighi"), 172

deforestation, 13, 21, 43, 66, 68,
   72–75, 129, 165
demography, 14, 37, 95, 128–
   29, 197, 199; of ethnic
   diversity, 172; Midwest
   urbanism and, 103;
   mining and, 96; race
   and, 131
Detroit: automobiles and, 161;
   hotdogs, 172; leisure
   classes, 41; lumber and,
   212; travel between UP
   and, 47, 80, 102–4, 116,
   128–29, 140
Detroit and Cleveland Steam
   Navigation Company, 42,
   102–4, 116
Devil's Kitchen, 77
Dickerson, Mary, 9, 167–68
Donahey, William: cookbook,
   9, 168, 185–87; newspaper
   column, 196, 248n76;
   Teenie Weenies and,
   167–69
Drummond Island, 44

Eames, Ray and Charles, 1–2,
   225n2, 225n3
ecology, 2, 176, 216; Leopold
   and, 4, 73, 75; picnic
   and, 6, 15, 20, 80–81;
   porcupine and, 6, 68;
   public policy and,
   208; succession and,
   166; water, 77, 81, 129;
   wilderness, 74
ecotone: definition of, 4
Edison, Thomas, 155;
   correspondence with,
   245n17
eggs: breakfast and, 54; deviled,
   24, 38, 44; hard-boiled, 38,
   165, 203; as ingredients,
   50–51, 84, 123, 148, 172,
   220, 222; supplies of, 30
Elizabeth II, Queen, 217
ethnicity: acculturation and,
   7; contradictions of, 6;
   and foods, 8, 25–26,
   29, 31, 96, 172, 202; of
   immigrant groups, 24,
   31, 37, 202; of picnics, 33,
   137; and singularity, 81,
   96, 201; tensions, 136; and
   women, 28, 29, 129. *See*
   also specific groups

family: automobiles and, 117,
   160–61, 170, 174–75, 181;
   camps, 162, 180, 221;
   cemeteries and, 81; eating
   outdoors, 3; economics
   and, 203, 206, 212–13;
   government relief and,
   196; housing and, 198;
   lore, 1, 123; migrations,
   22, 25, 33, 117, 202;
   mining, 27, 29, 135, 148;
   picnics and, 5, 21–22,
   33, 35, 43, 106, 117, 186,
   194–95, 201; race and, 34,
   47, 130, 132, 163; recipes
   and, 29, 50, 217, 219, 224;
   229n21; servants and,
   34, 171; tourism and,
   169, 197, 223; trains and,
   137–38; vacations and, 73,
   103–4, 106–8, 117–18, 173

sturgeon, 97
Sugar Loaf Rock, 42, 78

Tahquamenon Falls, 44, 180, 221
Tarver, Robert (Robert Voelker), 203, 206
tea. *See* coffee and tea
Teale, Edwin Way, 180, 207–8
Thoreau, Henry David, 79–80, 252n58
Tocqueville, Alexis de, 5, 75, 80, 92
tomato soup, 196, 237n89
tourism: attitudes towards, 223; automobiles and, 14, 161–62, 178, 180; growth in, 14–15, 42–43, 102–3, 171–72; maps and brochures, 169; promotion in UP, 13, 165–66, 169, 212; seasonality of, 167, 197; steamships and, 102; trains and, 138, 141, 146; water and, 104; wilderness access, 103, 146, 158, 162, 211
trains: Copper Range Railroad, 134–35, 139–40, 142; foods and, 35, 128–30, 199; gendered, 140; impact of, 14–15, 127–29, 132, 141–42, 144; picnics and, 5, 12, 14, 129–30, 133, 135–39, 166–67; steamships and, 128; travelers and, 41, 45, 126, 131, 141, 197. *See also* Iron Mountain: Railroad; tourism: trains and
Tranquility Grove (Hingham, Massachusetts), 21, 228n6

trout, 88, 97, 100, 129, 147–48, 206–8
Tudor, Frederic, 113–14
Twain, Mark, 31, 35, 229n29, 230n39

Upper Peninsula Development Bureau, 169, 173, 197
urbanism: automobiles and, 180; cemeteries and, 81; escape from, 5, 34, 39, 104, 117; growth of, 103; impact of, 7–8, 174, 199; lack of, 8; wealth and, 41, 103, 164; wilderness and, 74–75, 104, 164

Vagabonds: campsites, 162; composition of, 155–56; description of, 155–56, 182–83; marketing and, 176; picnics and, 155–56, 159, 170, 183; vehicles, 156, 158–59, 182
Vertin Brothers, 33

walleye, 89, 97, 195, 206
watermelon: in cookbooks, 9, 232n76; Obama and, 231n71; pickles, 48–49; at picnics, 2, 17–18, 34–35, 49, 113, 117, 224; postcards of, 45–47; Teenie Weenies and, 187
White, Stewart Edward, 70, 111–12, 143–44
whitefish: abundance of, 97, 208, 214; commercial fishing of, 100, 106; decline in, 208; pickled, 33; smoked, 84, 178; as

taste of wilderness, 10, 214; and tourists, 43, 118–19, 214
Whitefish Lake, 54, 65, 204, 232n2; and Laughing Whitefish Lake Preserve, 234n38
Wilderness Act, 14, 74
Williams, Governor G. Mennen ("Soapy"), 217
women: associations, 28, 33, 110, 213; boats and, 106, 116, 197; and cookbooks, 31, 33, 201; as cooks, 9, 21, 35, 50, 160, 170, 183, 202; and domesticity, 160; and employment, 24, 198; enslaved, 59; and fishing, 209; and gender inequality, 9, 24, 164, 248n65; immigrants, 22; marriage and, 132; and mining, 27; Perfect Ladies Society and women, 164; as picnickers, 17–18, 23, 28, 110, 151, 170, 173; and servants, 24, 132; as shoppers, 174; as tourists, 169, 197
Women's Land Army, 197
Wordsworth, William, 140. See also *Song of Hiawatha, The*
Works Progress Administration (WPA), 9, 140
World War I, 108, 122, 136, 140, 145–46, 196, 204
World War II, 153, 174, 196, 197, 204, 205

Yooper, 9, 61, 202, 223

ABOUT THE AUTHOR

CANDICE GOUCHER is professor emerita of history at Washington State University and lives in Portland, Oregon. She is the author and editor of numerous books concerning world history, African history, Caribbean history, food studies, women's history, and more. She is also a recipient of the World History Association's Pioneers in World History Award. She is from Sault Ste. Marie, Michigan.